More Advance Praise for *On Friendship*

"Beautiful and wise, *On Friendship* will deepen your understanding of the friendships through which you live. Can a work of philosophy be a page-turner? This one is hard to put down. Here Montaigne triumphs over Aristotle, while theater emerges as the art that best illuminates friendship—which, as Nehamas shows us, is best appreciated as a work of art is appreciated, for what it is for us, individually and irreplaceably."

—Paul Woodruff, professor of philosophy and classics,
University of Texas at Austin

"*On Friendship* accomplishes the remarkable; Nehamas punctures standard pieties with clear-eyed realism about the risks of loss or corruption through our friendships, while saving every bit of our unshakeable sense that our friends remain immeasurably valuable, and of central importance in our lives. This deeply insightful book—the fruit of a lifetime's reflection—should be read not only by those who care about friendship in general, but by all of us who care about our friends."

—R. Lanier Anderson, professor of philosophy,
Stanford University

ON FRIENDSHIP

ALSO BY ALEXANDER NEHAMAS

Nietzsche: Life as Literature

The Art of Living:
Socratic Reflections from Plato to Foucault

Virtues of Authenticity:
Essays on Plato and Socrates

Only a Promise of Happiness:
The Place of Beauty in a World of Art

ON FRIENDSHIP

ALEXANDER NEHAMAS

BASIC BOOKS
A Member of the Perseus Books Group
New York

Copyright © 2016 by Alexander Nehamas

Published by Basic Books,
A Member of the Perseus Books Group

All rights reserved. Printed in the United States of America. No part of this book may be reproduced in any manner whatsoever without written permission except in the case of brief quotations embodied in critical articles and reviews. For information, contact Basic Books, 250 West 57th Street, New York, NY 10107.

Books published by Basic Books are available at special discounts for bulk purchases in the United States by corporations, institutions, and other organizations. For more information, please contact the Special Markets Department at the Perseus Books Group, 2300 Chestnut Street, Suite 200, Philadelphia, PA 19103, or call (800) 810-4145, ext. 5000, or e-mail special.markets@perseusbooks.com.

Designed by Trish Wilkinson
Set in 11.5-point Adobe Caslon Pro

Library of Congress Cataloging-in-Publication Data

Names: Nehamas, Alexander, 1946– author.
Title: On friendship / Alexander Nehamas.
Description: First Edition. | New York : Basic Books, 2016. | Includes
    bibliographical references and index.
Identifiers: LCCN 2015041476 (print) | LCCN 2015042413 (ebook) |
    ISBN 9780465082926 (hardcover) | ISBN 9780465098613 (ebook)
Subjects: LCSH: Friendship.
Classification: LCC BJ1533.F8 N44 2016 (print) | LCC BJ1533.F8
    (ebook) | DDC 177/.62—dc23
LC record available at http://lccn.loc.gov/2015041476

10 9 8 7 6 5 4 3 2 1

For Tom

Contents

INTRODUCTION

IN THE PAST FEW YEARS, I HAVE HAD OCCASION TO travel to Greece, where I was born, on a more or less regular basis. The reasons for my trips were professional, the trips themselves were short—three days at most—and my schedule, crowded. But whenever I could, I would spend at least one evening in Athens in the company of a group of friends who have kept up the most striking relationship since our graduation from high school over fifty years ago.

Most of the group were boarders—some of us for as long as ten years. The school was academically rigorous and the boarding department was particularly regimented: all our activities—waking, washing, entering the dining room, studying, going to bed, and many others—were controlled by loud electric bells that usually gave us just enough time to get to our next task, and we were punished whenever we were late. Some of the boys were, like me, from Athens, where the school was located. Several came from other parts of Greece and a large number came from abroad, where their families had moved for one reason or another. Our dormitories gave us little privacy, we all belonged to the same section of our class, and we were also under constant supervision. All of that drew us very close to one another—many of us spent weekends and part of our vacations at one another's homes—and we formed intense and long-lasting friendships (and equally intense if not always as long-lasting breakups and antipathies).

My friends were to spend much of their lives together. Right after graduation, I left Athens to study in the United States, where I have been living since then, and it was a while before I was in touch with them again. I was amazed at how easy it was to rejoin their group and how relaxed and comfortable they all made me feel as soon as I did. I suspect that that was in part because, as we were reacquainting ourselves with one another, I recognized in them some of the most characteristic features I remembered them having when we were still in school. One, now a surgeon, is still the funny man of the group, his spontaneous sense of humor quite unchanged even after all these years; another, who always loved flying, has a son who is a pilot for a commercial Greek airline; a third has remained blindly devoted to the soccer team he followed in school and never misses a single game—and I am sure that they recognized similar features in me as well. Every one of us, of course, has also undergone many changes, and at least some are to the good. Most important, we can appreciate what we once were and liked about each other without the insecurities, the resentments, and the competitiveness of adolescence: our interactions are now easier, milder, and more consistently affectionate, even if they are less dramatic or passionate than they were at the time.

The group meets regularly, usually on Sunday evenings; some play cards, others just to see one another and talk. They go out to dinner together, especially (though not exclusively) when they welcome—as they always do—old classmates like me, who live abroad. Often, these dinners become elaborate affairs at someone's home, and their wives, who are also friends with one another, join in. Some spend family vacations together, others (husbands and wives both) have become godparents of some of their friends' children. Although originally they may have begun to keep in touch in order to keep their past alive and still enjoy thinking back to it, as they (and I with them) often do, their friendship has gradually become much more than an opportunity to wax nostalgic: the activities I have mentioned, and everything that goes with such close and protracted contact, have had nothing less than a profound, all-embracing effect on the shape of their lives and the lives of their families.

To say that their friendship has had an effect on their lives is to say that it has had an effect on themselves. When I realized that these people are who they have come to be, at least in part (and it is a large part) because of their friendship, I also realized that friendship, even when motivated by a desire to regain a common past, is also crucial in forging a different future. Who we are is to a great extent determined by our friends, whose role in our life is more pervasive and all-encompassing the closer our relationship happens to be. Our friendships are not inert. My classmates' friendship spreads out within their life: it suffuses it. Every friendship of ours is more or less closely connected with everything else about us: every one of our friends, the more so the more intimate we are, influences the direction our life takes, just as our life's direction influences our choice of friends. Friendship is crucial to what most of us come to be in life.

In this book, I hope to show why that is. What is needed, first, though, is a more complex picture of friendship itself. Friendship—and here I mean close friendship, not the indiscriminate kind that is so easily forged through Facebook (which will always have the unfortunate distinction of turning "friend" into a verb)—is a bond that, ever since people began to think about it, has been consistently praised as one of life's greatest gifts. Robert Burton's tribute is typical:

> "As the sun is to the firmament, so is friendship to the world," a most divine and heavenly band. As nuptial love makes, this perfects mankind, and is to be preferred . . . Take this away, and take all pleasure, joy, comfort, happiness, and true content out of the world; 'tis the greatest tie, the surest indenture, strongest band . . . A faithful friend is better than gold, a medicine of misery, an only possession.

And so is Ralph Waldo Emerson's:

O friend, my bosom said,
Through thee alone the sky is arched,
Through thee alone the rose is red,
All things through thee take nobler form,
And look beyond the earth.

While Charlotte Brontë's words to Ellen Nussey give us a sense of how deeply a friendship can affect a whole life: "Why are we to be divided? Surely, Ellen, it must be because we are in danger of loving each other too well—in losing sight of the *Creator* in idolatry of the *creature*."

Such an attitude originates with Aristotle, whose ideas about *philia*, which is universally taken to be equivalent to friendship, are still crucial to every effort to understand this relationship. *Philia* was for Aristotle a great and pure good: it is something, he explains, that no one would want to live without, no matter what else one already possesses in this life, and the tradition that follows him, with very few exceptions, has also taken friendship to be one of life's greatest possessions.

Yet the Aristotelian tradition, which has been so influential that it informs commonsensical views to this day, has tended to turn away from friendship's darker, more painful, and more compromising sides. In praising friendship, we often forget that the everyday interactions of friends are much more often than not commonplace and trivial. We forget as well the grief that comes with the end of a friendship. We ignore the fact that friendships, even good friendships, can sometimes be quite harmful. And we overlook the fact that even the best of friendships sometimes conflict with the morally right thing to do—when loyalty to a friend, for example, takes precedence over discharging one's duty to others. Friendship, I will argue, has a double face.

That it can lead us into danger or immorality is one feature of friendship's true complexity. Another was driven home to me by my reunions with my school friends. My meetings with them occur within a context significantly different from the context of many of my other relationships, and I found myself behaving and thinking differently in the company of these friends than I do in the company of others. For example, although the group includes, among others, engineers, journalists, business executives, and other professionals, no one among them is an academic. So, to speak to them as I speak without a second thought to my students and colleagues would be completely out of place. A tone of voice, a specific vocabulary, a mode of conversation that is perfectly natural with some friends can be affected, pedantic, or patronizing to others. Issues that you would always confront directly with one group suddenly take a second seat with another. We adjust to our different relationships, and what some particular friends see of us is very different from what is evident to some others:

> We have as many sides to our character as we have friends to show them to. Quite unconsciously I find myself witty with one friend, large and magnanimous with

another, petulant and stingy with another, wise and grave
with another, and utterly frivolous with another. I watch
with surprise the sudden and startling changes in myself
as I pass from the influence of one friend to the influence of another.

What your friends are like when they are in the company
of others, for instance, can often make you, as we say, "like
them less": you notice features of theirs that they have no
reason to manifest when you are together.

If different friendships bring forward different aspects
of ourselves, we will have to ask what exactly it is that
seems different, depending on the relationship in which it
is manifested. What is it that all our friends love, what we
often call "the self"? Is there such a thing? And if there is,
is it just the combination of all our different, and sometimes incompatible features or is it something distinct
from, over and above, everything that our friends see in
us? In this way, an investigation of friendship's double face
will not only lead to a more realistic picture of its nature,
but to some of the most important questions of all.

The first part of this book examines what has been said
about friendship and how the arts have represented it
through the centuries. We will find that both philosophy
and art reinforce our attitude toward friendship but also
that they bring to light features of it that have not yet
been examined closely enough. The second part is my attempt to come to terms with friendship's double face—to
show that despite the dangers and disappointments it

brings in its train, which may actually be the other face of its pleasures and benefits, friendship remains a great good. That both ideas can be true at the same time can lead us to a better understanding of our friendships and—to the extent that our friendships make us what we are—of ourselves.

We begin, as we must, at the beginning: with Aristotle, who remains at the foundation of every serious discussion of friendship.

PART ONE

Chapter 1

"A FRIEND IS ANOTHER SELF"
Aristotelian Foundations

NONE OF US WOULD EVER WANT TO LIVE WITHOUT friends, according to Aristotle, even if we had every other good in the world. Aristotle wrote a long time ago—in the fourth century BC—but time has done little to cast doubt on his praise of friendship: friends may have enemies; friendship itself does not. Some of us think of our friends as a kind of mirror in which we can see and come to know ourselves as we couldn't possibly do on our own, as another self. Others believe that the essence of friendship lies in the ability of friends to be completely open with one another and share their most intimate secrets. And everyone is aware of its indirect benefits, especially the willingness of friends to help one another personally, professionally, and financially in their hour of need, often sacrificing their own welfare, sometimes even their own life, for their friends' sake.

Aristotle has always been not only the inspiration of most of our philosophy of friendship but also of much of our common sense about it. His influence has been immense, both through his own writings directly and through Cicero's dialogue *On Friendship*, which disseminated Aristotle's views during much of the Middle Ages, while Aristotle's texts were lost and before they were rediscovered and became available again in the West.

To be sure, there are exceptions—but they are few, as we will see. On the whole, and to an extent unparalleled in a field that sometimes considers agreement a form of discourtesy, the philosophical tradition is overwhelmingly on Aristotle's side, from whose discussion of *philia*— which is almost always translated as "friendship"—it has inherited two central ideas. The first is that friendship is an unalloyed good, a flawless sort of love and one of life's greatest pleasures, making every life in which friendship plays a part a better life than one without it. Companionship is a basic human need. Without it, even Paradise is robbed of its pleasures, as Milton's Adam laments to God:

> *With me I see not who partakes. In solitude*
> *What happiness? Who can enjoy alone,*
> *Or all enjoying, what contentment find?*

David Hume followed suit: "A perfect solitude is, perhaps, the greatest punishment we can suffer. Every pleasure languishes when enjoy'd apart from society." For Ralph Waldo Emerson, friendship is nothing less than "a select and sacred relation, which is a kind of absolute, and which even leaves the language of love suspicious and common, so much is this purer, and nothing is so much divine."

The second Aristotelian idea that philosophical thought about friendship has incorporated without any qualification is that the three kinds of *philia* that Aristotle distinguishes are three distinct kinds of friendship. Some of us, Aristotle says, are attracted to one another because we have something to gain from our relationship, some because of the pleasure we provide for one another, and some are drawn to one another's *aretê*, or "excellence"—or, more often, "virtue," which, as we will see, has a meaning to Aristotle that is different from our own. A business association would be a case of the first kind and a love affair of the second. But it is the third kind of *philia* that is, for Aristotle, the best: a perfect good. Cicero followed Aristotle almost to the letter: "Without virtue," he wrote, "friendship cannot exist at all," and without such "true and perfect friendship" life would not be worth living. The virtuous have no need of the friendships of "ordinary" people, who, in line with Aristotle's view, find in it at best "a source of pleasure and profit."

Ever since that time, Aristotle's ideas about *philia* have dominated the philosophical approaches to friendship with uncanny consistency, as if friendship has remained the same, whether among the boisterous citizens of classical Athens and republican Rome, the isolated Cistercian monks of twelfth-century England, the French partisans of the religious wars of the sixteenth century, the retainers of the Elizabethan court, the scions of the Scottish Enlightenment, eighteenth-century Prussians, nineteenth-century transcendentalists, or contemporary analytical philosophers. Compared to disagreements about reality or justice,

knowledge or beauty, the discussion of friendship constitutes an isolated area of calm in philosophy's roiling waters.
The exceptions to this consensus are, again, very few. When
Nietzsche, for example, wrote in his autobiography that an
unprecedented burst of creativity—four major works and
several minor ones composed within a few months—made
him feel "grateful" to his whole life, he was most profoundly
isolated, and yet there is every reason to believe that his
happiness was genuine.

Whether it is possible to live well without any friends is
an open question. What is certain, though, is that good
friends do sometimes make life better and happier. Do
they always do so? Can't good friends, sometimes not even
through a fault of their own, draw us into dangerous or
harmful adventures? If they do, does that show that they
were bad friends or not friends at all in the first place? Aristotle would simply dismiss these questions because he
and, by extension, the philosophical tradition make a very
strong assumption about the nature of friendship: only
good people can be friends. Genuine or perfect *philia*, he
tells us, is limited to the virtuous: bad people can never be
friends, good friends can never be bad people, and no
friendship between them can ever cause harm. And although modern philosophy has acknowledged that less
than perfect people—most of us—are capable of genuine
friendship, it has agreed with him that friendship is always
to the good, a good, as we will see, it has identified with
morality. That, too, is a purely benign view of friendship: it
faces the same questions we just asked of Aristotle.

Can bad people be good friends? Can good friends harm each other? Does friendship belong to morality or not? These are questions that will occupy us throughout this book, which aims to present a more complex and nuanced picture of friendship. The first step to answering these questions will require asking one that may not seem directly relevant to them: Are Aristotelian *philia* and modern friendship equivalent?

PHILIA, FOR ARISTOTLE, IS UBIQUITOUS. IT IS NECESSARY not only for rich and poor, young and old, male and female alike, but for animals as well. It unites families, political parties, social and religious organizations, tribes, even whole cities and entire species. It can exist between individuals of the same age, with the same social, financial, intellectual, or moral standing, or between superiors and inferiors: parents and children, men and women, rulers and ruled, gods and humans. Through *philia*, the ignorant are connected to the wise, and the beautiful to the ugly. Erotic love is one of its kinds. It arises among travelers and soldiers and governs the relations between host and guest and, perhaps most surprising, between buyer and seller.

That is an extraordinary range of relationships. What is it that holds these seemingly disparate bonds together? Aristotle cites three features that characterize every case of *philia*. First, *philia* requires *philêsis*—a word as badly translated by its common rendering as "love" or "affection" as *philia* is by "friendship": "love" is much too strong a term for the feelings of debtors and creditors, members of social clubs, or citizens of the same state for one another; "affection" is much too weak for the attachment of parents to their children, the passion of lovers, and the deep devotion of friends. A broad and generic term, *philêsis* covers a huge variety of positive attitudes, ranging from a merchant's cool appreciation of profit to the most blazing erotic passion. It is provoked by everything that we care for to whatever degree. And what we ultimately care for, according to Aristotle, comes down to three fundamental objects: practical benefit, pleasure, and virtue.

Second, though it requires *philêsis*, *philia* is a reciprocal relationship, whereas *philêsis* is a feeling we can have for inanimate objects and need not be reciprocated in any way. I can care for many inanimate objects—wine is Aristotle's own example—but none of them can care for me in return. Only another person can.

Third, although my wish for what is good for my wine is a wish that it taste as good as possible only so that *I* can enjoy it more, if you and I are *philoi*, I must care and wish good things to you for your sake and not, or not only, for my own—and you must feel the same way about me. Aristotle calls this mutual care "good will." And when I bear you good will, I do so either because of the practical benefits I derive from our relationship, or because of the pleasure our interaction gives me, or finally because I am drawn to your virtues—courage, justice, temperance, magnificence, wisdom, and the other features that are necessary to make a life a good and happy one.

If, then, I care for you; if I wish you good things for your sake, not only for mine; and if, moreover, you feel the same way toward me, we are bound to each other by *philia* and are each other's *philos*.

The idea that our feelings for some people may sometimes make their well-being as important to us as our very own, that for them to do well is also for us to do well, that their successes and failures are also ours, is absolutely essential to friendship as we understand it today. Since, at least at first sight, that idea seems essential to *philia* as well, it has made it tempting to think that *philia* is the Greek equivalent of friendship and explains why the two have been so often identified with one another.

Of the three kinds of *philia* Aristotle distinguishes, however, only the bond that draws people to each other's virtue is "perfect" or "complete," the paradigm of *philia* for him and for friendship for the tradition that follows him. The pursuit of pleasure or benefit leads to lesser, inferior relationships, worthy of being considered *philia* only to the extent that they "resemble" and share some of their features with that perfect sort. Importantly, in Aristotle's view no relationship between two people can be based on their admiration of each other's virtue unless both are virtuous in the first place. In regard to his contemporaries, Aristotle didn't need to be the great observer and anatomist he was in order to have no illusions about them. "Such *philia* is rare," he concedes, "for there are few such people," although that fact seems not to have disturbed him at all: he seems perfectly happy to limit virtue to Pericles, the great Athenian statesman, "and those like him."

If all three kinds of *philia* were kinds of friendship as well, the rarity of the bond of the virtuous would not be a

problem. For, in that case, the other two kinds, less demanding and more appropriate to the rest of us, might fill
the gap. But can they? Does the appreciation of pleasure
and profit generate genuine, even if imperfect, friendships?

If our relationship were based on benefit or pleasure it
would count as a friendship, even if not ideal, if I loved
and wished good things for you for your own sake. But
Aristotle also says that "those who care for each other wish
each other good things insofar as they love each other."
That means that if we are bound to each other through
virtue, I will wish good things for you to the extent that
you are virtuous; if through pleasure, to the extent that you
provide me with pleasure; and if through practical benefit,
to the extent that you are useful to me. And in the latter
two cases, Aristotle tells us, I would not care for you for
yourself but only on account of the pleasure or benefit you
provide me. If, for example, I care for you because you can
introduce me to the right people, I don't care for you for
yourself, that is, because of the kind of person you are: I
don't care for you but only for the benefit you bring me;
our bond is imperfect. Only the bond of the virtuous is
perfect because for Aristotle it is our virtues that make us
who we truly are. It is our virtues, and only our virtues,
that express our essential nature, and so only if I am drawn
to your virtues do I care for you as you really are; only then
am I capable of wishing you well for your own sake.

There seems, then, to be a tension—if not an outright
contradiction—between what Aristotle first says about
philia and what he adds immediately afterward. Let's recall that he begins by saying that good will is to wish good

things "for the *philos'* sake"; he adds that it is to wish good things for our *philos* "on account of" his virtue, the pleasure or the benefit he provides; and he finishes with the claim that *philoi* wish each other well "insofar as" they are virtuous, pleasant, or beneficial. But despite the similarity of these accounts, Aristotle points out a major difference between benefit and pleasure on the one hand and virtue on the other:

> Those who care for each other on account of benefit don't care for [each other] in themselves but only insofar as they obtain some benefit from them; so too in the case of pleasure: these people don't care for those they find entertaining in themselves, but on account of their being pleasant to them . . . Such relationships, then, are incidental: people are not cared for insofar as they are who they are but only insofar as they provide either benefit or pleasure.

So, if your virtue is what draws you to me, I wish you well on account of your character and therefore on account of who you really are; but if it is pleasure or benefit, I wish you well on account of features—your sense of humor, your looks, your financial resources, or your social position—that are all, as far as Aristotle is concerned, incidental to your rational essence, which makes you what you are.

That means that imperfect *philia* is not focused on the other person at all: "Those who love for benefit are fond of the other on account of what is good for themselves, and those who love for pleasure on account of what is pleasant for themselves," and such relationships collapse if either one of us no longer provides pleasure or benefit. Even more: "Those who are *philoi* on account of benefit part as soon as their interests separate, for they were not *philoi* of each other but of gain," while erotic *philoi* separate "as soon as that for the sake of which they were involved is no longer there, for they did not care for each other but for things they happened to have—things that are not permanent."

In short, Aristotle says both that every kind of *philia* requires wishing good things *for the philos' sake,* and also that in pleasure- or benefit-*philia* we don't really care about our *philos* at all but for our pleasure or benefit instead. Can we make sense of these seemingly contradictory views?

Actually, we can. Let's first suppose that I wish good things to my barber, Tomas, insofar as he cuts my hair well. For Aristotle, that would be to bear him good will because of one of his incidental features, since he can stop being of use to me—by leaving town, for example—without changing at all in himself: and if that happened, our *philia* would end as well. But if I wish him well insofar as he is virtuous, my good will is based on Tomas's essence, or who he really is. I then care for him, in today's terms, "as a person" and not for this or that feature of his. Since the benefit I derive from Tomas does not depend on who he is as a person but on the occupation he happens to have, Aristotle would say that I don't care for Tomas himself but for the benefits he provides instead. Not so, though, if what matters to me is his virtue: since his virtue constitutes who Tomas is, to care for him on its account is not to care for his virtue *instead* of caring for Tomas himself.

Consider, second, that there are all sorts of good things I can wish for you if our relationship is based on benefit or pleasure: more money, a good marriage, winning a prize. I can be happy for you even if I get no added benefit or pleasure from your good fortune—so long as you continue to provide me whatever prompted our relationship in the first place. Since I get no benefit from your new riches or your marriage, that shows that I wish you well not only for my own sake but for yours as well. But other good things can happen to you that are contrary to my own interests: your new riches may introduce you to a new social circle and cause you no longer to care for my welfare. Since I value what benefits you only to the extent that it either promotes or at least does not conflict with my own interests, I will neither wish such things for you nor help you obtain them. In relationships of pleasure or benefit, what determines what I will or will not wish for you ultimately depends on my own interests. So, I will wish you well even if your welfare adds nothing to mine: that's why I wish you well for your sake and not only for mine. But I still won't wish you well for your *own* sake.

That's something that only virtuous *philoi* can do. If our relationship is based on benefit or pleasure, something may be pleasant or beneficial, and therefore good, for one of us but not for the other: if that happens, our relationship will collapse. But if we are joined through virtue, nothing that is good for one of us can ever be bad for the other. For when I wish you well insofar as you are virtuous, every good thing I wish you will either augment or at least not interfere with your virtue: otherwise it wouldn't be a good. But nothing that happens as a result of your becoming a better person can ever harm me or, as far as Aristotle is concerned, conflict with my interests. And since anything that serves virtue, if done for the right reasons, is itself virtuous, anything I do for you will be, in addition to any beneficial or pleasant consequences it may have for us, itself good—a virtuous act in its own right. As long as we are both virtuous, nothing we wish or do for one another can be bad for us. In the end, I wish all my *philoi* well *for their sake*, and not only for my own; but only if I wish you well on account of your virtue do I wish you well for your *own* sake, as the person you are and not for what I can get out of you.

Perfect *philia* also differs from its imperfect varieties because the bonds of virtue are, if not always permanent, at least very long-lasting. A virtuous character, according to Aristotle, is unlikely to undergo serious change; by contrast, wealth, power, and beauty can disappear without warning, and so relationships that are based upon them are also likely to be short-lived. It is sometimes thought that "friendship is eternal if it is true friendship; but if it should ever cease to be, then it was not true friendship, even though it seemed to be so." That is an exaggeration. Aristotle recognized that even the *philia* of the virtuous may sometimes come to an end—extraordinary circumstances can sometimes erode even the virtues—without thinking that such an end shows the relationship to have been a sham.

When friendships break down, they often generate the suspicion that what had appeared to be a real friendship was all along masked selfishness. As a result, it seems to us essential that if I wish you to do well for your own sake, I will be willing to rate my own interests below yours if that becomes necessary, and the extent of my sacrifice is often a measure of the depth of our friendship. But no such sacrifice is possible in Aristotle's scheme. That is clear if our *philia* is based on pleasure or benefit: I will end it as soon as I realize that your good is incompatible with mine. But it is also true, perhaps surprisingly, that even virtue-*philia* doesn't ever require a sacrifice: every good thing I might wish for you promotes your virtue and nothing that happens as a result of your becoming a better person can be either painful or harmful to me. Even if I give my life for you, Aristotle believes that far from harming myself, I end up with an even greater good than life: nobility (*to kalon*). With very rare exceptions, virtue-*philia* can't ever hurt those it connects to each other: it is almost an object of veneration for Aristotle.

Since I will sever any relationship of pleasure or benefit if I no longer obtain what I wanted, what ultimately matters for me is what I was able to get out of it. That doesn't make those relationships selfish or exploitative, since I am glad to provide whatever the other participants desire as long as it doesn't interfere with my own plans, though it does make them *instrumental*. But friends, we believe, are people who love each other, as we say, for themselves and not just for what they can get out of their relationship. The fact, then, that both pleasure- and benefit-*philia* are instrumental makes it clear that they are not friendships. We therefore cannot identify Aristotelian *philia* as a whole with modern friendship. In particular, whether based on benefit or pleasure, *philia* does not correspond to what we take friendship to be.

But virtue-*philia*, of course, does. It has a deep connection to our relationship with our closest friends. Both Aristotle's virtuous *philoi* and our own close friends love one another "for themselves," both are attracted to one another's character, and both expect their relationships to be, if not permanent, at least long-lasting. But there are other similarities as well. Although one does not enter into it for what one can get out of it, virtue-*philia* brings with it both benefits and pleasure. So does friendship: one can rely on one's friends in times of need, and their company is overwhelmingly enjoyable—although Aristotle doesn't seem to focus his discriminating eye on the sorrows and troubles that friends can cause one another. Like virtue-*philia*, friendship is immune, or at least resistant, to slander: virtue-*philoi* (we might as well call them friends from now on) trust one another, and it takes much to undermine their faith in each other. Friends influence the shape of one another's life: they spend much of their time together, do things they would not have done had they been alone, and affect each other's character deeply. Theirs is a complex and demanding relationship, which one can have only with a few people: "It is impossible to have the perfect sort of *philia* with many people." Friends don't dispute about who has done what for whom, and their relationship makes claims on them in its own right: one should still care for one's friends even if they have undergone serious changes—provided, though, that they have not become "incurably" vicious. Friends, finally, in Aristotle's famous formulation, "are disposed toward each other as they are disposed to themselves: a friend is another self."

But precisely because virtue-*philia* is so close to friendship, we should pause before we follow Aristotle, as many have done, in emphasizing the connection between friendship and virtue, especially, as we do today, its moral variety. That is partly because Aristotelian virtue, as we have seen, is much broader than moral virtue. But that is not the main reason. More important, Aristotle allowed only a small group of Athenian men to love one another (and sometimes, in a qualified sense, their wives) as friends love one another. But friendship is both much more common and more fraught with risk than he imagined.

Aristotle's scheme, in which friendship is limited to a rarefied few, turns out to be at odds with what we know through experience. We are all of us mixtures of virtues and vices, and all of us are aware that even our best friends have their shortcomings. True, it is unlikely that we can be friends with people we consider evil. But we often have no trouble excusing our friends' failings, both trivial and, often, serious.

NEVERTHELESS, IN ARISTOTLE'S BOND BETWEEN friendship and virtue there is a deep insight that it is important not to lose.

In Euripides' *Iphigenia in Tauris*, Orestes and his friend Pylades travel to Tauri, a town in the Crimea, in order to bring its sacred statue of Artemis to Athens. At Tauri, they are captured by the locals and brought to Artemis' priestess. As it turns out, the priestess is actually Orestes' sister Iphigenia, thought to have been sacrificed to Artemis by their father Agamemnon so that the Greek ships could sail for Troy but whom the goddess had secretly snatched from the altar at the very last moment. Iphigenia, of course, doesn't recognize her brother, any more than he knows who she is. Custom in Tauri required a human sacrifice to Artemis, but when Orestes has to choose which of the two is to be the victim, he refuses to allow Pylades, his "best and dearest friend" to die in his place—partly because, he explains, "I am the captain of this misadventure, / and he the loyal shipmate who stayed by my side," revealing that their friendship, whatever else it involves, is also based on Pylades' courage and loyalty—his virtues.

In the first instance, this represents Orestes' own view of Pylades, whose friend he would not be if he found nothing admirable in his character. Aristotle makes just this point when he writes that we are all drawn to what is good or pleasant "for us"—what we, as a matter of fact, find good and pleasant. But, he continues, what is good or pleasant for us is not necessarily what is good or pleasant in itself—naturally or objectively good or pleasant. And since he believes that virtue is the only thing that is good and pleasant in itself, he claims that only those who find virtue attractive are drawn to what is objectively good and pleasant. The rest of us, drawn to wealth, honor, or some other of "the goods that people usually fight over" or, we might add, taking the wrong feature to be a virtue, are not. Orestes, then, cannot truly be Pylades' friend unless Pylades' loyalty really is a virtue and not something that merely seems like a virtue to him.

Aristotle is absolutely correct: we can't be friends of people in whom we find nothing to appreciate. He also believes, though, that only a few features—the virtues— can be truly admired. Many recent philosophers have followed him but, as we shall see, they have, for many complex reasons, identified virtue almost exclusively with morality. They conclude, as a result, that "friendship is a moral good by its own nature [and] the life with such a good is, to that extent, an intrinsically moral life."

But that can't be right. Experience shows that morality is often irrelevant to, or even in conflict with, our love for our friends—not to mention the fact that most of us are much less clear about the nature of moral virtue than about the fact of our friendships. Also, not only do we love our friends despite their shortcomings but, some- times, we love them because of them: think of the self- importance or the forgetfulness that makes your friend so dear to you and so irritating to everyone else. That is part of what we mean when we say that we love our friends "for themselves": for Aristotle, that is to say we love them for their virtues. I think he is wrong, but reversing his view in some respects can point us in the right direction.

The virtues exist objectively for Aristotle, and recognizing them in another is the spark of friendship: I want to be your friend because of the virtues that you already possess. But although we can agree that friends love one another for features they admire, we need not think that these must be only the virtues of morality or even the broader range Aristotle had in mind. Your sense of humor may well be crucial to our friendship, although for Aristotle it is an accidental feature of your personality and could only lead to a pleasure-*philia*; the same is true of your taste in music, books, clothes, and who knows what else. At the same time, the features I admire in you are, *for me*, but not necessarily for others, part of who you are: I may think that you losing your sense of humor has turned you into a significantly different person and destroyed our friendship, even though this loss—and your having a sense of humor at all in the first place—may be irrelevant to other friends of yours. What draws me to you may even be just what someone else may find indifferent or even unattractive: "Why is a certain peculiarity, a certain imperfection, indifferent or baneful in one person but enchanting in someone else?" Finally—here comes the reversal of Aristotle's view—we are more likely to be friends not because we recognize in one another some independently acknowledged virtues but because we take the features we admire in one another, whatever they are, to be virtues, whether or not they are such in the abstract. Your willingness to take orders and your ability to execute them unquestioningly, for example, might well make us friends if we belong to the same criminal gang: even the vicious have friends.

Transforming Aristotle in that way preserves much of what he says about the best kind of *philia*. But it also raises further questions. What is the difference between loving you for yourself and loving you for your generosity, your good looks, your sense of humor, or (a favorite philosophical example) for your yellow hair? Why can't I say that I love you for your money? Why is it that whenever I try to explain why I love you, no matter how much I say, I always feel that I have left the most important thing unspoken? How, if at all, is friendship related to virtue and morality? And what is that most important thing, the self, which seems to be the only real object of our love but is always left unspoken? Aristotle had a substantive conception of human nature: he identified it with our virtues. That allowed him to say that to love our friends for themselves is to love them for their virtues and that friendship, inseparable from virtue as it is, can never lead us astray. But most people today would not accept Aristotle's view of human nature: in fact, we can't even seem to agree whether there is such a thing as a human nature at all—or, if there is one, on what it is. And without such a conception, what can we say about friendship?

ACCORDING TO MODERN PHILOSOPHY, THERE ISN'T much worth saying about friendship at all, in part because many modern philosophers adopted Aristotle's answers despite disagreeing with him on human nature. But another reason can be found in what happened when Christianity, rather than pagan philosophy, presented itself as the best guide to the good life.

A crucial aspect of Aristotle's account was that whether perfect or imperfect, whether based on virtue, benefit, or pleasure, *philia* had always been a partial and preferential relationship. Those to whom one pledged oneself were by necessity few and a vanishingly small segment of the world and were to be treated differently from everybody else. But that created a serious problem for Christian thought, which distinguished sharply between the partiality of *philia* or *amicitia,* on the one hand, and the universality of Christian love—*agapê* or *caritas*—on the other.

That friendship is a partial relationship may seem so perfectly natural to us that it hardly seems worth mentioning, but it posed a deadly serious problem for Christian theology because it was in direct conflict with Christianity's radical and, at least in its origins, subversive ideal of universal love. When Jesus announced that the commandment to love one's neighbor as oneself was second only to the obligation to love God with all one's heart, soul, mind, and strength, he did away with the old idea, both biblical and pagan, that the neighbor, as one might have expected, was part of one's own—one's own family, neighborhood, tribe, state, or religion.

That idea, like the principle of helping one's friends and harming one's enemies that often went with it, was repugnant to the doctrine (though often not to the practice) of Christianity. Christian love is supposed to be a reflection of the love of God. The love of an infinite being, who loves everything and everyone unconditionally, translated into the earth's finite realm, becomes love for everyone God loves. And that is absolutely everyone—including, in particular, one's enemies—in loving whom one ultimately loves God himself. Friendship, though, unlike Christian love, involves loving some people more than the rest of the world, toward which, though not necessarily ill-disposed, friends may remain more or less emotionally indifferent. Friendship and Christian love seem profoundly incompatible with each other, and their conflict underlies the continuing clash between the partiality of friendship and the universal claims of both religious morality and—as we will see in the next chapter—its modern philosophical descendants during the Enlightenment and beyond.

There have been exceptions. The suspiciousness with which the monastics and ascetics of the early Christian era viewed friendship contrasts sharply with the popular story of Saints Perpetua and Felicitas, martyred and dying together as they exchanged the kiss of peace during the third century BC, and with the remarkably moving poems St. Paulinus of Nola (354–431 AD) wrote to his friend Ausonius. Here is part of one:

> *Through all chances that are given to mortals,*
> *And through all fates that be,*
> *So long as this close prison shall contain me,*
> *Yea, though a world shall sunder me and thee,*

Thee shall I hold, in every fiber woven,
Not with dumb lips, nor with averted face
Shall I behold thee, in my mind embrace thee,
Instant and present, thou, in every place.

The official attitude of early Christianity toward friendship, however, was crucially shaped by St. Augustine's metaphysical and practical misgivings about it. Augustine (354–430 AD) was of course as keenly aware of its pleasures as he was aware of every earthly delight. Here is how he describes his own relationship to his circle of friends in the years before his conversion:

> We could talk and laugh together and exchange small acts of kindness. We could join in the pleasure that books can give. We could be grave or gay together. If we sometimes disagreed, it was without spite, as a man might differ with himself, and the rare occasions of dispute were the very spice to season our usual accord. Each of us had something to learn from the others and something to teach in return. If any were away, we missed them with regret and gladly welcomed them when they came home.

Augustine clearly loved his friends for themselves. But after his conversion, it was precisely in that kind of love that he located a temptation to sin and not, as the ancients had thought, an incitement to virtue. He certainly believed that we must love everything on earth—not only friends and enemies but the rest of God's creation as well.

Yet these were to be loved not for themselves but only as a means to the love of God. For whatever is good and beautiful in the world (and that, for Augustine, is everything) is simply a reflection of God's own love and goodness, and we should use it to remind ourselves of his own far greater splendor. The only object of true love, the only thing that can be loved for itself, for its own sake, is God himself. "What madness," he writes, "to love a man as something more than human! . . . to love a man who was mortal as though he were never to die." To love human beings in that way is to treat them as gods: it is the sin of idolatry.

Augustine may have removed friendship from its pagan pedestal, but as a means to the love of God, he still found a suitably limited place for it in the Christian world. The nineteenth-century philosopher Søren Kierkegaard, in whom Augustine's reservations found their most extraordinary expression, would have none of it. To him friendship was a form of sensuality, a species of self-love, a virtue of paganism, a "glittering vice." The only genuine love is love of the neighbor, a love that refuses every distinction: the neighbor is the "next" human being and "the next human being is every other human being . . . When you open the door which you shut in order to pray to God, the first person you meet when you go out is your neighbor whom you *shall* love." Christian love is addressed to absolutely everyone: "Love of one's neighbor . . . is self-renouncing love, and self-renunciation casts out preferential love just as it casts out self-love." Kierkegaard saw, correctly, that friendship is a matter of personal inclination and choice and it is

just for that reason that he concluded that it is an enslave-
ment to passion. He takes charity, by contrast, to be a
moral obligation and for that reason a manifestation of
freedom.

Within the Christian tradition, by far the warmest welcome to friendship was issued by the theory and practice
of the Cistercian monasteries of twelfth-century Britain—
by St. Bernard of Clairvaux, St. Anselm, and, especially,
St. Aelred, abbot of the Monastery of Rievaulx. Aelred,
although sensitive to the practical and sensual dangers of
close relationships, especially within a monastic setting,
was passionately devoted to friendship despite its pagan
pedigree: "Nothing more sacred is striven for, nothing
more difficult is discovered, nothing more sweet experienced, and nothing more profitable possessed . . . and
scarcely any happiness whatever can exist among mankind
without the friendship of the spirit." Deeply influenced by
Cicero, Aelred adopted the Roman author's definition of
amicitia as "mutual harmony in affairs human and divine
coupled with benevolence and charity." He also followed
Cicero, and through him Aristotle, and gave their three-
fold classification a Christian turn. The "spiritual friendship" he praised was not to be confused with its "carnal"
and "worldly" forms: "The carnal springs from mutual harmony in vice; the worldly is enkindled by the hope of gain;
and the spiritual is cemented by similarity of life, morals,
and pursuits among the just."

Although Aelred also agreed with Cicero and Aristotle
that only the virtuous can be genuine friends, he devised

an ingenious yet moving way of reconciling pagan and Christian doctrine. Before the Fall, he wrote, when human nature was still unsullied, to love the virtuous was in fact to love everyone, as charity requires, since everyone was virtuous then. Before the Fall, friendship and charity coincided, but

> after the Fall of the first man, when with the cooling of charity concupiscence made secret inroads and caused private good to take precedence over the common weal, it corrupted the splendor of friendship and charity through avarice and envy . . . From that time the good distinguished between charity and friendship, observing that love ought to be extended even to the hostile and perverse, while no union of will and ideas can exist between the good and wicked. And so friendship which, like charity, was first preserved among all by all, remained according to the natural law among the few good.

In friendship, Aelred saw nothing less than an anticipation of heavenly bliss, the earthly aspect of "the eternal enjoyment by which we shall enjoy one another in heaven, as the angels enjoy one another, in pure unity of mind."

Aelred's trusting and generous nature, so obvious in his writings and in the accounts we have of his life, allowed him to believe that some human beings were good enough to justify their friendship for one another without transgressing against the love of God. But the Cistercian influence on the rest of Christianity did not survive the twelfth century. Even St. Thomas Aquinas, who offered in the following century an Aristotelian defense of friendship in his *Summa Theologica*, thinking of it as closely connected to virtue and repeating the Aristotelian distinction between "friendship for the useful, for the delightful, and for the virtuous," was unable to integrate it smoothly into Christian doctrine, which, on the whole, continued to view it with suspicion. That suspiciousness, as we shall see, was inherited, for secular reasons, by modern philosophy. It is now time to leave the ancient and medieval worlds behind and follow friendship in its modern guise.

Chapter 2

"A SORT OF SECESSION"
The Emergence of Modern Friendship

IN JANUARY 2001, HIS LAST MONTH AS PRESIDENT, BILL Clinton offered an unconditional pardon to the financier Marc Rich. Rich had been living in Switzerland as a fugitive from American justice since 1983, having been indicted for evading more than $48 million in taxes and charged with sixty-five counts of tax fraud and various other offenses. He had also been charged with illegal oil trading with Iran in 1979–1980, when the two countries were involved in the hostage crisis at the American embassy in Tehran that occupied much of the Carter presidency. Although granting pardons is an absolute prerogative of the president according to American law, Clinton's decision was universally criticized because his only reason for the pardon seemed to be Rich's ex-wife's generous contributions to Clinton's presidential library. Clinton's action was a case of pure patronage and became the subject of a serious investigation. As it turned out, no evidence of a direct connection between Mrs. Rich's gifts and the pardon could be established, and Clinton escaped yet another bout with the US judicial system.

In October 2005, Clinton's successor, George W. Bush, nominated his personal lawyer, Harriet Miers, for a seat in the United States Supreme Court—a decision the *New York Times* described as "very much in character with the president's tendency to reward familiarity and loyalty over independence and a reputation for excellence." Bush's choice was universally ridiculed, and when Miers's judicial record—or rather its absence—became an embarrassment even to the US Senate's most conservative members, Bush withdrew his nomination and eventually named another judge in her place. It would not be an exaggeration to say that both President Bush and Harriet Miers were literally laughed out of court. Ability and achievement, not friendship or other personal connections, are supposed to determine how one advances in society.

Yet in 1623, James I of England named George Villiers, who had risen through the ranks of the British nobility at an unprecedented pace, Duke of Buckingham. In virtue of his new title, Villiers, who only seven years earlier had been a commoner, became not just the single most powerful man in England, as he already was, but also the highest-ranking British subject outside the royal family. Though remarkable in many ways, Villiers owed his advancement much less to his abilities than to his good looks and charming manners, which had completely captivated the king's fancy. Pathetic and arrogant at the same time, James had long ago confessed to his privy councillors, according to Sir Francis Bacon, that he "loved the Earl of Buckingham more than any other man, and more than all those who were present—and not, as they might have supposed, because of any defect in his nature: 'For Jesus Christ had done just what he was doing . . . and just as Christ had his John, so he, James, had his George.'" By 1624, Buckingham's income from the gifts, lands, and privileges with which James had showered him was officially £20,000 per annum "and quite possibly a good deal more"—certainly not much less and perhaps considerably more than the £30,000 allocated to the entire British navy, of which he was then the lord admiral, and which consisted of no fewer than thirty-five ships.

The details of Buckingham's relationship to James remain tantalizingly ambiguous, but it is clear that, whatever else they may have been to each other, they were also friends. Yet unlike the cases of Clinton and Bush centuries later, no one disputed the king's (or anyone's) right to favor one's political or financial supporters or reward one's friends. Buckingham himself did not always have an easy time of it. Increasingly, he came to be excoriated in the popular ballads of the time: he was likened both to Piers Gaveston, the notorious (if perhaps misunderstood) favorite of Edward II, and to Hugh Despencer, Gaveston's successor in Edward's favor, prompting James, when he learned of it, to exclaim, "If he Spencer, I Edward II . . . I had rather be no king than such a one as King Edward II." The main reason for Buckingham's unpopularity, though, was his corruption, the extraordinary extent of which nevertheless did not prevent him either from retaining James's favor or from becoming the favorite of Charles I as well once the Prince of Wales inherited his father's throne. Buckingham's case was unusual only because of the direct involvement of the king, the magnitude of his rewards, and the extent of his own corruption. In all other respects, it was quite typical of his time.

Which is to say that, in early modern Britain, friendship was inseparable from favoritism, patronage, and clientage. It was mainly through one's friends—through their personal, financial, and political support—that one achieved worldly success:

> In this lost world . . . it was through gifts, not salaries, that one hoped to make one's fortune; through patronage, not open competition, that one endeavored to make one's way in life; and through the praise of loyal friends, not impartial critics, that one aspired to establish an enduring reputation.

As the historian Keith Thomas has pointed out, friends were fundamentally of three kinds: "relatives by blood and marriage, who were informal providers of aid and advice . . . allies, backers, associates: persons on whose support one could rely in times of need; . . . [and those who embodied] the more general social friendship which arose out of propinquity. This, too, was usually of a practical kind." In all these cases, "friends were valued because they were useful. One did not necessarily have to *like* them."

This stark picture, which identifies friendship in early modern Britain (and many other parts of Europe) with

Aristotle's benefit-based *philia*, needs to be qualified: even though one did not have to like one's friends, it is certain that many actually did. Yet, even qualified in this way, the picture nevertheless strikes us as thoroughly foreign. We might sometimes describe people who help us in various ways as friends: "A friend can get me tickets to the concert" is true even if we are never in touch except when I need tickets or she needs help with her Greek. Still, it is difficult for us to imagine that relationships based above all on financial interests, political expediency, and public advancement could have much to do with friendship, especially close friendship as we understand it today. What happened to the nature of friendship between James I's time and our own?

ARISTOTLE'S CONCEPTION OF FRIENDSHIP WAS STILL dominant during the early modern period. Although the Aristotelian tradition did acknowledge that *philia* included private relationships, the connection between virtue and public accomplishment in the ancient world was close enough that the relationships of the virtuous were played out, for the most part, in the open. These relationships, moreover, were closely associated with the public domain of politics and statesmanship, which throughout antiquity as well as during the early modern period was regarded as the sphere of higher human activity, in contrast to the private realm of household and family. Aristotle's view is characteristic: "Even if the good is the same for an individual and for a city, that of the city is obviously a greater and more complete thing to obtain and preserve. For while the good for an individual is desirable, what is good for a people or for cities is nobler and more godlike." Politics was inseparable from military affairs: according to Aristotle, again, "The activity of the practical virtues is in politics or war," and Cicero, too, connected friendship and war: true friendship, he writes, brings with it both honor and glory.

At the very end of the sixteenth century, however, friendship began to be transformed from a public into a private good. The transition is marked by the contrast between two works that appeared within a few years of each other.

One is Edmund Spenser's *The Faerie Queene*, whose first three books appeared in 1590 and were issued again, with the addition of three more, in 1598. The poem is, among many other things, an allegory of the various virtues. Each one of its books is devoted to a particular virtue, in the following order: Holiness, Temperance, Chastity, Friendship, Justice, and Courtesy. There is an (imprecise) echo of Aristotle in Spenser's distinction between three kinds of love,

> to weet
> *The deare affection vnto kindred sweet,*
> *Or raging fire of loue to woman kind,*
> *Or zeale of friends combynd with vertues meet,*

but what is most important for us to note is the place of friendship within Spenser's catalogue of virtues:

In the first three books of the *Faerie Queene* Spenser is primarily interested in the virtue of the individual as such: his holiness, his temperance, his chastity. . . . Beginning with the Fourth Book he turns to a more definite study of the individual in relations to other individuals. With his classical background it was reasonable that he should put friendship next. Aristotle had upheld the thesis that all social relationships grow out of friendship.

FRIENDSHIP IS FOR SPENSER A UNIVERSAL FORCE, THE daughter of Concord and the sister of Peace, and provides the ground of Concord's ability to hold not just individuals but groups, states, even the whole universe together:

> Concord she cleeped was in common reed,
> Mother of blessed Peace and Friendship trew;
> . . . .
> By her the heaven is in his course contained,
> And all the world in state unmoved stands,
> As their Almightie maker first ordained,
> And bound them with inviolable bands;
> Else would the waters overflow the lands,
> And fire devoure the ayre, and hell them quight,
> But that she holds them with her blessed hands.
> She is the nourse of pleasure and delight,
> And unto Venus grace the gate doth open right.

For Spenser, as for several ancient thinkers, friendship "encompasses the harmonious order appearing in the relations of the planets, the placement of the elements, and the safety of commonwealths, as well as the bonds uniting groups and individuals." Although Aristotle had rejected the relevance of this cosmological view to his ethical concern with *philia*, for him, too, *philia* belonged primarily to the domain of the public. And it is Aristotle's conception of *philia* that underlies Spenser's poem, addressed as it was to "an aristocratic and upper-middle-class audience in a self-consciously archaizing manner, thereby participating in the decorative revival of feudal trappings that characterized Elizabethan courtly ritual." But while Spenser was, so to speak, trying to consolidate the past, Michel de Montaigne was constructing the future. His great essay on friendship was published in the first volume of his *Essays* in 1580, to which two more volumes were added in 1588, and reissued with the revisions Montaigne had been making to his copy of the second edition until his death, in 1595.

"Of Friendship" is an effort to account for Montaigne's close and intense relationship with Étienne de la Boétie, whose untimely death deprived him of one of the greatest joys in his life. It is a strange essay and also, apparently, a failure. It hardly touches La Boétie's life, character, and accomplishments, as we might naturally have expected, and nowhere else in the *Essays* do we find a concrete picture of the man. Never at a loss for words on any subject, Montaigne seems to have almost nothing to say about the person who was by far the most important in his life. He tells us that, had he lived longer, La Boétie's "natural gifts" (whatever they were) would have enabled him to produce much better works than his youthful treatise, *On Voluntary Servitude*. He describes him as "infinitely" more virtuous and capable, and a better friend, than he himself could ever be. And he defends La Boétie's politics by saying that although, truthful as he was, he had meant the apparently subversive ideas of his treatise seriously, he was also "religiously" devoted to the laws of his land, a perfect citizen who despised civil unrest. That is ludicrously inadequate as an explanation of Montaigne's exorbitant claims for La Boétie's virtues and the unique perfection of their friendship; and the rest of the *Essays*, which mention him quite sparsely, give us no further help.

On a descriptive level, La Boétie remains a cipher for reasons we shall discuss later. Everything Montaigne tells us about him is generic and vague, and fails to give him even a hint of the extraordinary individuality with which Montaigne himself emerges through the *Essays*. What Montaigne does emphasize, again and again, is the private nature of their relationship, a friendship that is theirs and theirs alone: it "has no other model than itself, and can be compared only with itself." It binds them to each other and to no one else; it cannot even be extended to a third person, "for this perfect friendship I speak of is indivisible: each one gives himself so wholly to his friend that he has nothing left to distribute elsewhere." Theirs, he makes clear, is a friendship that had nothing to do with public considerations or political achievements. If anything, this friendship effectively removed Montaigne himself from the public sphere, which he abandoned (though perhaps less so than he claimed) in order to devote himself to writing. Retiring to his library and surrounded in great part by the books La Boétie had left him in his will, he originally undertook the *Essays* for the sake of their friendship, in order to give his friend the "place" for which he had asked Montaigne as he lay dying.

Montaigne tells us that he and his friend became completely intertwined—so intimately, in fact, that at some point they ceased being two:

> I know his soul as well as mine . . . Everything actually being in common between [us]—wills, thoughts, judgments, goods, wives, children, honor, and life—and [our] relationship being that of one soul in two bodies, according to Aristotle's very apt definition, [we] can neither lend nor give anything to each other.

That one soul is the soul we come to know in the *Essays*, present in every bit of it, and a soul no one else can possess. For friendship, the *Essays* intimate, obtains only between individuals in all their particularity. Montaigne refuses to detail the proper character, behavior, and obligations of friends in general as traditional authors on the subject from Aristotle on had done, because he knows that no friendship can provide a pattern or example for others to follow: "It has no model other than itself." Example, in any case, he considers "a hazy mirror, reflecting all things in all ways," and the function of Montaigne's own example, the self-portrait that emerges from the *Essays*, is most equivocal: those who might want to learn from him would have to imitate his own manner of learning from others, "by contrast rather than by example, and by flight rather than by pursuit." To imitate Montaigne is to be as different from him as he was different from those who had served him as his own examples.

By giving friendship a place in the private realm and removing it from the arena of war and politics, which were all male prerogatives, Montaigne's approach made friendship theoretically available to women as well, despite the fact that his personal view of the matter continued to fit the ancient mold. He wrote that if a genuine friendship between a man and a woman (he fails to imagine that two women could also be friends),

> free and voluntary, could be built up, in which not only would the souls have this complete enjoyment, but the bodies would also share in the alliance, so that the entire man would be engaged, it is certain that the resulting friendship would be fuller and more complete. But this sex in no instance has yet succeeded in attaining it, and by the common agreement of the ancient schools is excluded from it.

In this case, his practical opinions didn't manage to track his theoretical insights. But the turn away from a public conception of friendship, as philosophers and writers from Aristotle to Edmund Spenser had taken it, had been most forcefully made.

OF COURSE, MONTAIGNE DID NOT BRING ABOUT SUCH A monumental shift by himself, and in a single essay, no less.

The place of friendship in the private realm was cemented gradually, in large part through the broad economic, political, and philosophical developments of the eighteenth century. In particular, as the sociologist Allan Silver has argued, the "abhorrence of instrumentality in personal relations and the theoretical sundering of the personal and the impersonal . . . was seminally formulated by the Scottish Enlightenment," that remarkable intellectual, literary, and scientific movement centered in Glasgow and Edinburgh, whose main figures included among others the philosophers David Hume and Adam Smith, the poet Alice Rutherford, and James Watt, the inventor of the steam engine.

Crucial to the removal of friendship from the public realm was the emergence of the market, which opened a gap between instrumental transactions on the one hand and personal relations on the other, setting interest and affection apart. In pre-commercial societies, where danger is ever-present, Adam Smith wrote, family members, who, after one's own self are "the natural objects of [one's] warmest affections," find it necessary to band together primarily for practical considerations, particularly "for their common defence." According to the historian Lawrence Stone, early modern Britain, which was still a pre-commercial society, saw an "extraordinary amount of casual inter-personal physical and verbal violence." Friends—allies, clients, or patrons—were likely to abandon you when it suited them; families, organized on the principle that those outside them were not to be trusted, presented a closed and violent front to the outside world. Murder and physical violence were much more likely to occur between families than, as is often the case today, within them: "The family was more a unit for the perpetration of crime . . . than a focus for crime . . . [making it] tempting to argue that the family that slayed together, stayed together." Naturally, other, more humane relationships also existed: Alan Bray, for example, has documented the existence of deep, long-lasting friendships among both men and women, some of them passionate, during that period. But these relationships, which were often sanctioned by the church, were intensely private, and as far as we can tell, they were almost exclusively limited to the aristocracy.

In commercial societies, by contrast, issues of practical interest belong to the public domain of the market while our ties to those closest to us in the private realm are rooted in love and friendship. These relationships, although they have practical aspects as well, always contain a core that is detached from instrumental considerations. It is only as our relations stretch further into the public domain and extend to progressively larger circles of people that they become progressively attenuated into relations of contract and exchange.

Smith's approach to affection was different from Aristotle's. To him, affection is founded on sympathy, our ability to imagine ourselves in the place of another and share their feelings, if perhaps less intensely, when they find themselves in happy or unhappy circumstances. It is on sympathy that morality is grounded, for, by sharing in another's feelings, we come to understand our commonalities and treat others as we would treat ourselves. Smith was optimistic enough to hope that commercial relations might, ideally, be capable of uniting individuals into a civil society that would be not only economically but also morally justified and in which, overcoming the doubts Immanuel Kant was to express some years later, affection might one day apply universally. That raised the hope that affection, and with it the claims of friendship, might in the future be reconciled with the demands of morality. But Smith's hope, which was central to the Enlightenment's aspirations, was to be crushed by the increasing weight of the market's reliance on behavior and institutions that were not just independent of, but directly antithetical to, affection and friendship.

Even under ideal conditions, though, such a hope would be in vain: affection, from the most intense to the most casual, can only reach so far. Aristotle had already pointed out that it is extremely difficult to spend a lot of time together, as friends must, with more than a few people. Not only impractical, devoting oneself seriously to a large number of people is also psychologically costly and confusing. Not only that: it is a fact that we can feel affection only for people with whom we are directly connected, to whom we are related as one individual to another. A direct connection doesn't always require a face-to-face meeting. It can also be established through letters or portraits, sometimes even through a third person's account of what someone is like: what is always needed is a concrete conception of another person. Friendship—unlike charity and like erotic love—can't be impersonal. You can't love all the virtuous, whoever they happen to be. You might wish to become a friend of those who share your interests, but you can't actually become their friend unless you get to know and like them, which is not at all guaranteed by a similarity of concerns. In all its forms, love is addressed to particular individuals. We say that we like our friends for their "particular" features or for "the way" they exhibit them because love is focused on what distinguishes each one of us from other people, not on what we have in common with them. It is impossible to love someone who is no more to us than an abstract presence.

The range of friendship is necessarily and, in the case of close relationships, severely limited: friends recognize in one another something they don't find in the rest of the world. We choose our friends, as C. S. Lewis saw, because (though not only because) we "have in common some insight or interest or even taste which the others do not share," which is why every friendship is also "a sort of secession, even a rebellion . . . a pocket of potential resistance." The essential partiality of friendship is the most fundamental obstacle to modeling our social and political relationships, as Smith and others had hoped to do, upon it.

SMITH'S IDEAL—THE POSSIBILITY OF A POLITICS THAT is based on private friendship, the hope that friendship and "secession" needn't necessarily go together—has nevertheless reemerged among philosophers of different stripes in recent years. In *The Politics of Friendship*, for example, Jacques Derrida points out that the Aristotelian tradition has located genuine friendship only among men with significant public achievements, socially and intellectually superior both to women and to men of average status and abilities, not to mention slaves and "the wicked." He also remarks that the traditional account of "the friend" depends on a collateral understanding of "the enemy" and an unbridgeable distinction between them. Derrida is deeply suspicious of that distinction, which, in line with his overall scheme, reflects the binary distinctions (physical/mental, speech/writing, I/other, original/copy, and others) that underlie, by his account, the traditional "logocentric" or "metaphysical" approach of Western philosophy. Throughout his book, he gestures toward a new conception of friendship, which, freed from its exclusionary commitments, might provide the basis of a new politics of democracy.

Derrida doesn't have much to say about what such a politics would look like. In this he is not alone, and the reason, I suspect, is that little can in fact be said about it: however valuable friendship may be, it can't be generalized as its application to politics would require. Even if the members of small political movements can be friends, such a bond is bound to break down when applied to the state at large. Even if, unlikely as it is, the distinction between friend and enemy might one day be overcome, the contrast between those who are friends and those who are not will not.

Smith's hope has also received new life as a result of Carol Gilligan's widely influential book, *In a Different*

Voice. Gilligan, a psychologist, argued that, for women, care, which focuses on particular individuals, is considerably more important than impartial justice, the main concern of men. Her thesis, which she modified in subsequent work, inspired feminist philosophers to look for ways of supplementing, or even replacing, the "dominant theories" of morality with what has come to be known as "an ethics of care." The feminist argument is that, by relying exclusively on justice, impartiality, and general rules, traditional moral philosophy has ignored the value of care, interpersonal connections, and contextual flexibility that are important to women, though by no means necessarily limited to them. That is true. But the question is whether these two approaches to human life can be combined in the political realm without generating irresoluble conflicts.

We care for people who for one reason or another matter to us more than the rest of the world. The relation of a mother to her child, who is comparatively or totally powerless, unable to pursue its own interests without her help, is paradigmatic for this approach to morality and politics. As the philosopher Virginia Held remarks,

> Every person starts out as a child dependent on those providing us care, and we remain interdependent with others in thoroughly fundamental ways throughout our lives. That we can think and act as if we were independent depends on a network of social relations making it possible for us to do so. And our relations are part of what constitutes our identity.

By itself, that is not new. It is the guiding idea of "communitarian" political theorists and philosophers, sometimes inspired by Hegel, who reject several views that accompany liberal thought. According to liberalism, individual identity is largely independent of interpersonal and social relations, and the principles of justice that govern social and political behavior are more or less common to all political unions. Communitarians, by contrast, argue that different societies may well have different standards of justice because these are molded by the nature, history, and values of each. Individuals are enmeshed in their society, and their identity is essentially connected and, to a large extent, generated by their social and cultural context. They also believe that political argument and criticism can't proceed from outside each community but must take account of the ways and traditions that inform each particular society. What is new in feminism is that it envisages more complex and less stable relations than the traditional lists—family, neighborhood, clan, tribe, church, and nation—of communitarian thought, which often rank women and members of various minorities below men. It appeals instead to smaller, less formal, and less hierarchical communities, like support groups or circles of friends: it is there, the argument goes, that much of human identity is forged.

We all in fact belong to several different overlapping communities—some hierarchical, others not—that are essential to our identity. Some of our relationships to these communities are "ascribed," that is, not the result of a choice on our part, for example, relationships based on age, family background, sex, race, and ethnicity. Others are "achieved," that is, chosen in light of our abilities and the contingencies of our situation: occupation, for instance, is one; marriage (in the West, today) is another; friendship another still. Feminism pays particular attention to friendship because it can be deeply liberating for those who don't fit well into society's existing structures: friendships can be agents of social change.

However, the usefulness of taking private friendship as a model for moral, political, or social relations more generally is limited. If we must know directly the individuals we care for, impartiality has to take priority when we are facing groups too large and complex to be sustained by the bonds of personal affection and commitment. If we can ever hope to extend fundamental—human—rights to everyone in the world and expect them to do the same for us, we *have* to try to think impartially. Bias and prejudice may always lurk in our attitudes—it is exceedingly difficult to be aware of all the things we value or abhor as a result of the particularities of our situation—but that is a reason to think harder about ourselves in light of what we come to know about these others.

But another sort of bias—if, of course, "bias" is the right word for our commitments to those, and only those, who mean the most to us—is absolutely inevitable: these are commitments that we neither can nor should want to avoid. Some, like helping our friends before thinking about strangers, are perfectly conscious. Others may be beyond our control: friends, for example, tend to be more charitable regarding one another's defects and more generous regarding their virtues than might seem "rationally" appropriate; friendship, which, as we will see, on occasion conflicts with morality, can also conflict with our epistemic standards. And although we may want the moral and political principles of a just state to apply to everyone, we would never want the principles that underwrite our own friendships, however perfect these are, to govern the relationships of others, even if it were possible for them to do so. That friendship can be a sort of secession or rebellion is not one of its problems but one of its virtues: it can "provide social support for people who are idiosyncratic, whose unconventional values and deviant life styles make them victims of intolerance . . . Out of the unconventional living it helps to sustain there often arise influential forces for social change." But friendship, even—or especially—now that it is firmly in the private realm, simply cannot serve as the bedrock of a new, more just kind of politics.

OVERALL, MODERN MORAL PHILOSOPHY, ROOTED IN the Enlightenment, has disagreed. Modern philosophers have discussed friendship in one of two contexts. We just explored the first: that of the possibility of a politics grounded in friendship. The second is broader and more influential. To many modern philosophers, the main issue surrounding friendship is the fact that it often comes into conflict with considerations of morality, justice, and impartiality. When it does, moralism—the view that moral (and political) values are the most important or even the only values of life—dictates that its values always take precedence. But it is sometimes impossible to decide which type of consideration should receive priority.

We encountered Søren Kierkegaard in the previous chapter urging the superiority of the Christian love of one's neighbor to any form of friendship. We must agree that, as he puts it, being preferential means to make distinctions. For him to distinguish one person from the rest of the world, to love one in preference to others, is "a mockery of God." On that, however, we must disagree. Making distinctions, far from being a blemish, is one of friendship's glories, and its equivocal hues resist the best efforts of our philosophy to paint it over with the stark monochromes of morality. Moralism, which permeates both current philosophy and public discourse, is, as we shall later see, not true to life.

C. S. Lewis thought that modernity rejected the ancients' seriousness about friendship because of "Romanticism" and "the exaltation of Sentiment." But neither Romanticism nor the exaltation of sentiment can account for its neglect; the ancients weren't nearly as otherworldly as Lewis thought, and Tennyson's *In Memoriam*, which he considered the last major poem of our time devoted to friendship, is hardly short on sentiment. Rather, it was the exaltation of a new kind of reason, common to everyone, which, before Romanticism came into the picture, made friendship an unlikely subject for modern philosophy. Modern moral thought centered its attention on the impartial principles that govern our obligations to one another in the abstract, our duties and responsibilities to the world at large and, in so doing, turned away from the narrower, partial, and preferential relationships of which friendship was often the emblem.

The central and liberating aspiration of modern moral and political philosophy, especially since the Enlightenment, has been to make every human being morally salient to every other. Its task has been to overcome and render irrelevant the specific differences that earlier times anchored in nature and used to justify the inhuman treatment of others. It is a task that is far from complete, in both theory and practice. "Christian" and "Muslim," "Uighur" and "Han," "Sunni" and "Shia," even "male" and "female" are categories still powerful enough to support and justify the most extreme forms of cruelty and oppression. The moral treatise that will convince the world to move beyond them is still unwritten, and whether it can ever be written is very much an open question, especially since the two main schools of modern moral philosophy have diametrically opposed conceptions of morality.

Kantianism holds that moral value depends on acting for the right reasons, whatever the consequences; Consequentialism locates moral worth in acting with the aim of bringing about the best possible outcome for the greatest number of people. Despite their differences, however, they are at one on a more fundamental issue: all moral behavior must be impartial and universally applicable. To treat others impartially, we must not give preference to some people over others because of specific or idiosyncratic features they share with those others only and not with everybody else. Moral decisions must be made only on the basis of those characteristics that every human being shares with every other—it is these features that give us all the same rights and obligations. For the Kantians, the common feature that joins human beings together is rationality; for the Consequentialists, it is our need and desire for well-being. Nothing short of these two features—being, for example, male or female, Sunni or Shia—is a relevant moral consideration. Sunnis should not be treated in a particular way—whether for good or ill—simply because they are Sunni; to treat them morally, we must abstract from all ethnic and religious features and consider only what we would do for any human being that is part of an oppressed group.

Friendship, however, is inconceivable without thinking that it is perfectly all right to treat some people differently from the way we treat everyone else, to give them preference and pride of place, simply because they are our friends. How could such an inherently partial relationship fit within a modern conception of morality any more than it fits political aspirations? Not that efforts to find it a place within morality have been lacking: both Kantian and consequentialist philosophers have tried to devise ways to include friendship among the moral goods. But, in the end, the unashamed preference we give our friends is likely to seem like an avatar of tribalism to modes of thought that require that we treat those closest to us as we would treat a stranger—or, to put the point more positively, to treat strangers as we would treat our own. The relationship of friendship to morality remains uneasy, and its role in moral philosophy is secondary at best. That's partly why it has been mostly a marginal issue for modern philosophy, which has generally assumed that the realm of morality exhausts the range of values that are important to human life.

But that, again, doesn't quite match our experience. The philosopher Harry Frankfurt puts the point well:

> For most people, the relevance of their moral obligations . . . is quite limited. What morality has to say concerning how to live and what to do is important, but its importance is often exaggerated; and in any case there are other important things to be said as well. I think that philosophers need to pay more attention to issues . . . that have to do with what people are to care about, with their commitments to ideals, and with the protean role in our lives of the various modes of love.

"Protean" is just the right word for love's role in our lives. It comes in the most various forms and has the most disparate effects upon us, by no means all of them good. Friendship is one of these forms and its own effects are much more complicated than envisaged by the Aristotelian tradition, which counts friendship as a moral virtue. On this question, C. S. Lewis is open-eyed and realistic: "Friendship (as the ancients saw) can be a school of virtue; but also (as they did not see) a school of vice. It is ambivalent. It makes good men better and bad men worse." Lewis was worried because friends are sometimes so impressed by their particular differences from the rest of the world in some respect or other, as friends sometimes are, that they consider themselves superior to others in every way and subject to different rules: "A circle of Friends can come to treat as 'outsiders' in a general (and derogatory) sense those who were properly outsiders for a particular purpose": they then turn into a claque and become oblivious to their own faults.

The danger that friendship may lead from legitimate distinction to illegitimate exclusion is real and the cause of many problems for both individuals and groups, both young and old. But friendship can also be "a school of vice" in another, more urgent way. A friendship may sometimes not simply permit or encourage but actually *require* attitudes or actions that can't be morally justified. The ethical problem has not one but two dimensions. When morality and preferential relationships are juxtaposed, they can conflict not only in how they evaluate the purpose of an activity but also in how they evaluate the means to achieve it: strict moralists might disapprove of my saving my friend rather than a stranger from drowning or, assuming they approve of my goal, may disapprove of the fact that I do so just because my friend is my friend and not because I can justify my choice by appeal to a moral principle. Similar thoughts have led two contemporary philosophers to make the point, which is too obvious to have been so blithely ignored, that friendship may sometimes involve immorality without for that reason ceasing to be valuable in its own right: "A friend helps you move house; a good friend helps you move a body."

As we all know, friendship and morality are not always at odds: a relationship based on immorality may only seem like a friendship but in reality be "mere collusion and cynical self-advancement." A particularly disturbing case is the relationship between Kim Philby—who, over thirty years of working for MI6, betrayed Great Britain to the Soviet Union and caused the death of no one knows exactly how many people—and his fellow spy, Nicholas Elliott. Philby used Elliott as a source of information that he passed on to the Soviets, but his affection for Elliott, according to the best evidence we have, seems to have been genuine. Their friendship extended to each other's family; they clearly enjoyed their many times together, which were by no means confined to discussing secrets that Philby was gathering for his own purposes; they told each other as much about themselves as their class background allowed; and they did each other favors: there was genuine feeling there. Was Philby just lying when he said that, contrary to what people thought, he was never laughing at his friends all the time that he was deceiving them? "I have always operated on two levels," he continued, "a personal level and a political one. When the two have come into conflict I have had to put politics first. The conflict can be very painful." And was Elliott, while interrogating Philby just before Philby's escape to Moscow in 1963, simply trying to draw him out when he said, "I understand you. I've been in love with two women at the same time. I'm certain that you were in the same situation in politics: you loved England and the Soviet Union at the same time"? It's impossible to think of Philby as a *good* friend to Elliott, whom he certainly used in the most shameful manner; but it also seems possible that he genuinely loved him. Is that believable? I can only say that it isn't unbelievable.

Even if Philby's deception was too deep and repulsive to coexist with friendship, not every friendship is canceled by immorality. Sometimes, a friendship that depends on immorality may still, for all that, be genuine and worthy of admiration, a genuine good for the people it binds to each other. We will examine such a case in Chapter 6. For now, we must turn to some other crucial features of friendship that complicate our overwhelmingly benign conception of it. These have been overlooked by most of our philosophical and historical approaches to friendship, but they emerge clearly through its various representations in the arts.

Chapter 3

A STRUCTURE OF THE SOUL
Friendship and the Arts

LONG BEFORE ARISTOTLE WAS EVEN BORN, HOMER'S *Iliad*, the story of the Greeks' siege of the city of Troy, had made the friendship of Achilles and Patroclus famous throughout the Greek world. And to this day, their devotion to each other is still at the heart of our everyday attitudes toward friendship—in our sense of its nature, of the acts that sustain or destroy it, of its importance to life. The relationship between the two heroes may not exhaust our picture of what friends can do for each other, but it still anchors our imagination and gives wing to our aspirations. It is still at the heart of our culture, even for those who may never have heard of it: it provides a standard that determines how genuine their own commitments to their friends happen to be. Achilles' desperate reaction to the utter catastrophe of Patroclus' death is paradigmatic: it has become the most extreme example of what one friend can expect of another and, in its extremity, it inspires our own behavior when we confront the slighter emergencies that everyday friendships inevitably involve.

The situation Achilles finds himself in is anything but a slight emergency, of course. Furious because he has been slighted in the division of Trojan plunder among leaders of the Greek armies, Achilles withdraws from the fighting. He allows Patroclus, to whom he gives his own armor, to enter the fray and advises him not to be reckless. Patroclus, however, does not heed Achilles' advice, risks more than he should, and is killed by Hector, the Trojan champion. Upon learning of his friend's death, "a black cloud of grief came shrouding over Achilles"—a grief matched, in fact outdone, only by his thirst for revenge: "You talk of food? I have no taste for food—what I really crave is slaughter and blood and the choking groans of men!" Almost mad with the pain of his loss, Achilles vows to avenge Patroclus, despite knowing full well the gods' decree that, were he to do so, his own end was sure to follow. But with Patroclus, whom he had loved as his "own life," gone, he feels that he has nothing more to lose: "My own death, I'll meet it freely." He challenges Hector to a duel, hurls himself upon him like a wild, bloodthirsty beast, drives his spear through Hector's neck and, contrary to every chivalric and religious custom of the time, desecrates his dead body by dragging it behind his chariot and leaving it unburied, fodder for dogs and vultures.

Achilles eventually understands that his brutal treatment of Hector's corpse had gone far beyond what revenge required, and he tempers his savage behavior. When

Priam, the king of Troy and Hector's father, comes to his tent and, on his knees, begs him to let Hector's family give him a proper burial, he realizes that the old man's grief for his dead son is of a piece with his own mourning for his friend. And so he and the old man weep together for their dead, and Achilles returns Hector's body to Priam, remaining alone with his pain and the knowledge that his own life is soon to end.

Achilles and Patroclus are not the only example of mythical or historic friends faced with questions of life and death. The Bible has given us the story of David and Jonathan, whose "soul was knit with the soul of David" and loved David "as himself," and on whose account he defied his own royal father, who actually tried to kill him for his disobedience. Greek tradition tells us that when Phintias, sentenced to death by Dionysius, the tyrant of Syracuse (fourth century BC), asked for leave to go home and settle his affairs, his friend, Damon, gladly offered to be executed in his place if Phintias failed to return. But Phintias did return, at the very last moment before Damon's execution, after escaping from the pirates who had abducted him in the meantime, causing his delay. His return saved Damon's life but also Phintias' own because, amazed by the friends' loyalty, the tyrant spared them both. In the medieval *Song of Roland*, when Roland's friend Olivier dies at the hands of the Saracens, Roland confesses, "Now that you are dead, it grieves me to remain alive," and, "full of grief and overcome with rage," he rushes madly at the enemy and loses his own life as a result. And there are similar episodes in the ancient Sumerian epic of Gilgamesh, the Greek tale of the tyrannicides Harmodius and Aristogeiton, the medieval romance of Amis and Amile, and many others: the mythology of friendship thrives on such sacrifices.

Different as they are from one another in so many ways, these stories all converge on one point: their heroes are *literally* heroes. They are larger than life, uncommon characters able to act in ways closed to most of the rest of us. They display their love for each other in battles or other extreme misfortunes and adversities, and they always stand ready to sacrifice themselves for each other's sake. When their relationship is hierarchical—Gilgamesh, Achilles, David, and Roland are superior in strength and standing than their companions—the lesser of the two usually dies and the one who remains, though overcome by grief, is spurred to new exploits and often meets his own death in the effort to avenge his friend. When the friends are equal, they may die together like Harmodius and Aristogeiton, or, like Damon and Phintias, they may both survive as a reward for their courage.

Heroic narratives generally unfold against a specific political or military background that was obvious to their original audience, though not often to their later readers. As one classical scholar has argued, in Achilles and Patroclus, we can see "a specific cultural formation, a type of heroic friendship which is better captured by terms like comrades-in-arms, boon companions, and the like." Perhaps that is right: such relationships may be possible only within a particular context, which is not available today, and we shouldn't think of them as paradigms of every kind of friendship. But even if we do, they are uncommonly rare and involve such extraordinary characters and events that our own friendships, no matter how important they may be to us, are bound to seem trivial in comparison. Moreover, they are essentially relationships between men, yet men—and warriors in particular—are (it goes without saying) not the only people who can be friends: women are friends with other women or with men, children are friends with one another or with adults, old people befriend each other or the young, and so can a good many others for whom such extreme sacrifice may be unthinkable. In any case, very few of us—including many present-day warriors—are likely to find ourselves in such demanding circumstances. And yet, dying for the sake of one's friend may perhaps be the noblest expression of friendship, and a friendship that leads to it may make the friends' lives altogether worth living.

What is it, though, that makes Achilles, Roland, and the rest capable of such an extraordinary sacrifice? How did they come to be so totally devoted to their friend? None of their stories has very much to say about the history of their friendships, their origin and development, their texture, the ordinary tangles of emotions, attitudes, motives, activities, and relations that may gradually lead to—or, for that matter, away from—the joyful embrace of self-sacrifice for another's sake. And one might say that they don't need to do so: the friends' sacrifice is on its own enough to demonstrate the depth of their love, whatever exactly it is that led up to it. Do we really need to know anything else?

Yes, we do, if we are to understand friendship more generally. First, since very few of us are ever going face the possibility of dying for our friends, we need to turn our attention to the less exalted and much more common manifestations of friendship that will never make such a demand of us. Second, because, as we will see, friendship depends less on what friends actually do than on the motives out of which they do it—motives that emerge gradually through the ordinary, seemingly inconsequential interactions of which all friendships, from the most casual to the most intense, consist.

Central as it may well be to our idealizations, the epic—and the war story more generally—is not the first place to look for a fuller understanding of friendship because it focuses exclusively on climactic events. But friendship, in its more everyday versions, is represented in other art forms as well. By looking at some of them and, through them, at some of friendship's less glamorous and extraordinary moments, we may form a different picture of its nature and importance.

AROUND THE YEAR 1524, THE FLORENTINE ARTIST Jacopo Pontormo composed a portrait of two men, one of whom is holding a page of a Latin manuscript while the other is pointing at it (Figure 1). The manuscript is legible. It is a page from Cicero's tribute to friendship, the dialogue *De Amicitia* ("On Friendship"), and the painting has

FIGURE I. JACOPO PONTORMO,
*Two Men with a Passage from Cicero's
"On Friendship"* (c. 1524)

come to be known as *Two Men with a Passage from Cicero's
"On Friendship."* Giorgio Vasari, the chronicler of Italian
Renaissance painting whose *Lives of the Painters* appeared
a few years after Pontormo painted this portrait, identified
one of the men as the son-in-law of the prosperous Florentine merchant Beccuccio Bicchieraio but confessed that
he never determined who the other man was. He also tells
us that the two men were Pontormo's friends. Beyond that,
though, the work is surrounded by unanswered questions.

Expanding on Vasari's account, one art historian has
suggested that the picture is a celebration of "Pontormo's

own circle of friends, perhaps . . . a group of men, including Pontormo, who read the classics together." Another points out that Cicero's *De Amicitia* is a fictional dialogue between Gaius Laelius, the great Roman general, orator, and man of letters of the second century BC, and his two sons-in-law: so, if one of the men in the picture is Beccuccio's son-in-law, why not the other as well, since we know that, as a matter of fact, Beccuccio had two married daughters? Looked at that way, the painting is a visual re-enactment of Cicero's dialogue, the two men addressing "the person who corresponds to the speaker of the words on friendship to which they point, that is, their father-in-law, in this case not Gaius Laelius but Beccuccio Bicchieraio." According to the first interpretation, the painting is a document of Florentine republican humanism, a celebration of the friendship that joined together one of the circles of Florence's educated elite. According to the second, it is, instead, a gesture of familial solidarity.

I mention these interpretations because, despite their sharp differences, both take it for granted that the painting is, in one way or another, about friendship. And although there is no reason to think that it isn't, asking if there is a reason to think that it is yields a surprising answer.

To see why, it will help to compare Pontormo's portrait with two other works. Anyone familiar with Western representational painting can tell at a glance, without any further information, that one represents an erotic episode (Figure 2) and the other a killing (Figure 3). The visual features of these paintings alone can show much of what they are about with considerable accuracy. And anyone with a little knowledge of iconography can be quite certain that the first picture portrays Mars, spent after an encounter with Venus, while the second is of Judith beheading Holofernes.

FIGURE 2. SANDRO BOTTICELLI,
Venus and Mars (c. 1485)

FIGURE 3. CARAVAGGIO,
Judith Beheading Holofernes (c. 1598)

What, though, would we able to say about the next two pictures (Figures 4, 5), no matter how well-versed we were in the history of art, just by looking at them?

One thing we certainly would *not* have reason to say is that every one of them is a picture of friends: none of their visual elements encourages such an interpretation. And why not? Because nothing these people are doing characterizes friendship any more than it characterizes a whole slew of other human relationships. Without their titles—Raphael's *Self-Portrait with a Friend* (Figure 4) and Ernst Kirchner's *Two Friends* (Figure 5)—we simply would not know what to make of them.

FIGURE 4. RAPHAEL,
Self-Portrait with a Friend (1518–1519)

FIGURE 5. ERNST KIRCHNER,
Two Friends (Zwei Freunde) (1924)

So too with Pontormo. We know what to make of his painting—to some extent, anyway—because of Cicero's text, which is not, strictly speaking, one of the portrait's visual features, and Vasari's account, which has nothing to do with its appearance. Standing next to another person (Figure 1), draping an arm over someone's shoulder (Figure 4), or embracing (Figure 5)—none of these actions suggests, on its own, that the people involved are friends. In Raphael's portrait, one friend rests his hand on the other's shoulder, as friends do—but only sometimes.

Some friends embrace each other, as they do in Kirchner's work—others, as in Pontormo's, don't. And sometimes a kiss, far from being an expression of friendship, is nothing less than the kiss of death (Figure 6). "We picture lovers face to face," C. S. Lewis once wrote, "but friends side by side; their eyes look ahead." Pontormo confirms it, but Degas shows that they don't have to (Figure 7). "Men and women can't be friends," says a popular commonplace, but Titian had no trouble including a woman in his *Self-Portrait with Friends* (Figure 8). "Friendship and sex don't mix," says another commonplace, yet Bernard Faucon's title for his obviously erotic *Les Amis* (Figure 9) needn't be ironic at all: friends is what these two boys may well be.

FIGURE 6. GIOTTO,
"Kiss of Judas," detail from *The Life of Christ* (1303–1305)

FIGURE 7. EDGAR DEGAS,
Portrait of Friends in the Wings (1879)

The visual features of painting depict gestures, looks, the disposition of bodies, attitudes, feelings, emotions, actions, and situations. But no gesture, look, or bodily disposition, no attitude, feeling, or emotion, no action and no situation is associated with friendship firmly enough to make its representation a matter for the eye. The natural and conventional signs of sexuality are many, but their range is limited. We don't need to know the title of Botticelli's *Mars and Venus* in order to tell that it has to do with sex. But friendship is different: it has no sure signs. In

FIGURE 8. TITIAN,
Self-Portrait with Friends (c. 1550)

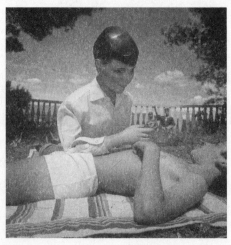

FIGURE 9. BERNARD FAUCON,
Les Amis (1978)

painting, friends can be of any age or gender, passionate or cool, affectionate or reserved, absorbed in each other or in their own interests: friends can be doing just about anything together.

And as in painting, so in life. It is as difficult to tell whether two people are friends by looking at them as it is difficult to tell that their portrait is a picture of their friendship by looking at it. This may seem a trivial point, but it represents a deep truth—a truth whose importance Plato was the first to notice in the fourth century BC. In his *Laches*, a general suggests to Socrates that courage is the willingness to stand your ground against the enemy. That, Socrates concedes, is true enough of infantry soldiers, but it can't possibly be true of the cavalry, whose common tactic of retreating in order to draw the enemy forward before turning to the attack does not put their courage in doubt. That, he argues, shows that neither standing your ground nor retreating is in itself an indication of courage. Each is only a way of behaving that may or may not manifest courage, depending on its context and the motive with which it is undertaken. For courage is not a mode of behavior but the capacity to know when the brave thing to do is to stand your ground and when it is to retreat, when to persist in an effort and when to give up, when it is worth risking your life and when it is not. Courage, like every other virtue, is not a form of behavior but a structure of the soul.

And so is friendship. Like courage, it can be manifested in all sorts of different, even conflicting, ways of behaving. Whether a particular way of acting is an indication of friendship or not depends on the motives with which one behaves as one does. Should we tell our friends, for example, that people are saying terrible things about them behind their back? Perhaps, if it's you they are talking about, the right thing for me to do is to tell you; but you, knowing how deeply I already doubt myself, might do the right thing as a friend by hiding the truth from me. Just as both standing your ground and retreating can be signs of courage in different contexts, so both revealing the truth and hiding it can, in their place, be just what a good friend should do. The reason is not the behavior they involve but the context in which we engage in them—our reasons for acting as we do. That makes it impossible to know without further information, simply by observing two people interacting, whether they act in friendship or not. Even dying for you—that staple of our mythology of friendship—does not necessarily show that I am your friend. To take an example from literature, in the closing pages of Charles Dickens's *A Tale of Two Cities*, as they are being carted to the guillotine, a young seamstress recognizes Sydney Carton, who is sacrificing himself instead of Charles Darnay. When she asks him, "Are you dying for him?" Carton replies, "And for his wife and child." That, along with what we know of him more generally, shows that he is sacrificing himself not out of friendship for Darnay, not as Damon was willing to die for Phintias, but out of love for Lucie, Darnay's wife: he dies *for* Darnay—in his place—but not *for his sake*: that, he does for Darnay's wife and child. More than that: someone may die for you without having any concern for you as a person at all.

Consequentialists, as we have seen, believe that what makes an action morally right is the extent to which it contributes to the well-being of the greatest number of people: by and large, they have no use for the special and preferential treatment that friends accord each other. Nevertheless, a committed utilitarian may be ready to die for you as a matter of duty, if your life would add more to the overall welfare than his own (or kill you, if the opposite were true), and would be willing to do so for anyone else in the same position.

As paintings show, then, one reason that two people's behavior on any one occasion can't reveal whether they are friends is that no specific mode of acting is associated with friendship closely enough. Another reason is that whether an action expresses friendship or not depends crucially on the context within which, and the motives out of which, it occurs. To discern an action's motive we must place that action within a wider context, fitting it into a pattern that accounts for its particular character. But that is where painting reaches its limits: friendship, like the pattern of behavior it exhibits, takes time to manifest itself, and painting is not suited for the representation of time.

For example, my offer to help you may seem like an act of friendship until my further actions reveal that it really was a self-interested calculation; what, on the other hand, may seem like selfishness on its own can well turn out to express a deeper understanding between two friends. It takes time to realize that the behavior of two people fits into a pattern that is brought about by their friendship for each other. Not only that: it takes time, of course, to realize that our own feelings for another person have been transformed into friendship—it takes time for a friendship to be established in the first place. And since painting has trouble depicting subjects that are extended in time, we can discern friendship in painting only with the help of the sort of information supplied by a title, a conventional symbol, or a third-person account.

Not everyone believes that friendship only emerges in time. Montaigne seems to date the beginning of his close and intimate friendship with Étienne de la Boétie from the very first moment the two met: "At our first meeting . . . we found ourselves so taken with each other, so well acquainted, so bound together, that from that time on nothing was so close to us as each other." But, as the late Polish poet Wislawa Szymborska wrote, "Every beginning / Is only a sequel, after all. / And the book of events / Is always open halfway through." Even Montaigne seems to concede this, since although he emphasizes "the precipitancy of our mutual understanding, so promptly grown to its perfection," he also acknowledges that their meeting had been long prepared for: he himself had already read and greatly admired La Boétie's treatise, *On Voluntary Servitude*, and both had "sought each other before we met because of the reports we heard of each other." Aristotle was more nearly right when in the *Nicomachean Ethics* he pointed out that friendship requires

time and familiarity. As the saying goes, [two people] cannot know each other until they have eaten the proverbial salt together; nor can they accept each other or be friends until each has shown himself to be worthy of love and gained the other's confidence. . . . For though the desire for friendship arises quickly, friendship itself does not.

Nothing, he adds, is more characteristic of friendship than the friends' need and desire to spend a considerable part of their life together. Time is of the essence here: whether a relationship is a friendship or not—and whether or not we can know that it is—depends on how long it has lasted so far, how long it will continue in the future, and, most important, for what reasons.

PERHAPS, THEN, WE SHOULD TURN TO LITERATURE, especially its narrative varieties, which have no problem with events that take time to unfold, for a more accurate representation of friendship. Moreover, literature can establish the relationship between two people simply by mentioning it: "Mr. Bingley," Jane Austen writes in *Pride and Prejudice* when she first introduces her character, "was good looking and gentlemanlike . . . but his *friend* Mr. Darcy soon drew the attention of the room." But here is a curious fact—unexpected and startling to me when I first became aware of it: I was struck by how rare it is to find a novel of the first rank that takes friendship as its central subject.

That may be an exaggeration. Friendship is everywhere in the novel, and it is essential to it: it furthers the plot, creates verisimilitude, and illuminates character; it is particularly important to literature written by women, and for women. Many of the works I am about to mention involve various friendships—some, even among their protagonists. Still, none of them is *about* friendship, as the *Odyssey*, *Robinson Crusoe*, and *Ivanhoe* are, among other things, about adventure, resourcefulness, and fidelity; *Paradise Lost*, *Crime and Punishment*, and *The Stranger* about human imperfections, limitations, and responsibilities; the *Aeneid*, *The Red Badge of Courage*, and *All Quiet on the Western Front* about bravery, loyalty, and war; *Middlemarch*, *War and Peace*, and *Buddenbrooks* about family life in town or country; *Pride and Prejudice*, *Carmen*, and *Wuthering Heights* about love and desire; *Madame Bovary* and *Anna Karenina* about adultery; or *Wilhelm Meister's Apprenticeship*, *Great Expectations*, and *Portrait of the Artist as a Young Man* about education and culture.

My list is inevitably selective and one-sided. It is not impossible for a novel to be about friendship as its fundamental theme. It is only that narrative in general and the novel in particular are not especially well suited for treating it in the proper detail, though for reasons other than those that are an obstacle to painting. By contrast, friendship is the central subject of some great lyric poems. Horace, praying for Virgil's safe journey to Greece, thinks of his friend as "half of my soul"—an image connected to, but not exactly the same as, Aristotle's "another self," which we meet again in Bacon and Montaigne. "Precious friends hid in death's dateless night" bring about tears and moans and grief to the speaker in Shakespeare's Sonnet 30: "But if the while I think on thee (fair friend) / all losses are restored and sorrows end." "Half my life I left behind"—another development of Horace's image, is how Tennyson feels about the death of Arthur Hallam, who, unlike Virgil, did not return safely from his journey abroad. And not only lyric poetry: as we shall see in this book's Part 2, drama in its various forms—theater, film, and television—may well be friendship's ideal medium.

Even though it is limited to the novel, my skepticism about the place of friendship in literature is radical, sweeping, and irritating enough to provoke immediately a search for counterexamples. Some are obvious and well-known— Mark Twain's *Huckleberry Finn*, James Joyce's *Ulysses*; others less so. For example, in *Truth and Beauty*—a memoir that, like all memoirs, has the structure of a novel—Ann Patchett recounts her friendship with the writer Lucy Grealey. Grealey's face was marred by a dehumanizing and humiliating deformity, which she tried to correct by a series of debilitating surgeries and to forget through drugs and abject sex. But the focus of *Truth and Beauty* and the source of the book's power is not the two women's friendship: it is Lucy Grealey herself, incessantly suffering, impossibly demanding, and desperately reaching for life—a life almost redeemed by the success of her own memoir, *Autobiography of a Face*, a success that still did not prevent her from dying a few year later from a heroin overdose. In *Huckleberry Finn*, Huck and Jim do, for a while, become friends and equals, but Twain, when he is not falling victim to his own prejudices, focuses his gaze more on Huck's recognition that this black man is as fully human as he is himself, and less on his characters' friendship in its own right. As for Joyce's Leopold Bloom, uninspiring as he sometimes can be, he is more Odysseus to Stephen Dedalus's Telemachus than Achilles to his Patroclus—and, anyway, he has enough of his own problems to worry about.

Nothing is more central to the novel than the depiction of intimate human relationships that span large tracts of time, sometimes entire lives. Why, then, has friendship been less common as a subject in the novel's accounts of everyday life than it is in everyday life itself? Perhaps the beginnings of an explanation lie in William Hazlitt's observation about the most common needs that friendship satisfies:

> In estimating the value of an acquaintance or even a friend, we give a preference to intellectual or convivial over moral qualities. The truth is that in our habitual intercourse with others, we much oftener require to be amused than assisted. We consider less, therefore, what a person with whom we are intimate is ready to do for us in critical emergencies, than what he has to say on ordinary occasions.

Hazlitt reminds us of the sheer pleasure we get from having friends and interacting with them and emphasizes the calm valleys rather than the rugged peaks of friendship. Montaigne says something similar, though in a different register, when he compares erotic love, "more active, more scorching, and more intense . . . an impetuous and fickle flame, undulating and variable, a fever flame, subject to fits and lulls," with friendship's "general and universal warmth, moderate and even, besides, a constant and settled warmth, all gentleness and smoothness."

Hazlitt and Montaigne are both right. The fact is that despite the immense weight of the epic tradition that associates friendship with extreme situations and extraordinarily passionate feelings—with sacrifice, death, mourning, and revenge—friendship, in modern times, has become, for better or worse, a milder affair. Ordinarily, friendship is manifested in the most, well, ordinary situations—situations that all but the friends themselves are likely to find almost always inconsequential and often irredeemably boring. What could be more mundane than the friendship between Catherine and Isabella in Jane Austen's *Northanger Abbey*?

> They called each other by their Christian name, were always arm in arm when they walked, pinned up each other's train for the dance, and were not to be divided in the set; and if a rainy morning deprived them of other enjoyments, they were still resolute in meeting in defiance of wet and dirt, and shut themselves up, to read novels together.

Just so, to take for a moment an example from a different medium, most of the interactions that gradually transform the characters of Clark Gable and Claudette Colbert from squabbling chance acquaintances into lovers in Frank Capra's film, *It Happened One Night* (1934), are in themselves insignificant—sharing food, hitchhiking, devising decent sleeping arrangements, and the like. "Lovers," though, is too flat a term for what they become, for as Stanley Cavell points out in his analysis of the film,

> what this pair does together is less important than the fact that they do whatever it is together, that they know how to spend time together, even that they would rather waste time together than do anything else—except that no time they are together could be wasted. Here is a reason that these relationships strike us as having the quality of friendship, [marking] the ascendancy of being together over doing something together.

Being together rather than doing something together: that is surely part of what distinguishes friends from mere acquaintances and people from whom we expect something specific. And though being together is always manifested in doing something or other together, not *every* doing something together will do; or rather, since, as we have seen, no particular type of situation is characteristic of friendship, absolutely *any* doing something together will do—but only if it is part of a series of incidents through which, collectively, friendship is established, cemented, and expressed.

What, then, distinguishes those series of incidents that manifest friendship from others that don't? Although we shall see that it is impossible to answer that question in a way that is both sufficiently general and genuinely informative, one thing is certain: most of the incidents that make up such a series in the normal course of events are bound to be unimportant, not only in literature but in life itself. In literature, because if the characters in a narrative engage in activities that are significant in their own right, it will seem at least as likely that what draws them to each other are these activities themselves and not the attractions of friendship: they would seem to be doing something together rather than being together. In life, because, by and large, friends—good friends at least—share significant parts of their lives with each other and most of the activities of which life consists are, for better or worse, unimportant. In literature, it is only against a background of mundane shared events that, when the extraordinary occurs, the characters' extreme reactions can be seen to spring from friendship and not from duty, ambition, or recklessness. In life, it is through little incidents that friendship is established, even if it sometimes finds expression during life's most urgent moments.

Of course, mundane events and interactions don't belong only to the representations of friendship: every novel, whatever its subject, lives on the insignificant. What could be less consequential, for example, than the "unhistoric acts" of the characters who populate George Eliot's England—characters like Dorothea Brooke, whose "full nature, like that river of which Cyrus broke the strength, spent itself in channels which had no great name on earth"? But no story that consists of merely insignificant events will ever make for absorbing reading; unredeemed insignificance is a bore. Indeed, Eliot creates Dorothea precisely in order to endow her acts with significance, in order to trace the growth that springs to life when the river's waters finally find their way into the earth: "That things are not so ill with you and me as they might have been, is half owing to the number who lived faithfully a hidden life, and rest in unvisited tombs."

Yet if the events that express friendship in a novel are to serve their purpose, they must be represented, and received, *as* insignificant—they must not make a difference, except inadvertently, to you and me and sometimes even to the friends themselves. But in order to give you some reason to believe such a thing, I must first qualify what I claimed earlier: that there are no great novels of friendship. That is not quite true. There is, quite ironically, at least one: Gustave Flaubert's *Bouvard and Pécuchet* (his *Sentimental Education* is often said to be another)—ironically, because Flaubert has nothing good to say about either friends or friendship.

The novel is the story of two copy clerks who leave Paris for the country, where they hope to devote themselves to various worthy projects. It is not at all a kind or generous book. In his letters, Flaubert confessed that he was counting on it to help him "spit . . . the gall that chokes me—that is, to speak some truths. By this means I hope to purge myself. . . . Stupidity now crushes me so hard that I feel like a fly with the Himalayas on its back! No matter! I will try to vomit my venom into my book. This hope soothes me." And in order to lift the weight of stupidity from his own shoulders, Flaubert transferred it to his characters, whose chance meeting in the Luxembourg Gardens gradually blossoms into a serious friendship. We don't learn exactly what attracts them to each other in the first place. It's true that

> their personal tastes were complementary. Bouvard smoked a pipe, was fond of cheese, and his espresso daily. Pécuchet took snuff, and only a bit of preserves for dessert, and dipped a cube of sugar into his coffee. One was confident, rash, generous; the other discreet, pensive, frugal.

But Flaubert is aware that we are as often drawn to our friends by our similarities as we are by our differences. Instead of providing an explanation of the clerks' friendship, this observation prompts him to ask a question that will eventually become our own as well: "How can one explain why any two people hit it off? Why is a certain peculiarity, a certain imperfection, indifferent or baneful in one person but enchanting in someone else?"

Whatever it is that first brings them together, Bouvard and Pécuchet decide to put copying other people's ideas behind them and try out their own. They successively take up agriculture, chemistry, medicine, history, archaeology, literature, aesthetics, politics, love, and much else besides. And although, unfortunately, they are completely incompetent, they are as completely undaunted. When each one of their efforts ends in abject and miserable failure, they immediately move on to a new task with a light heart, only to see it founder in the very same way.

Bouvard and Pécuchet have to be friends if the story of their doomed projects is to make any sense, for only friends—very close friends—could have tolerated, much less remained fond of, each other through these successive disasters. And only very good friends could ever, like them, finally renounce their absurd ambitions and still want to spend the rest of their lives together. This they do, but instead of searching for new things to learn they take up once again the only activity they ever mastered—copying—and devote themselves to reproducing whatever falls in their hands: manuscripts, tobacco packets, old newspapers, or lost letters. More important, only such a repetitive series of events, dispiriting as it is, could have presented a convincing display of their friendship.

But is it possible for a novel to give a satisfying representation of friendship that is also interesting? Flaubert was tortured by that question, worrying that his novel would be a total failure exactly because of its repetitiveness: "The reader won't read me—the book will put him to sleep from the start. . . . There are no quotable excerpts, no brilliant scenes, just the same situation over and over . . . I'm scared it might bore people to death." In fact, the novel has actually been hailed by some as a modernist, by others as a postmodernist masterpiece. Mark Polizzotti, a recent translator of the novel, insists that "boring it's not, once we've accepted the ground rules." Nevertheless, *Bouvard and Pécuchet* is far from a joy to read: "It is aesthetically stubborn in its constant refusal to grant readers the narrative flow they traditionally crave. And it requires a stubborn reader, one willing to suspend normal expectations and able to confront both repetitious effects and a vomitorium of predigested book-learning." To Polizzotti, its repetitiveness is "a huge part of its comic effect," but that strikes me simply as special pleading. And his advice to "think of the Three Stooges' head bonks and nose tweaks, or Laurel and Hardy's fine messes: the more we expect them, the funnier they become" seems to concede exactly what we are going to find as we go on, namely, that the action of drama is better suited to the representation of friendship than the narrative of the novel.

There is a particular kind of novel, though, that offers a different perspective on friendship: the fabulous adventures of Don Quixote, which are not exactly a novel but a picaresque, are a case in point. On the one hand, Sancho and Quixote remain indissolubly servant and master throughout, the hierarchical nature of their relationship as fixed and unchanging as their individual characters and the work's repetitive plot, while Quixote's monomania makes it hard to find in him the mutual recognition that friendship has always seemed to require. What's more, their relationship is in the service of their adventures; had the book been primarily about friendship, it would have been their adventures that were in the service of their relationship. Nevertheless, Sancho and Quixote do achieve a sort of harmony of wills: the warmth, understanding, and even the occasional conflicts between them come as close to a depiction of friendship as most narrative works are capable of.

Cervantes's mock-heroic characters and the structure of his work have not disappeared. They survive in the protagonists of the modern detective-story series—Arthur Conan Doyle's Holmes and Watson, Rex Stout's Nero Wolfe and Archie Goodwin, Ian Rankin's John Rebus and Siobhan Clarke, and many other pairs: their relationships replicate the warmth, the mutual dependence, the hierarchical order, and sometimes the conflicts that are essential to Sancho and Quixote. The books in these series (*The Hound of the Baskervilles*, *The League of Frightened Men*, *Set in Darkness*) are all novels in their own right, but the series to which they belong are as a whole the contemporary descendants of the picaresque, turning each individual story into something like a long chapter of a single but very long work. Their heroes remain mostly unchanged by their adventures. They complete one task only to embark on the next, their characters remaining stable over the course of many years. Their friendship is indicated through the same minor occurrences time and time again: Holmes playing his violin while Watson enjoys his pipe, Wolfe reading at his desk or tending to his orchids while Archie needles him into accepting a commission, Rebus and Siobhan having yet another drink at the Oxford Bar on Edinburgh's Young Street. The key here is the repetition of the insignificant: it may make a single novel, like *Bouvard and Pécuchet*, almost impossible to read, but it is a source of delight when it connects one novel in a series with another. It is not an accident that readers of detective stories often describe each new entry in a series as an opportunity to meet "old friends" again: the characters' habitual mannerisms and the repetitive narrative structure generate a reading that is itself a repetitive experience, replicating some of the actual features of friendship in everyday life.

THE PHILOSOPHICAL TRADITION, BY AND LARGE, considers friendship a crucial element in the good life, an unadulterated boon, a moral good. The epic shows the magnitude of the sacrifices friends may make for each other's sake. Painting establishes that friendship isn't necessarily expressed in the extreme situations of the epic, but that, on the contrary, it involves all sorts of behavior, much of it completely ordinary. If painting also inadvertently shows that friendship is manifested over time, in the novel we see that the ordinary behavior of friends involves repetitive, inconsequential, and sometimes ridiculous interactions. But the novel shows something else as well, which sets it squarely against the philosophical tradition: that friendship need not be an inherently beneficial relationship or a moral good.

Consider, for example, Frederick Moreau, the hero of Flaubert's *Sentimental Education*. At an early age he forges what turns out to be a lifelong friendship with a schoolmate, Charles Deslauriers:

> One day a servant called [Deslauriers] a pauper's brat in the middle of the junior-schoolyard; he went for the man, and would have killed him but for the intervention

of three of the masters. Deeply impressed, Frederick embraced him. From that day on, their friendship was complete. The affection of a senior doubtless flattered the younger boy's vanity, and the other gratefully accepted the devotion offered to him.

What Frederick admires as brave and honorable, Flaubert gives us every reason to consider impetuous and excessive, an expression of Deslaurier's pugnacious aggressiveness that had already prompted his schoolmates' "mute" hostility. Even leaving aside the questionable role of vanity in cementing their friendship, it is clear that Frederick is inspired not by recognizing Deslaurier's excellence but by mistaking his behavior. At best, his friendship springs from what he wrongly takes to be a virtue in Deslauriers, not by the boy's real virtue (supposing he had any).

And yet, though anything but excellence of character binds these two questionable characters to each other, theirs is and remains a serious and genuine friendship, capable of surviving their various separations and adversities as well as their mutual disappointments and their quarrels. Flaubert drives that point home in the closing scene of the novel, which finds them both back in the village where they had grown up, seated in front of a blazing fireplace, "reconciled once again by that irresistible element in their nature which always reunited them in friendship." As they look back over their lives together, they recall a long-ago Sunday when they skipped church, curled their hair and put on in their best clothes, made bouquets from flowers stolen from Frederick's mother's garden, and, carefully taking a roundabout route, paid a visit to the village brothel, "the secret obsession of every adolescent." No sooner had Frederick entered the house, however, than he lost his nerve: he stood there, unable to move, mortified and speechless for some time. Eventually, he managed to turn around and ran off, followed by Deslauriers, who, penniless as usual, lacked the means to stay on his own. Having thrown caution to the winds, they were seen leaving the brothel and provoked a serious local scandal. Their reminiscence ends with these words and so does the novel:

> They told one another the story at great length, each supplementing the other's recollections; and when they had finished:
>
> "That was the best time we ever had," said Frederick.
>
> "Yes, perhaps you are right. That was the best time we ever had," said Deslauriers.

There is no virtue in these men, nor has there been any for a long time. They are simply two trivial characters who reveal and revel in the banalities that sustained their friendship—a close and genuine one—through all their adventures, their errors, and their changes of fortune.

Despite such scenes, friendship is not the central theme of *Sentimental Education*. Frederick's relationship to Deslauriers serves, like his listless efforts to pursue a career of some sort and his endless changes of mind and heart, as one more illustration of his unengaged passage through life. The true place of friendship in the arts is not in the novel but in drama, which can give center stage to the mundane expressions of friendship and capture their repetitive form without the complications that beset the novel's efforts to do so. We will look at drama in the second part of this book. And we will ask why we consider friendship a great good, although it is most often expressed in the most trivial and commonplace actions and sometimes leads us into immoral, even criminal behavior. Friendship is much more complicated and ambiguous than the picture we have derived from philosophy and the arts we have looked at so far. It is its complexities and ambiguities that will occupy us from now on.

PART TWO

Chapter 4

"AND SO ON"
Why Do We Love Our Friends?

A YOUNG WOMAN AND HER FIANCÉ ARE PLANNING their wedding. "How many friends have you got in all?" she asks him as they are trying to decide on their wedding's guest list. He answers:

> I have no idea. Ten really good ones. Ten more peripherals. A score or so right at the outside edge, virtual acquaintances. A few left over from school, a few more from college, a few picked up at work, perhaps an ex in there somewhere. One or two borrowed or stolen from other friends. An ex-flatmate or two. Not as many mates as I used to have, that's for sure.

A little later, he asks her in turn, "How many varieties of friends are there?" and she replies:

> Oh, loads. For a start there are friends you don't like. I've got plenty of those. Then there are friends you do like,

but never bother to see. Then there are the ones you really like a lot, but can't stand their partners. There are those you just have out of habit and can't shake off. Then there's the ones you're friends with not because you like them, but because they're very good-looking or popular and it's kind of cool to be their friend. Trophy friends. . . . Then there are sports friends. There are friends of convenience—they're usually work friends. There are pity friends who you stay with because you feel sorry for them. There are acquaintances who are on probation as friends. There are—

"Enough!" he finally interrupts her.

ENOUGH INDEED. WIT ASIDE, HOWEVER, THIS CATALOGUE of friends in Tim Lott's novel *White City Blue* is not at all unlike the elaborate, though unstable, taxonomies of social scientists, who classify friendships according to age, class, gender, degree of kinship, social context, and dependency relations. The five stages of friendship between the ages of three or four and early adulthood are supposed to be distinct, but their boundaries are so porous that they are constantly running into one another. Adult friendships are equally nebulous and differ according to age and gender, class, education, and many other factors. There are fair-weather, heart-sink, dangerous, fossil friends, and "frenemies"—not to mention friends who know each other only through the virtual spaces of social media. Some friendships echo family relationships; others, professional, academic, sporting, or religious connections. And there are a great many other types.

To be sure, there are still fewer friendships than there were "instincts" in the 1920s, when more than 6,000 may have been "identified"! But the number of *particular* kinds of friendships is still large enough to suggest that we are thinking about them in the wrong way. Faced with this explosion of distinctions, the sociologist Fred Pahl concludes: "Despite the very large literature generated by developmental and social psychologists . . . it does appear, happily, that friendship has eluded their grasp . . . Friendship, more perhaps than any other aspect of our social lives, has eluded the attempts of social scientists to be classified and codified."

According to Pahl, types of friendship are bound to proliferate as long as we try to account for friendship by the patterns of behavior to which it gives rise. But, as we've seen, in painting most strikingly, there is just about nothing that friends can't do together. That means that our behavior is never, on its own, enough to determine whether it springs from friendship or not. Any attempt to account for friendship by describing the activities to which it gives rise misses the most important point: what defines a friendship is not the particular actions and activities that friends engage in but the motives with which they perform them as part of their friendship.

Aristotle understood motive to be at the heart of *philia*, and his approach may help impose some order on the many types of behavior that characterize friendship in different contexts. Although his scheme might not accommodate Tim Lott's "umfriends"—as in "This is my, um, *friend*"—Aristotle did find in all varieties of *philia* a mutual concern of various levels and intensities, and a shared desire to benefit not only oneself but one's *philos* as well. Just so, to the extent that it expresses friendship, every one of the relationships I have mentioned so far is accompanied by a degree of affection and goodwill.

Still, however important the willingness to help may be to friendship, what separates my friends from the rest of the world is not that I am moved to do good things for them that I am not moved to do for others: most of us do all sorts of good things for all sorts of people who aren't our friends. Philosophical accounts of friendship typically begin with a formula like this one: "If *x* loves *y* then *x* wants to benefit and be with *y*." True enough, as far as it goes—but it doesn't go far enough: our desire to do well by our friends is part and parcel of our love, but not by any means its most salient feature.

To go further, we may try to follow Aristotle on *philia* and start by saying that our close friendships are based in virtue, or its more ambivalent modern analogue, character, while our less intense, more occasional, and relatively casual friendships are based either on practical benefit or pleasure. For Aristotle, though, *philia* based on either benefit or pleasure is purely instrumental: those who engage in such a relationship "are not attracted to each other but to the beneficial [or the pleasant]," and if their relationship stops providing either pleasure or benefit, it is immediately terminated. That means that our close friendships, in which we *are* attracted to each other and not to what our friends happen to provide us with, must differ in kind from our less involved relationships: "In the best friendships," a philosopher writes, "the central feature of the friendship is simply that the friends love, and wish each other well, as ends in themselves, whereas in lesser friendships, the central feature is the instrumental or means value of each to the other." That difference is crucial. The contrast between loving our close friends as "ends in themselves"—for what they are, "for themselves"—and treating all the rest as means to our advantage or enjoyment is radical: it makes them so different in kind from one another that it implies that the latter two can hardly be considered friendships at all.

We have said, and will say again, in more detail, that what is essential to friends is their motive for behaving as they do—that they do what they do *out of* friendship, out of their love for each other. I can give the same present to my friend and to someone else but only my gift to my friend is motivated by love and a desire to make him feel good and not out of politeness, social convention, obligation, calculation, or even a goodwill that ranges far and wide but is not friendship. It is also impossible—or, if possible, pathological—to love someone because they are rich. Unlike *philia*, which does come in three distinct kinds, friendship does not: it comes in many *degrees*. Like every kind of love, it ranges from mild affection to stormy passion and, in all cases, it involves what, for lack of a better term, we describe as loving our friends "for themselves." The problem is that we don't yet know what that means. That is what we need to understand.

IT TURNS OUT TO BE SURPRISINGLY DIFFICULT TO DO SO. In order to capture the complexities of the situation, I must begin by admitting what is in fact the case: most of my connections to other people are instrumental; not to put too fine a point to it, I *use* other people for my own purposes—just as everyone else does. I know what I want from them and my interest in them is exhausted by the specific qualities that allow them to perform their particular function. Montaigne says it best:

> The religion of my doctor or my lawyer cannot matter . . . I scarcely inquire of a lackey whether he is chaste; I try to find out whether he is diligent. And I am not as much afraid of a gambling mule driver as of a weak one, or of a profane barber as of an ignorant one. . . . For the familiarity of the table I look for wit, not prudence; for the bed, beauty before goodness; in conversation, competence, even without uprightness.

What Montaigne wants from such relationships has little or nothing to do with the particular person who provides it. Montaigne is after those qualities—benefits and pleasures, in Aristotle's terms—*in and of themselves*. He has little or no interest in the particular people who happen to embody them: he would be satisfied with any lackey who was as diligent as his current servant and would immediately replace his barber if a more competent one came along.

And so would I. When I needed to have my hair cut, I searched for a competent barber. Beyond being competent and relatively pleasant, it made no difference to me who the barber happened to be: any equally qualified barber would have done just as well. When I found Tomas, whom we first met in Chapter 1, what mattered to me was not Tomas the barber as a person but—in Aristotle's terms— Tomas the barber as a barber. But that does not mean that my instrumental interest, which was centered on what Tomas could do for me, made our relationship, as some might think, exploitative: it wasn't, at least as long as both of us derived something (ideally of equal value) from it. It was, however, what the sociologist Georg Simmel was the first to call an "impersonal" relationship:

> The delivery man, the money-lender, the worker, upon whom we are dependent, do not operate as personalities because they enter into a relationship only by virtue of a single activity such as the delivery of goods, the lending of money, and because their other qualities, which alone would give them a personality, are missing.

In an impersonal relationship all that matters is how well the job is done. Of course, I also tried to treat Tomas with the decency that, ideally, I would extend to as many people as possible. But exactly because it doesn't matter to me who these people are—I would want to treat them decently whoever they happen to be—to treat Tomas in that manner was not, beyond some minimal degree, to treat him as an individual: I treated him as I would (like to) treat every human being.

But some impersonal relationships can gradually develop into something else, and I gradually found myself becoming concerned with aspects of Tomas's life that were not directly connected to his professional role and taking an interest in what we call his "personal" life. That, as the very word reveals, turned our relationship into something more than impersonal—and for that reason it was no longer purely instrumental, either.

Before our relationship took that turn and as long as it remained impersonal and purely instrumental, I knew exactly how to answer you if you asked me why I liked Tomas: I would have said something like, "I like the way he cuts my hair" or, to make things perfectly clear, "I don't like Tomas *himself* (though of course I don't dislike him, either): I only like the way he cuts my hair." As long as my feelings were not primarily directed at my barber himself but at a particular ability he shared with others, I could say exactly why our relationship mattered to me. It mattered because he was a good barber—good at cutting my hair. But as soon as our relationship developed into something closer and I was no longer concerned merely with how well he cut my hair, I could only answer your question by saying, "I like the way he cuts my hair and I also like *him*."

The second part of my answer, though, is no answer at all. You asked me why I like Tomas, and I told you that . . . I like him, which immediately provokes the further question, "And why *do* you like him?" Here now is a most intriguing point: although I had no problem with your question before, once my relationship with Tomas became personal, *I no longer know how to answer it.* Once I came to like Tomas *himself* and not just what he could do for me, I could no longer explain exactly why that was so. It certainly isn't *just* because I like the way he cuts my hair—but, then, what else is it? True, I could tell you that I like him because he is kind, entertaining, or interesting, and so on, but such attempts at explanation can go only so far. They are disappointingly vague and they explain much less than we might think. Would I leave Tomas, for instance, if a kinder or more entertaining barber came along? Would I even replace him if a *better* barber came along? And why don't *you* prefer him to your own barber if, like me, you find him wittier than your own?

Try as we might, our best efforts to explain why we like someone are invariably vague, imprecise, and finally unsatisfactory—banal and incomplete, always leaving out what we strongly suspect are the most essential reasons for our feelings. When it comes to any of my friends—and once I have come to like *him*, my barber is my friend, however casual—it is impossible for me to say (because, as we shall see, it is impossible for me to know) exactly why I like them or, in the case of my close friends, why I love them. What I like about them cannot be separated from their person and, for that reason, it makes my friendships completely different from my impersonal relationships. In particular, that means that I can't replace one friend with another in the way I can replace those with whom my relationships are impersonal: no one but my friend herself can play her role in my life. When my relationship with my barber became personal, even if it never became very intimate, my loyalty to him no longer depended purely on his talents. And although I may value the intelligence of another friend, I will not give her up when someone still more intelligent comes along. It is not just intelligence in the abstract that matters to me here: what matters, as we say unhelpfully, is *her* intelligence, her *particular* intelligence, or the *way* her intelligence manifests itself. My friend, as we say, equally unhelpfully, matters to me not just for her features but for herself.

We are then left with the question, What is the difference between my friend's features and my friend herself? After all, her features are hers and no one else's; don't I, in loving her for her features, love *her* as well?

Perhaps the answer is that to love your friends is to be attracted not to one or more of their features but to every single one of them—to love them for everything they are. Yet, first, many of our friends' features are irrelevant to our relationship, and, second, I suspect that most of us have friends whom we love not because of, but despite, the defects they, like everyone else in the world, inevitably have. Here, again, is George Eliot:

> Among our valued friends is there not some one or other who is a little too self-confident and disdainful; whose distinguished mind is a little spotted with commonness; who is a little pinched here and protuberant there with native prejudices; or whose better energies are liable to

lapse down the wrong channel under the influence of transient solicitations?

Nor again do our friends possess, as Aristotle thought, an essential nature, constituted by only some of their features, which establish who they really are—their self.

But if neither a special group of our features nor all of them together constitute who we are, what does? What is "the self" that we so intimately feel we are? Think, for example, of a friend who no longer matters to you, not because you found out things you don't like about her or because you had a falling out but because, as it so often happens, you lost your interest in each other over the years. Think, too, of the features that attracted you to her in the first place. She may still be just as intelligent or kind as she was when you were close, but you are now indifferent to her, and neither her intelligence nor her kindness can rekindle your love. But if these had been part of your reasons for loving her in the first place, and they haven't changed, why don't they make a difference still?

Or consider a scene from the television show *The L Word* in which a woman asks her former partner why she no longer loves her and receives the reply, "Yes, I love you, I do . . . I love who you are . . . I love how you stand in the world, I love your talent, I love your passion, I love your anger. But you and I are so fundamentally different . . . " Even when it is perfectly true, such a response is no consolation. Its words notwithstanding, it is a way of saying, "But I don't love *you.*" That is why it is perfectly (and perhaps more) correct to say not "I love *who* you are" but "I love *what* you are." And here is something very strange: "I love your talent" is here a way of saying "I don't love you"; yet, earlier on in the relationship, it would have been a perfectly reasonable, if superficial, way of saying "I love you" instead. How did love for the friend's talent become irrelevant to love of the friend? It is tempting to answer that it is not our friends' attractive features that inspire our love but our love that renders their features attractive.

But that conclusion is not quite right: the relationship between our love for our friends and their features is more complex than that. Again, although I might abandon an impersonal relationship if my needs are better served by another, I would not abandon my friend just because someone with more of what I prize in her comes along. But we must be careful here: that is true not only of my close friends but also, to a different extent in different cases, of my more casual friends, to whom I am bound by weaker bonds. As long as I like Tomas and not just what I can get from him, our relationship is not purely instrumental or impersonal: it is not as strong or passionate as my closest relationships, but it does involve genuine affection for Tomas and not just an appreciation of his abilities. In other words, it is not that our casual friendships are instrumental while our close ones are not: no friendship is purely instrumental but, also, no friendship is completely *un*instrumental. Best friends do "love, and wish each other well, as ends in themselves." But they can also use one another if the need arises; "lesser" friends may often use each other but they also, necessarily, "love, and wish each other well, as ends in themselves." And when a friendship's instrumental aspects come to the fore, even the closest of friends become replaceable: if you need an operation and your best friend is a decent surgeon but the greatest specialist in the world is available, you would do well to ask your friend to assist in your operation instead of taking the lead. Instrumentality does not separate one kind of friendship from another; it sets friendship as a whole apart from a vast range of other relationships. We love *all* our friends, not just our closest ones, "for themselves" and not only for the specific things that they can do for us. "Instrumental friendship"—whether based on advantage, pleasure, or anything else—is a contradiction in terms.

When our relationship is primarily instrumental, I know exactly what I want from you in advance, and anyone who can provide it for me will do. In an instrumental relationship, nothing much changes about me if someone new assumes your role in my life: the desires I already had continue to be satisfied as well or better. When our relationship, though, is not instrumental, when love is involved, I actually *don't* know what I want from you, and it isn't clear which features of yours account for my love. When a new friend enters my life, so does a truly new relationship, and it gives us both something we can't find anywhere else. When we become friends we are both changed, as the Bible reminds us: "Iron sharpeneth iron; so a man sharpeneth the countenance of his friend." I can have the same relationship with several barbers, but neither Tomas nor I can have *our* friendship with anyone else. Nor, for that matter, can *any* other two people have a friendship like ours: in contrast to a concrete role, which several people can occupy, our friends' roles in our life are inseparable from who they are. No one else, no matter how many features you share with them, can possibly have *your* place in my life, even if your place is as small as our friendship is casual.

"A PLACE": THAT IS JUST WHAT ÉTIENNE DE LA BOÉTIE, on his deathbed, asked Montaigne to give him in 1563: "My brother, my brother, do *you* refuse me a place?" Montaigne did not understand; perhaps he thought his friend was delirious: he told La Boétie that he "was still breathing and speaking, had a body, consequently he had his place." But that was not what La Boétie was after: "'True, true,' he answered me then, 'I have one, but it is not the one I need; and when all this is said and done, I will have no being left." Montaigne, at a loss, could only assure his friend that God would give him a better place soon. It took him almost a decade to begin to formulate what he took La Boétie's entreaty to have been: a plea for a place in Montaigne's own life, for their friendship to remain alive after his own death and play a continuing role in what Montaigne was to become.

His book of essays, Montaigne tells us, is "consubstantial with its author, concerned with my own self, an integral part of my life": "I am myself the matter of my book." If his best and most intimate friend was to have a place in his life, it should be reflected in his place within the *Essays* themselves. But just where in Montaigne's life was La Boétie's place? And how could the *Essays* reflect it? It took him several efforts and another decade to find the right answer.

The *Essays* represent the kind of communication Montaigne might have had with La Boétie, regaling him with the sort of stories, incidents, and thoughts that one would share with one's close friends—stories, feelings, and thoughts that range from the most trivial and mundane to the most serious and profound and that, in the process, express their author's personality. But La Boétie was dead; each of the *Essays'* readers assumes his role as the friend to whom Montaigne reveals himself. And in order to communicate the central place that La Boétie held in his life, Montaigne located his essay on friendship, whose hero is La Boétie, at the center of the first volume of the essays. Since what was to become that first volume was all he was planning to write at the time, the essay would have been the centerpiece of the whole work, and the *Essays* would have revolved around it. In addition, Montaigne also included in the essay the text of La Boétie's political treatise, *On Voluntary Servitude*. In the self-deprecating manner that was so characteristic of him, Montaigne likened himself to a painter, who always chooses the best spot—the middle of the wall—for his painting and fills the empty spaces around it with "grotesques" of various kinds. His own essays, therefore—"grotesques and monstrous bodies, pieced together of divers members, without definite shape, having no order, sequence or proportion other than accidental"—would form the background against which La Boétie's book, like the painter's central work, would allow Montaigne's readers to see for themselves the extraordinary quality of his friend's mind and personality.

While Montaigne was making these plans, La Boétie's treatise was published in part and used by the Protestant side in the religious wars of France. Concerned not to antagonize the Catholic establishment and eager to find common ground between the warring factions, Montaigne changed course. Having announced at the beginning of the essay that he would include the book, he declares at its end that he ultimately felt it would be better to leave it out. And so, although he left his own text intact and preserved its opening exhortation to "listen a while to this boy of sixteen," he removed it and at the end of the essay gave us not La Boétie's text but only an explanation of its absence.

Although Montaigne officially explained his reversal by his desire not to inflame political tensions, he had other reasons as well. Had he included *On Voluntary Servitude* in the *Essays*, he would have allowed his readers to take it up on their own, read it for themselves, and come to know its author through it. Many of his readers, though, were unlikely to be as enthusiastic about La Boétie's book as Montaigne had been, despite his explicit reservations; in that case, his attempt to manifest his feelings for his friend would have fallen flat. Publishing the treatise, therefore, would have undermined Montaigne's ultimate purpose, which was to account for his love and give substance to his lament that when La Boétie died, "I was already so formed and accustomed to being a second self everywhere that only half of me seems to be alive now."

The text of La Boétie's book would have represented Montaigne's effort to give an explanation of his feelings for his friend. It would have been as if he were saying, in effect, "Read his work: *That's* why I loved him as I did." The main thesis of *On Voluntary Servitude* is that only the voluntary submission of the ruled gives their rulers the power to act as they will and that the ruled can withdraw their consent when their sovereign becomes tyrannical. The essay has become important to the tradition of civil disobedience, but at the time Montaigne seems to have realized that, despite its virtues, it couldn't serve his purpose. It would have been perfectly possible, perhaps likely, that even if his readers had liked the treatise they could still have asked themselves, "*That's* why he loved him? Because of a good book?" How could that possibly be enough to justify Montaigne's extravagant claims for his friend's virtues and the depth of their love for each other?

It couldn't. Still, Montaigne didn't immediately abandon the effort to convey what La Boétie was like and what drew him so powerfully to him through his friend's writings. And so, "in exchange for this serious work," his next essay offered a group of La Boétie's sonnets, "gayer and more lusty" than the treatise. The poems appeared in both editions of the *Essays* that were published during Montaigne's lifetime. But he crossed them out in the "Bordeaux Manuscript," a copy of the second volume, heavily annotated in his hand, on which all subsequent editions of the *Essays* are based. The sonnets, however good they were, would have done no better than the treatise: "He loved him so because he was a decent poet?"

Montaigne never again tried to account for La Boétie's virtues by citing his works. Montaigne, in fact, was the first philosopher to realize a truth that is absolutely central to love and friendship: that any effort to explain why we love particular people by citing their virtues, their accomplishments, or anything else about them is bound to fail. And here is why.

The greatest part of Montaigne's classic essay on friendship describes a variety of personal relationships—the link of master to servant, the bond between fathers and sons, the ties of siblings and lovers, marriage, and paederasty (in discussing which in the context of friendship, Montaigne shows that he is still close to Aristotle, but in condemning which he parts company with him). Montaigne claimed that none of these can do justice to his extraordinary friendship with La Boétie: a friendship that led to "the complete fusion of our wills." He also came to realize that the complexity of their relationship—its "quintessence," in his word—could never be explained by a list of discrete "considerations":

> It is not one special consideration, nor two, nor three, nor four, nor a thousand: it is I know not what quintessence of all this mixture, which, having seized my whole will, led it to plunge and lose itself in his; which, having seized his whole will, led it to plunge and lose itself in mine, with equal hunger, equal rivalry.

Yet even if Montaigne can never know what that quintessence is, he still leaves open the possibility that that such a "mixture" may account for their friendship. The last phrase, which gives La Boétie an equal role in their relationship, only appears in the Bordeaux copy. It suggests that the difficulty is not only Montaigne's own but La Boétie's as well (also, by implication, a difficulty for anyone who has a close friend—and, I would add, anyone who has a friend at all). In the first edition, we find him conceding defeat: "If you press me to tell why I loved him, I feel that this cannot be expressed." I understand him to be saying here that his love could not be expressed in general terms—"considerations"—since he still thought that La Boétie's sonnets might give an accurate picture of his friend. But when, in the Bordeaux Manuscript, he excises the poems and abandons that effort as well, he expands that original sentence with what has become the most moving statement about friendship ever made: "If you press me to tell you why I loved him, I feel that this cannot be expressed *except by answering: Because it was he, because it was I.*" This extraordinary statement signifies total resignation. Montaigne is hereby giving up on the possibility of ever saying anything genuinely revealing about his friendship with La Boétie. Which raises the question: Has Montaigne, then, failed to give his friend a "place" in the *Essays* after all?

I think the only possible answer is: not at all. On the contrary, it is precisely by virtue of this most famous non-explanation that Montaigne brilliantly redirects our attention from this or that distinguishable aspect of both his friend and himself to the irreducible experience of the two of them *together*. In effect, he says: "Look at me, and at him, for the answer to your question."

But how can we do this? Where can we find the two friends together in order to look at them as Montaigne directs us? In the substance of his essays. "It is myself that I portray" in this book, Montaigne tells us, and that self is inextricably tied to his friendship with La Boétie. Montaigne described La Boétie and himself as "one soul in two bodies," and it is that single soul that the *Essays* portray. The *Essays* are the very "place" he has secured for his friend, even though—or precisely because—he has left out his friend's own work. La Boétie's place is his contribution to what Montaigne eventually became—what *The Essays* reveal him to be, virtues, defects, and all—and that is a contribution we can determine only by describing Montaigne himself.

But to describe Montaigne himself we must interpret the *Essays*: that means that who he is can't be under Montaigne's complete control because it also depends on his readers and what they make of him. That is always in question, since different readers are bound to have different reactions to his work. No reading, however, will ever be able to separate out what is due to Montaigne and what to La Boétie, for they are tied together by a Gordian knot: a knot so complex and intimate that it could only be unraveled by hacking through and destroying it. The two have become inextricably connected: "In the friendship I speak of, our souls mingle and blend with each other so completely that they efface the seam that joined them, and cannot find it again." By contrast, both La Boétie's treatise and his sonnets were detachable parts of the *Essays*. Including them as discrete objects would have given the impression that we could understand and appreciate

La Boétie's virtues simply by reading these two works. It would suggest that La Boétie had made a contribution to Montaigne's life and character that could be removed and described independently of describing Montaigne himself, as if La Boétie's "place" in Montaigne's life, just as in his work, could be emptied and filled in by someone else

But Montaigne knew that La Boétie's contribution to his life was unique: no one else could have had the same place within his life, and for that reason their relationship could only be described in terms that applied to both of them and to them only. Perhaps, then, he was not boasting when he claimed that their friendship "has no model but itself, and can be compared only with itself." For no friendship—not just its best exemplars—can in fact be compared to any other: every friendship is a unique combination of two souls, impossible to duplicate.

MONTAIGNE IN EFFECT TELLS US THAT HE COULD NEVER account for his love of La Boétie by a list of his features, however complex. With that in mind, we return to our question: What is it for me to love you for yourself?

I thought of an answer to that question, perhaps surprisingly, when I read a short but brilliantly suggestive discussion of metaphor by the philosopher Stanley Cavell. Cavell wanted to know what we do when we try to explain what a metaphor means. His starting point was that we do not try to explain metaphors in the same way we try to explain literal statements. When asked to say what a metaphor means, he wrote, "[I will try] to put [the] thought another way, and perhaps refer you, depending upon who you are, to a range of similar or identical thoughts expressed by others." When Aristotle, for example, writes, "Those who wish good things to a friend for his sake are friends most of all," we can express his thought in different words. In this particular case, the thought is that the most crucial feature of true friendship is the desire to see good things happen to one's friend independently of one's own welfare. We could also find this same thought, put in yet another way, in Cicero: true friends, he tells us, love one another and "'to love' means nothing but to cherish the person for whom one feels affection, without any special need and without any thought of advantage." But metaphors don't allow for this kind of explaining: we can neither put the thought another way nor find it expressed by someone else in different words. Instead, we *paraphrase* them, and the paraphrase of a metaphor has a very special feature.

Here, for example, is Cavell's paraphrase of Romeo's declaration, "Juliet is the sun": "Romeo means that Juliet is the warmth of his world; that his day begins with her; that only in her nourishment can he grow. And his declaration suggests that the moon, which other lovers use as an emblem of their love, is merely her reflected light, and dead in comparison; and so on." The first thing to note here is that the paraphrase is itself full of metaphors each one of which may require, in certain circumstances, its own paraphrase. The second is a contrast between metaphors and similes. If Romeo had said "Juliet is like the sun" instead of "Juliet is the sun," we would have expected him to go on to say, or to let the context show, in what specific ways the two are alike. Similes are open ended, yet when they are expanded, they are closed: when Charles Dana writes, "A ship is like a lady's watch, always out of repair," we know the full details of what he proposes to communicate: ships need constant attention. But metaphors don't create the expectation that they will be amplified, nor do they establish their meaning once and for all. They stand alone, and it is up to their audience to find what they can in them; as Cavell puts it, "The over-reading of metaphors, so often complained of, no doubt justly, is a hazard they must run for their high interest." Third, the possibility of over-reading also shows that metaphors are open ended, though in a distinct—and for our purposes, useful—way. The "and so on" with which Cavell ends his paraphrase of "Juliet is the sun" is a necessary part of every paraphrase, significant and ineliminable. It signals that the work of paraphrase is never finished: "It registers what William Empson calls the 'pregnancy' of metaphors, the burgeoning of meaning in them."

Unlike a simile, a metaphor can stand on its own; any attempt to paraphrase it, though, is bound to be incomplete. This "and so on" reveals that I am aware of its incompleteness; it speaks to my sense that if I were to spend more time with the metaphor, I could come to see in it things I am unable to envisage now. Although I will make that effort only for the metaphors that matter to me—and these will inevitably be different from the metaphors that matter to you—every metaphor presents that possibility to some degree or other. A metaphor that *can* be paraphrased without remainder, a metaphor whose meaning we can fully express in different words, belongs in a dictionary; it has become a cliché or turned into one of those countless expressions we use without a second thought and call "dead metaphors," which is itself a dead metaphor just like "the arm of the chair" or "the face of the clock" and the many other expressions it describes.

Unlike a dead metaphor, a living metaphor is inexhaustible. And since the full meaning of a living metaphor is always just beyond my grasp, the fact is that I can never fully know what it is, which tells me, in turn, that I can't use any words I already know to "put the thought another way"— to say, in these different words, what the metaphor means. No other words can do what a living metaphor does: a metaphor is irreplaceable. So too, we might add, with every work of art that matters to me: there is always more to find in it.

And so, also, with my friends. If our relationship is instrumental, I know what I want from you independently of who you happen to be. I can judge how well you serve my purpose and I can replace you with someone else who will do as well or better. Just as what matters primarily in literal discourse is the meaning the words communicate and not the words themselves, so in instrumental relationships what matters is the purpose these relationships serve and not the person who serves it: it is what you do, not who you actually are, that makes a difference to me: you are, so to speak, fungible. By contrast, if we are friends, who you actually are makes a tremendous difference: like a living metaphor, you are irreplaceable. And here perhaps is a further parallel with metaphor: Could our friends be irreplaceable because, just as with metaphors, we *never* fully know what their role in our life may be? Could our friends be, in the sense that metaphors are, inexhaustible?

Let me try to explain this notion by means of a story. Several years ago, a very good friend (I'll call him Tom, since that is his name) was visiting me at home in Princeton. On a cold, wet, gray November morning, as I was getting ready to drive my ten-year-old son to school, Tom decided to come along and, since we were in a hurry and he wasn't going to get out of the car, he threw a raincoat over his pajamas and jumped in. Traffic at the school yard, because of the rain, was even worse than usual and we were part of a long, slow queue of cars waiting their turn. When we finally came to the front, as I got out of the car to speed things up for those waiting behind me, I saw that one of my tires was flat. As I stood by the car, cold, wet, and horrified because I had no idea how to change it, under the eyes of the many annoyed parents in their cars behind us, Tom—in dark-blue pajamas, a gray raincoat, and bare feet—leaped out of the car and took over. Changing the tire turned out to be a complicated affair and, every few minutes, he had to stop working and move out of the way so that a few of the cars behind us could drive by.

A crowd gathered: the children mostly stared, fascinated; some adults offered to help, though there was nothing they could do; others just watched or made various jokes (one, a colleague of mine at the university, told me how lovely she thought Tom's outfit was). Of all that, Tom remained completely oblivious. He fixed the tire, drove with me to a garage, discussed the situation with a mechanic—still in pajamas, raincoat, and bare feet—and returned home ready to work while I collapsed in a useless heap.

If you ever were to ask me why Tom is my friend, that story would certainly be among the things I would tell you. I would also talk to you about his talent for dealing with practical issues and of the loyalty he manifested in his actions that morning. But that would miss the point, which I would try to capture further by emphasizing that, surrounded though he was by scores of well-dressed people about to go to their office or country club, his absurd outfit didn't give him a moment's thought. I would tell you that his down-to-earth practical sense coexists with a touching, spontaneous otherworldliness, which, like everything else I have mentioned about him, is completely in character. *And so on.*

Even that, though, would fail: it would fail to communicate that no one else could have done what Tom did that morning. And if you replied that fixing a tire in a silly outfit is not such a rare feat, nor something only a friend would do, I would say to you, unhelpfully, that only Tom could have done what he did in that "particular" way or, equally unhelpfully, that what mattered to me was not just what Tom *did* but who he *is*, which no list of his features, however long, could ever capture. It's not that I *don't* love my friend because he is practical: there is something right—but not *quite* right—in that way of speaking. For there are plenty of practical people in the world whose practicality leaves me more or less indifferent. Why, then, does it give me a reason to love *this* particular person?

Perhaps the answer lies not in my friend's features alone but in the relation between his features and mine. Perhaps, that is, the answer lies not just in Tom's practical efficiency alone but in the fact that he is practical and I am not. It could be this complementary contrast between us that accounts for our attraction to each other: "Opposites attract," as some ancients used to say, and many of us still do. But the problems of this view are obvious: Why should my practical friend not seek to avoid me and the chores and frustrations that come from my needs and shortcomings instead of liking me on their account, as he claims he does? Could it be, instead, that we are attracted to each other not by our differences but by our similarities—say, that both of us have similar academic inclinations and interests? "Like likes like," as some other ancients would have it. But how would that account for the fact that one of the main reasons of my friendship with my classmates from boarding school in Greece is precisely that none of them is an academic and our relationship allows me to leave that part of myself temporarily aside? It seems clear that neither similarities nor differences, which, after all, we share with everyone in the world, can explain why we love one another.

A story, like the story of Tom fixing the flat tire, may be more illuminating than any list of features because it is so much less abstract, but no narrative can stand on its own, either. To let you see how what happened that morning both sprang from my friendship with Tom and at the same time contributed to it, I would have to tell you still other stories, if only to establish some aspects of Tom's personality and show that what happened that particular morning was rooted in our long history together. But even a combination of stories, whatever detail and texture they may add to my original narrative's rough picture, will never be enough to explain—either to you or, for that matter, to me—why Tom and I are friends. However fine-grained, these stories will always describe something general or generalizable, something of which not only Tom but many others are capable as well. Inevitably, these stories will miss exactly what distinguishes my friend from these other people, why I am drawn to him and not to them instead. What matters, as Montaigne rightly observed, is "not one special consideration, nor two, nor three, nor four, nor a thousand: it is I know not what of all this mixture" that might explain it, if such a mixture could ever be fully described—but it cannot.

Lovers and friends who appreciate the inadequacy of such explanations can turn to lyric poetry, using it to transfigure our stories and our lame lists of features, however trite the verses we invoke may have become: "Shall I compare thee to a summer's day? / Thou art more lovely and more temperate." Transfiguration is exactly the point:

in using poetry, we abandon the realm of the literal and once again enter the domain of metaphor. What does it mean to be more lovely and more temperate than a summer's day? The sonnet goes on to tell us: It is to be unshaken by "rough winds" like "the darling buds of May"; it is to hold no "lease" that has "too short a date." But these are metaphors too, and each one must be in turn paraphrased and explicated, and each paraphrase and explication will end with another "and so on," which marks the unavoidable gap between what we can say about both the language and the people we love and the full extent of our feelings. Even the simple verses of a Broadway song— "If you're ever in a jam, / Here I am. / If you're ever in a mess, / SOS"—were I to use them to express my feelings for you, would reveal that gap the moment I tried to say exactly what they mean. Lyric poetry is useful for talking of love and friendship because it acknowledges that explaining these phenomena fully is a vain hope.

Lyric poetry and metaphor bring us into the domain of aesthetics, and I am tempted to say that there is indeed something aesthetic in my appreciation of Tom's actions in the school yard (it certainly wasn't moral). Aesthetic, in part, because what made it so touching is that although it revealed something quite new about him—I could never have predicted it—it also fit in so well with what I knew about him already. What Tom did *made sense*: once it happened, all I could say was, "Of course!" It was both new and fitting, it made him both more complex and more coherent: it manifested his style. Aesthetic, also, because nothing I say can guarantee that you would also see what I saw in his behavior: despite all my efforts, you might very well—and without being necessarily wrong—find the event ludicrous, even if you were there that morning. Thoreau said it best: "You know about a person who deeply interests you more than you can be told. A look, a gesture, an act, which to everybody else is insignificant tells you more than words can."

Immanuel Kant said something very similar about our relationship to beautiful objects. We can never say everything about them—there is always more to tell than we can express at any point. And nothing I can tell you about something whose beauty moves me, no reason I can give you for admiring it is ever enough to make sure that you, too, will be moved when you are exposed to it. There is, Kant argued,

> no rule in accordance with which someone could be compelled to acknowledge something as beautiful. Whether a garment, a house, a flower is beautiful: no one allows himself to be talked into his judgment about that by means of any grounds or fundamental principles. One wants to submit the object to his own eyes.

In the same way, nothing I can tell you about Tom's behavior in the school yard can make sure that you will see what I saw in it: "You had to be there," as we say in these situations. But even if you were, all you might have seen is a crazy person holding up traffic.

Just as we can't fully explain why something is beautiful, so we can't fully explain why we are friends with someone in a way that will make the grounds of our attraction obvious to another—and even to ourselves. Our efforts always leave something out. And it is what is always left out that we try to gesture toward when we say that it is not something *about* our friends that we love but our friends *themselves*. But the self that we love is always just one step beyond whatever we can actually articulate. And so we are faced with a choice between saying something that seems informative but is never enough of an explanation ("loyal, practical, unworldly, and so on") and saying something else that seems like an explanation but is completely uninformative ("the individual, in the uniqueness and integrity of his or her individuality").

ALTHOUGH NO LIVING METAPHOR CAN BE FULLY paraphrased, we are content to leave most of them incomplete and turn to other things. Some metaphors, though, won't let us go and we become their willing captive. These—and they are different for each one of us—move us with a promise that what we have not yet seen in them will be valuable in some way or other, that it will be worth our while to find what it is. And so we stay with them. They—and the works of art where we find them—become parts of our life: we love them.

This is also true of our friends. Some people matter to me because they provide me with things I already know I want and my interest in them, beyond a minimum of necessary respect, is limited to what they can do for me. Although I know that they have their own lives and loves and dreams, their sorrows and disappointments, that doesn't give me a reason to want to know them better and care about their lives and loves and dreams, their sorrows and disappointments. I am content to leave the matter there. They are means to my ends, and my interest in them ends, as we have seen, with their usefulness.

But other people matter to me not only as means but also as ends in themselves. I take their desires seriously in their own right, sometimes as seriously, sometimes even more seriously, than my own. I am ready to change my desires, to let their lives and loves and dreams, their sorrows and disappointments affect, and sometimes become, my own, and so I am willing, even eager, to change myself as a result of coming to know them. These are the people who—no matter how close or distant our relationship—have a place in my life that no one else can occupy, and I love them all. It's not, for example, that I like Tomas simply for his wit while I love Tom for himself. My feelings are directed at Tomas himself no less than, in his case, they are directed at Tom. The difference between love and affection or liking is, like the differences between our various friendships, only one of degree: Love is affection's deepest and most all-encompassing expression.

At no point do I shift my affection from my friend's features to my friend's "self": that is in place from the very beginning, even in the most casual friendship. If I care for my barber or for Tom and not just for my haircut or the condition of my house, what matters to me in both cases is

something more than our "ascribed"—that is, our professional or instrumental—relationship. That "something
more," which every attempt to explain my feelings for my
friends always leaves out, is what, in each and every case,
counts as their "self." It involves a commitment to the future, a sense that there is more to know here, and a promise
that what I still don't know will be worth learning. And so,
what counts as our friends'"self"varies with the nature, the
intensity, and the complexity of our relationships. My interest in Tomas (like his interest in me) extends to few ar-
eas beyond those covered by our professional connection,
and we keep silent about countless aspects of our lives that
are essential to my relationship with Tom, as many other
aspects of Tomas's life that I know nothing about are essential to his own close friendships.

Some subjects, though, may remain beyond the reach
of even our most intimate friends. Kant was not being
completely unreasonable when, in one of the dark moods
of his late years, he warned that there is always a need for
reserve,

> not so much for one's own sake, as for that of the other;
> for everyone has his weaknesses, and these must be kept
> hidden even from our friends . . . so that humanity
> should not be offended thereby. Even to our best friend,
> we must not discover ourselves as we naturally are and
> know ourselves to be: that would be a nasty business.

There are many things I might disclose to a physician, a
psychiatrist, or, if I were religious, to a priest or minister

that I would keep from my friends. Such precautions aside, however, there are almost no limits to the aspects of ourselves that enter our friendships. Our instrumental relationships are clearly circumscribed: our interest in each is focused on satisfying some explicit need or desire. But our interest in our friends goes well beyond whatever specific expectations we may have for our relationship.

Friendship, like every kind of love, requires more than an appreciation of what we already know our friends to be. It also makes, as I said, a commitment to the future. Saying "You are my friend" or, more generally, "I love you," is not only an expression of how I feel at the present moment. It is also, and crucially, a promise that my feelings will last longer than this present moment and an expression of my sense that our place in each other's life will in some way make life for both of us better than it would be otherwise. Our friendship reflects not only on what we have already found attractive about each other (think how little we may know about some people when we make such a commitment) but also on the sense that other things about us, things we don't yet know—even things that may come into existence only because of our friendship—will seem attractive to us as we come to know each other better: "Love is not an end but a process through which one person attempts to know another."

We saw earlier that friends are not primarily means to each other's ends but ends in their own right. That means that when I become your friend, I don't take my desires for granted. I submit myself to you, and I am willing to want new things, to acquire new desires, perhaps even to adopt new values as a result of our relationship. I can't know in advance what any of these will be, especially since you, too, are going to change through our friendship in ways neither one of us can anticipate. Our friendship promises—and continues to promise, as long as it lasts—a better future; but all that I can know about that future is that I can't approach it with anyone but you. To befriend someone else, to want to start desiring new things because of that friend's ("particular") needs and desires, would lead to a different future: it would turn me into a different person. The promise friendship makes can be very firm but, however firm it is, its fulfillment is never guaranteed: ready as I am to come to want new things and harbor new wishes because of your own desires and wishes, I also can't know what will become of me once these have a hand in shaping my life.

That commitment to the future—the hope for a better life that remains unknown for now—is exactly what every one of our efforts to explain the grounds of our friendships always and necessarily leaves out. That is why every explanation is so disappointingly thin. They all contain an implicit "And so on," an open end or ellipsis that reveals that the friendship is still alive. It is when this ellipsis disappears, when we feel that we know exactly why we are attracted to someone and that our future together will be just like our past, that we are in fact no longer attracted to them: "I love how you stand in the world, I love your talent, I love you passion, I love your anger," as *The L Word* put it—but I don't love *you*.

It's not that friendship involves two different attitudes or states of mind and feeling—the love I have for you now on the basis of what I already know about you, and the love I expect to have on account of what I may find about you in the future. Rather, I love you already because of what I imagine, however obscurely, that future to be. If ever that image of the future disappears, if one day you find yourself feeling that you already know everything that matters, that there is nothing more you want to learn about me—on that day our friendship will be over: it will have become a bore. Friendships can end for many reasons: quarrels, absences, new relationships. Each can play a role in the disintegration of a friendship, but what each really does is deprive friends of their desire to share their future with each other.

Because friends, as Aristotle says, spend a lot of their time together, the forward-looking element in friendship makes every relationship risky. When I approach you in friendship my hope is that you will make me wish for things I couldn't have even thought to wish for without you. I give you power over myself and trust you not to exploit it. I put my identity at risk because, despite the certainty that love inspires, it is impossible for me to know what our relationship will ultimately mean for me and whether it will be for good or bad. Nothing ensures that my feeling or my judgment is right, that I won't one day realize that you have actually been a disappointment, even a harm. Worse, nothing ensures that our relationship won't harm and degrade my judgment itself, making me feel happy to have become someone I would have hated to be, perhaps rightly, had you not come into my life.

All that is true of all my friends but, once again, it is a matter of degree. I am closer to some of them than I am to others, and I don't devote myself to them all with equal intensity. My interest in my casual friends spreads to fewer aspects of their personality and isn't strong enough to motivate the passionate involvement I have with those whose lives are inextricably connected with mine. But even with my casual friends, the sense that there is more to know, and that this more will be good, is always there. As long as that sense is alive, we remain friends and I love them "for themselves."

Aristotle believed that friends love each other for themselves when they love each other for their essence, for those features that make them who they are: their virtues (or as we might say, their character). But what I am arguing is that we don't need to accept this metaphysical justification in order to say what needs to be said about the love friends have for each other. Love always includes the desire to come to know our friends better, in ways and respects that go beyond our impersonal connections. It is a desire based on an unshakeable sense that coming to know each other better will be good for us both. We make this prospective commitment to our friends without knowing exactly what aspects of themselves will come to light through our friendship. We love our friends not just for what they already are—some of which we know, some not—but also for what they can be, at least partly as a result of our relationship. Our friends' "self" includes both what they already are and what they can be, and to love them "for themselves" is to love not only what they are not but also what they can become. Equally important, to love our friends for themselves is also to hope that we will love what we *ourselves* will become because of our relationship with them. But what any one of us may be in the future can't be known in the present, and this commitment to a still-unknown future that can't possibly be described is what every effort to explain why we love someone always leaves out.

The self, then, is elusive because it is always unfinished business. And not only that. It is also elusive because, since different aspects of our personalities are involved in our different friendships, to love all my friends for themselves is not to love the same thing in them all—whether that is a special set of features (their essence), or all their features together, or something else, a mysterious "subject" above and beyond them all. The self we love in each particular case consists of different features of our various friends and what we suspect, or hope, they can be as a result of our interaction. Moreover, my friends have other friends, whom they love for themselves, and the features these other friends are focused on are bound to be different from those that are important to me. According to C. S. Lewis, Charles Lamb said somewhere that if one of three friends (A, B, and C) should die, B loses not only A but also "A's part in C," while C loses not only A but also "A's part in B": "In each of my friends," Lewis observed, "there is something that only another friend can truly bring out." If I and someone else are both your friends, and love you for yourself, the self we love is bound to be at least a little different. For the same reason, my own self—the self my friends love—is different within each one of my various friendships.

Because of their desire to create a different, unanticipated future, friends give each other power over each other and put their respective identities in question. That, rather than the complex nature of persons or our limited capacity for knowledge, is the reason we don't ultimately know why we love our friends. We do love our friends for reasons we don't rightly understand, but when we approach another in friendship, we don't take ourselves for granted, either. We come to each other with a sense that our friendship will allow us to function at our best, improving what we already know of ourselves, engaging parts of which we have been unaware, and leading us to new features that, we hope, will be all to the good. However convinced we may be that everything will work out well in the end, our coming together is always a commitment to an uncertain future. Our lives and the lives of our friends are indissolubly mixed, the more so the closer we are, and our lives develop, for better or worse, in ways and directions made possible by our relationships with one another.

That I love you for yourself, because of who you are, is only a partial truth. It also matters who I happen to be. The full truth lies in Montaigne's nonexplanation: If you press me to say why I love you, I can only say, "Because it is you, because it is I."

Chapter 5

"NO SENSE OF HUMOR"
A Friendship Breaks Down

LIKE METAPHORS AND WORKS OF ART, THE PEOPLE who matter to us are all, so far as we are concerned, inexhaustible. They always remain a step beyond the furthest point our knowledge of them has reached—though only if, and as long as, they still matter to us. For where one of us may discover a whole new world, another may pass by without a second look. Worse, where we ourselves had once discovered a whole new world, we may now see only its ruins. We go through life immersed in a vast array of possibilities, unaware of most and mostly indifferent to those we are aware of. Our time and energy are limited, our obligations are heavy; we need to be on our way and we can't stop to look into everything we pass by. Yet every now and then we come across some people who invite us—sometimes compel us—to make time for them: people who promise to make a difference to our life, to draw us into new, exhilarating directions. Anticipating a future with such a promise fulfilled, we long to join our lives with theirs—sometimes for a short while, sometimes for very long—imbued with the certainty that things will be good with us both. No matter how strong, though, that conviction can prove baseless and the hopes it generates are often dashed. When that happens—and it happens often enough—little compares to the grief and disappointment of love that is met with aversion or indifference, or that turns out to have been prompted by deception or wishful illusion.

We can find a concrete illustration of this reality in Yasmina Reza's play *Art*, which, like all drama, can offer us a nuanced picture of friendship. Friendship, an embodied relationship, is intimately expressed in the looks, gestures, postures, and tones of voice that are crucial to dramatic representation but difficult to capture in the other arts. Drama can also depict the repetitive situations that are important to friendship without commentary—without, that is, the long and often boring descriptions that are necessary for the novel. Most important, though, *Art* draws a single frame around art, friendship, and loss, and in so doing casts light on all three.

ART IS ABOUT THE FRIENDSHIP AMONG THREE MIDDLE-aged, urban men and their love, or hatred, of a particular painting. Serge is a well-to-do dermatologist who has just bought, for a substantial sum, an abstract painting that is almost uniformly white. At least, it seems almost uniformly white—and nothing else—to his friend Marc, an aeronautical engineer, whose world is shaken by the idea that Serge could have spent so much for a painting Marc hates. He is convinced that Serge could not possibly love such a painting—or, worse, he suspects that Serge actually does. But where Marc sees white and white only, Serge discerns complexity and subtle coloration—not undifferentiated blankness but celestial light. Marc's harsh and sarcastic reaction to the painting hurts Serge very deeply. The tension the painting creates between them quickly spreads to the rest of their relationship, and their friendship begins to disintegrate. Their other friend, Yvan, whose professional life has been mostly a failure so far, is a mild man who hates strain and confrontation. Appalled by what is happening to Marc and Serge, Yvan keeps trying to intercede and help preserve their friendship. His efforts, though, only help to make things worse, and eventually everyone is furious with everyone else.

One question that animates the play is whether we can possibly love both people and works of art, which are not even animate objects, in the same way. As the philosopher Mary Mothersill once asked, "Isn't it pure gush to speak of falling in love with a novel? Can one be seduced by a poem or enamored of a melody?" She answered that we can:

Unless the absurdity is supposed to be self-evident, there must be an answer to the question, "Why not?" and it's not clear that there is any non-boring answer. ("A novel is not a person" is a boring answer.) Not everything is possible; for example, getting married and living happily ever after with a novel is not; but "falling in love" strikes

me as literal and non-hyperbolic in its application to aesthetic response within a certain range.

There are many things we can't do with works of art, even
if we love them: marry them, make love or fight with
them, be jealous of them, or go shopping together—
though we can, I believe, live happily ever after with them.
The reason, though, is not the difference between two
kinds of love but the difference between the two kinds of
things that we love: we can't marry our friends, either, but
that doesn't prevent friendship from being one of love's
paradigmatic instances. The love of art preserves the most
essential feature of the love between people: the exhilarating sense that things will go well with both of us, though
in ways we can't ever fully articulate, if they acquire a place
in our life. Interacting with works of art changes us in
ways we cannot anticipate completely; and it also changes
them because, ideally, our interaction, which consists in
interpretation, establishes new and previously unknown
features of theirs, and gives them to us and perhaps the
world with a new face.

Art opens with Marc addressing the audience: "My
friend Serge has bought a painting. It's a canvas four foot
by five: white. The background is white and if you screw up
your eyes, you can make out some fine diagonal lines." The
action then moves back in time, to the day when Serge
proudly unveils his painting for Marc, who examines it si-
lently for some minutes. When he finally speaks all he
asks is: "Expensive?" and when he hears what Serge paid

for it, he sneers, "You paid 200,000 francs for this shit?" Before speaking, Marc, like any good friend, had two choices: if he thought that the most important thing for friends to do is to spare each other's feelings, he could pretend that he liked or at least didn't dislike the painting and leave it at that; but if he believed that friends need above all to be honest with each other, he could say just what he thought of it. In fact, he chooses the latter, but he uses a scornful tone that suggests his motives may be darker than the simple desire to be truthful. Serge is shocked.

Refusing to humor Serge in any way, Marc insists on treating the whole thing as a joke. He pretends—perhaps in the hope that he might be right?—that Serge is perfectly aware that his painting is worthless and has bought it as a lark, infuriating him even further. Marc claims not to mind Serge's being "an exhibition freak" so long as he remains "a freak with a sense of humor"—as he would be, if only he, too, treated his painting as a joke. Serge, of course, does nothing of the sort. Crucially, Marc now shifts his criticism from the work itself to the significance of what it reveals about Serge's character. The decision to spend all that money for a nearly all-white painting, he says, indicates that Serge's sense of humor has abandoned him: "You can't have a laugh with him any more," he complains to Yvan a little later.

Serge, for his part, tries to explain away his friend's reaction: Marc is, after all, an engineer and knows nothing about modern art. Friends often disagree about such things without quarreling, and Marc is entitled to his opinion. It's not his opinion that Serge seems to hold against Marc but, generalizing again from a particular instance, the aspects of his character that it brings into view. Marc, he complains to Yvan, showed "no warmth when he dismissed it out of hand. Just that vile, pretentious . . . know-all laugh. I hated that laugh." Rather than Marc's philistinism, Serge minds the pretentious knowingness with which he brushes the painting aside and his lack of consideration for their friendship. Not what Marc said but "the way he said it," not what Marc did but what doing so "showed" about him, is what sticks in Serge's throat—just as Marc claims that what he finds intolerable is not that Serge spent all that money on the painting or that he disagreed with him on its worth but his humorlessness.

This pattern, of taking one another's words to mean "more" than they say and to manifest objectionable character traits, emerges several times during the play. It brings to the fore a crucial feature of the way friends construe one another's words and actions, both when their friendship is flourishing and, perhaps even more so, when it is in the process—as it is in *Art*—of falling apart. At one point, for example, when Yvan confesses that he has found the white painting rather moving, Marc lashes out savagely at him. He doesn't object to Yvan's confession itself, but to what the confession, which he sees merely as an effort to avoid a confrontation with Serge, demonstrates about Yvan's character: "You have no substance, Yvan. You're flabby, you're an amoeba . . . obsequious . . . dazzled by money." On yet another occasion, as things are going from bad to worse, Serge reveals that he has always found Marc's partner, Paula, "repellent": to explain what he means, he singles out the dismissive gesture with which she waves cigarette smoke away when it bothers her, blaming her not so much for the gesture itself but for what it expresses: "You can't tell if it's you or your cigarette that's getting up her throat . . . it reveals a cold, condescending and narrow-minded nature. Just what you're in the process of acquiring yourself," he tells Marc.

The play's repeated transitions from the particular to the general, from a single action to a character as a whole, are deeply convincing. The reason, which applies as well to the case of my own friend Tom, is that friends—and enemies, which is what Serge, Marc, and Yvan are in danger of becoming and indeed, at least for a while, are—see much more in one another's actions than those who are not personally involved; and what they see matters more to them than it matters to the rest of the world.

That was just how I, too, reacted to that school-yard incident involving Tom. Changing someone's tire is not itself a remarkable feat (if, unlike me, you know how to do it). Tom could easily have done it for someone else; a stranger could easily have changed mine. But where others saw merely a hindrance or a strange eccentric, I saw my friend. What I saw, moreover, had little to do with Tom's purpose. It's true that his action helped me greatly, but although that may have been his goal in the first place, it didn't account for the difference: I was grateful for his help, but I would have been equally (perhaps even more) grateful to a stranger who had come to my aid. It is not that his purpose was irrelevant. Had I known, say, that he was simply showing off, I would have been surprised and disturbed because such a purpose would have manifested aspects of Tom's personality that were both new and distasteful to me. Like the characters in *Art*, I would have complained not about his changing the tire (with which I would have been quite happy) but about what doing so revealed about his character. As things stood, his help was most welcome, but it was what it showed about his character, of which it was part and parcel, and about our friendship, of which it was a manifestation, that mattered to me; and it mattered much more than the specific action he performed.

In the interactions of friends, the character traits from which their actions proceed are at least as important, if not more so, than the goals with which they act. One philosopher has even argued that the purpose with which an action is undertaken is never enough to establish whether it is an act of friendship or not. According to this line of thought, an act of friendship must proceed from the right motive: it must be done *out of* friendship, out of concern for one's friend; what it aims to accomplish is never enough to establish it as an act of friendship. On the level of their behavior itself, Tom, an altruist, and a toady could have done the very same thing: any one of them might have changed my tire. But the altruist would have acted because that was the right thing to do and the toady because of the goodwill it would create on my part. Tom, though, did it because he is my friend—or, to keep to Montaigne's formula, because we are friends.

That is not to say that when we act out of friendship, thoughts like "I will do what she wants because she is my friend" figure explicitly in our deliberations. Our friendships permeate our personality, they structure our perception of the world, and in many circumstances enable us to act in a particular way without a second thought: they are part of the background that allows us to perceive directly that we must do something for a friend that we wouldn't do for someone else. Friendship is in that respect more like courage, generosity, or modesty than it is like justice. In order to act justly, we must establish that our course of action is in fact, at least according to our own definition, just: we must be aware that we are trying to be just, having something like this thought in mind: "I am doing this because it is the just thing to do." Even if such a thought isn't necessary, having it would not disqualify my action: it could still be just. Yet doing something in the awareness that it is courageous, with the thought "I am going to save my comrade's life because that is the courageous thing to do," far from expressing courage, is actually incompatible with it. If I were acting courageously, my thought, if I had a conscious thought at all, would be something like "This will save my comrade's life"; the action would simply seem the natural thing to do. It is only others who must appeal to its virtuous character in order to understand it: "She stood up against the oppressors because she is brave." So it is with friendship as well. "He helped Alexander because they are friends (or: out of friendship)" is what others would say of Tom; he himself must have simply noticed that people were waiting in the rain and that waiting for official help would be a waste of time. When, by contrast, I tell myself, "I will do what she asks because she is my friend," I admit that although I may doubt whether what she asked of me is right, I feel that loyalty requires me to do it.

What did I see when I saw my friend that morning in the school yard? I saw that Tom acted in character, manifesting several features of his on which our friendship depends: spontaneity, helpfulness, eagerness to solve problems, an extraordinary ability to focus, a disregard of dress conventions, and so on. "And so on" is again necessary because nothing I can say beyond "Well, that's Tom for you" could convey—and that only to someone who already knew Tom well—what I saw in his action: in a serious sense, I saw *all* of him or, at least, all that he is to me. Other acts, not only acts of friendship, can also manifest features of character: altruistic acts, say, can very well "be in character" as well. But what they manifest is relatively clear and not part of an open-ended list. They display a commitment to taking the interests of others in general seriously, perhaps as seriously as our own, and they join us to everyone else. Altruists treat everyone as they treat—or should treat—themselves and act as everyone else would act—or should act—in the same situation. This is clearly not a philosophically sophisticated account of what altruism is, but neither is the correct account of altruism the point here. Whatever the correct account turns out to be, it will explain fully what altruistic acts express and will apply in the same way to every altruist in the world: altruism goes hand in hand with the secularization of Christian love into universal respect: it is part and parcel of morality.

But the features we mention in trying to explain what a friend is like will seldom if ever apply in the same way to anyone else—that is the point of qualifying them not just as wit, kindness, or practicality but as the particular way our friend is witty, kind, or practical. Friendship differentiates us from the rest of the world. It requires, among other things, treating every one of our friends differently from the way we treat everyone else and in many cases differently from the way we treat our other friends, and depends on features that are distinctly our own.

To act in character is not to be predictable or unsurprising. Character is like style: that some artists have a distinct style doesn't mean that we predict what the works they will produce in the future will be like. Once they are produced, however, we will recognize that they were made by the same hand and perhaps delight in seeing how a particular style is manifested in a distinct and, for that reason, engaging work. Just so, one of the great pleasures of friendship is recognizing our friends' character in all sorts of new situations and actions that, although we could never have predicted them, make perfect sense once they have been performed. "That's just what Tom *would* do" does not mean that I could have ever known in advance how he would react to our situation that rainy day.

His behavior was surprising but, at the same time, totally (what else?) characteristic. It introduced new possibilities in our relationship.

FRIENDS CAN SURPRISE WHEN THEY ACT IN CHARACTER but they can also surprise—often in very jarring ways—when they act in ways that are drastically out of character. When they do, the friendship's basic presuppositions may be seriously threatened. That is the situation *Art* explores. For Marc, Serge's decision to buy the white painting is totally out of character, and that's why at first he tries to turn the whole episode into a joke. He seems to think that if Serge bought the painting on a lark—or if, at least, he says that he did—they could both treat the incident as a single, isolated event, an aberration with no significance for Serge's personality as a whole. Or again, they could take it as an expression of the sense of humor that Marc had earlier admired in Serge—a very surprising act that was still in character. In either case, the episode would fit smoothly into Marc's image of Serge and give him no reason to change his attitude toward him: it would not have changed Serge in Marc's eyes. But his efforts are unsuccessful: their only effect is to provoke Serge's resentment and anger and block Marc's two attempts to give a harmless interpretation to the event. Serge was serious when he bought the painting and his buying it shows something serious—and disturbing—to Marc.

From that point on, no matter how hard he tries, Marc can't keep the incident in what we might consider a sort of quarantine. He can't prevent what he takes it to show about Serge from spilling over into the rest of his friend's personality and so he can't help revising his view of his character—and the meaning of his past actions—in ways that make him, in his turn, resentful and angry. To him, the painting reveals a Serge he can no longer recognize: either Serge has somehow changed in intolerable ways or he has finally revealed his true nature, which, kept hidden so far, turns out to have been intolerable all along.

When a friendship is breaking down, everything acquires a new significance. Marc, who "can no longer have a laugh" with Serge, refuses to believe that Serge may have been laughing at himself for the enormous sum the white painting had cost him—"Crazy, or what?" Serge had asked, bursting into laughter, when he was discussing it with Yvan. Yvan relates the episode to Marc, who would have found the laughter natural in the "old" Serge, but now sees in it only the "new" Serge's cunning spinelessness: "He wasn't laughing because his painting is ridiculous . . . You [Yvan] were laughing at the painting and he was laughing to ingratiate himself." The white painting leaches into every aspect of Serge and Marc's relationship, affects the significance of everything they say and do, and shines a completely unflattering light on everything they have said and done. Everything that happens between them now grates on them both.

It is a common pattern in disintegrating relationships that when friends try to smooth things over, they only manage to sharpen their conflicts. During one of their several efforts to leave their quarrel behind, Marc offers Serge a sort of apology: "I'm too thin-skinned, I'm too highly strung, I overreact . . . You could say, I lack judgment," to which Serge replies, rather curtly: "Read Seneca," having already suggested that Marc could learn a lot from the Roman philosopher's treatise on the good life. Marc, trying to make amends, insists that he is thin-skinned because he "could easily have been annoyed" by Serge's superior tone, a reaction Serge himself calls "absurd." But Marc's effort backfires because when he says that Serge's pomposity doesn't bother him, he in fact implies that Serge *is* pompous. He also reveals, not quite inadvertently (as most of us do when we say such things), that it does in fact annoy him—if it didn't, he wouldn't have thought of it as pomposity; he might even not have noticed it at all. Serge, for his part, concedes, half-heartedly, that Marc may have been right; his tone was wrong: "When I said 'Read Seneca,' you thought you could identify a kind of superiority. You tell me you lack judgment and my answer is 'Read Seneca,' well, it's obnoxious!" But his effort to apologize fails because, needled by his "you *thought* you could identify a kind of superiority," Marc replies that what Serge said was in fact obnoxious. That inflames Serge, who now accuses Marc of lacking judgment: he should have understood that Serge hadn't said "Read Seneca," whose tone might have sounded superior, but "Read Seneca!" which didn't. Instead of a reconciliation, all they accomplish is an escalation of hostilities, which lead back to where the breakdown started, with Serge accusing

Marc of having lost his sense of humor. Soon, among other insults, Serge expresses contempt for Marc's ignorance of modern art, while Marc is equally scornful of Serge's pretentious attitude toward it. The common ground that had kept their friendship going for years has disappeared, and nothing is left in its place.

Another pattern in the behavior of friends whose relationship is breaking down emerges when Serge and Marc, in a subsequent effort to leave their quarrel behind, change the subject and discuss where to have dinner. When Serge suggests a particular restaurant, Marc responds with a catty comment about its cuisine—"Bit heavy, isn't it? Bit fatty, all those sausages." He immediately regrets his words and asks, in a conciliatory tone, "What do you think?" But at that point, neither one is willing to make a proposal— and certainly not a decision—which could give the other reason to complain about his choice, and each is keen to appear more flexible and ready to compromise than the other. So when Marc makes a concession—"I think the food's a bit on the fatty side, but I don't mind giving it a whirl"—Serge insists on being the one who gives ground—"No, if you think the food's too fatty, we'll find somewhere else"—and so on, back and forth. Their sparring is as funny on the stage as it is depressing in real life: at least one of them, probably both, will end up resenting whatever decision they finally make. Meanwhile, the peace-loving Yvan claims to be indifferent and glad to do whatever they want. That causes both Serge and Marc to turn on him, call him a coward and, when Yvan is naturally upset by their malice, pretend they had only been joking. And so Yvan, too, is accused of having lost his sense of humor.

Try as they may, the friends can't keep their feelings about the painting separate from the rest of their relationship. The reason becomes clear when Marc confesses, "I can't imagine you genuinely loving that painting . . . I love Serge and I can't love the Serge who's capable of buying that painting." He would rather believe that his friend has deceived himself than think of him as the kind of person who genuinely cares for such an object. Marc is facing once again the dilemma that confronted him earlier: If Serge really does like the painting, Marc must choose once again between the two equally depressing alternatives he has already faced. Either Serge, under the influence of his rich new friends, has become a "different," loathsome person, whom Marc must denounce if he is not to become loathsome himself; or the painting reveals that Serge had deceived him about his character, which had been loathsome all along, and that their friendship had always been a sham. In the first case, what might have been a genuine friendship has finally disintegrated. In the second, their relationship turns out to have been based on an illusion and had never been a genuine friendship at all.

When our friendship is strong, I am quite content with the idea that you may understand me better than I understand myself: we often depend on our friends to help us see things about ourselves that we can't recognize or admit on our own. But if our friendship is at risk, even the suggestion that I know you better than you know yourself will strike you as arrogant, overbearing, and obnoxious. That is just how Serge feels when Marc insists that Serge can't really like the white painting. His view is that either Marc should make a genuine effort to understand what it is that he likes about it or keep his criticisms to himself. After all, Serge confesses, he has never told Marc what he thinks of his partner, out of consideration for his friend's feelings: "When you asked me what I thought of Paula . . . did I say I found her ugly, repellent and charmless? I could have done," and launches his attack on her character based merely on the way she reacted to cigarette smoke. Merely? No, because in a friendship everything is interrelated and everything "shows something"—something good when the friendship is strong, something noxious when it is disintegrating. Not to mention the fact that in saying that he has not expressed his real opinion of Paula so far, Serge actually expresses it, which shows that he respects Marc's feelings as little as he accuses Marc of respecting his own.

Their anger reaches such an intensity that they come to blows, although the only one injured is Yvan, who tries to stop them. The scuffle seems to help their anger subside and, once again, they try to come to terms. But when a friendship is close to being in tatters, the most unimportant incident can acquire the greatest and most sinister significance.

After the fight, Marc confesses that what has really hurt him is that he feels that the white painting has replaced him in Serge's affections (a reminder that friends and works of art can play similar roles in our lives). That might have been the beginning of a reconciliation if Serge had tried to draw him out and perhaps show that it was possible for him to love them both. Instead, he claims that he can't understand what Marc is saying, asking Yvan to side with him (Yvan, though, has had enough: "I couldn't care less, you are both insane"). And so, instead of reconciliation, we get further aggression: "In my time, you'd never have bought that picture," Marc says, and when Serge asks, "What's that supposed to be, your time?" he answers, "The time you made a distinction between me and other people, when you judged things by my standards." Serge, rather sarcastically, questions whether there ever was such a time. Marc insists that there was, that Serge once treated him like "a man apart," proud to be his friend, but that he has now turned away from him: "I detest your independence. It's violence. You've abandoned me. I've been betrayed. As far as I'm concerned, you are a traitor." "I had no idea whatsoever," Serge scoffs, "really, it's come as a complete surprise to me—the extent to which I was under your influence and in your control."

Whatever we say in such a situation runs the risk of offending rather than reassuring. Whether we are aware of it or not, we may even *intend* it to be capable of both, intending it, that is, as a test of our friendship—an opportunity for the other to show goodwill by taking whatever we say in its reassuring rather than its offensive sense. But the charitable interpretation becomes excruciatingly difficult once we have begun to doubt our friend's character. We lose our bearings: "Now when we talk we can't even make ourselves understood." Perhaps it's time for the characters to face the facts: Serge: "So here we are at the end of a fifteen-year friendship." Marc: "Yes." Serge: "Pathetic."

BUT THE STORY DOESN'T END HERE.

It seems that the friends were not yet quite ready to face the facts. Instead of going their separate ways, Serge and Marc stay where they are and seem to relieve the tension between them by directing it against Yvan. They blame him for everything: he has been talking of nothing but himself, he is cowardly, he arrived late and ruined their evening; his "sheer neutral inertia has lured Marc and me into the worst excesses," Serge screams, and Marc excoriates him for his "finicky, subservient voice of reason . . . it's intolerable." They threaten not to attend his impending wedding, which they tell him is a big mistake, and urge him to cancel it. Yvan finally explodes. He bemoans his place in their friendship, his whole life in fact, and accuses them of betraying him: "I made you laugh . . . but come the evening, who was left solitary as a rat? . . . I'm not like you, I don't want to be an authority figure . . . I don't want to be self-sufficient, I just want to be your friend Yvan the joker! Yvan the joker!"

A long silence follows, broken by Yvan himself, who claims to be starving—"Haven't you got any nibbles?"— an abrupt change of subject that turns their attention to the mundane and actually helps calm things down. Serge offers him a bowl of olives (perhaps because they often signify the end of catastrophe and the arrival of peace). Yvan wonders how a simple "white square" could have possibly pushed them to such extremes and, when Serge once again insists that the painting is not white, Yvan bursts out laughing: "That's what it is, a piece of white shit! Let's face it, mate . . . What you've bought is insane!" Marc laughs along with him, happy to see him treat the painting as a joke: somehow, it seems that they have found their sense of humor again. While they are laughing, Serge leaves the room and returns with the painting. He tosses Marc a felt-tip pen and urges him to have at the painting. Marc first hesitates but eventually—to Yvan's (and the audience's) horror—he traces one of the white diagonals in the painting with the pen, and turns the blank canvas into a picture of a mountain slope, on which he draws a little skier with a woolly hat (Figure 10).

By giving Marc the pen and allowing him to deface it, Serge, too, turns the painting into a joke: he seems to care more about Marc after all. An uneasy truce is established and, after another silence, the three of them finally go out to dinner.

A few days later, we find Marc and Serge cleaning the painting, erasing both skier and mountain slope, restoring the picture to its original more or less pristine state while Yvan tells the audience that they both attended his wedding as his witnesses. Things seem to have taken a turn for the better, and along with the painting, their friendship, too, is in the process of being restored: the pen, it has turned out, was filled with washable ink. But Serge tells us

FIGURE 10. "THE LITTLE SKIER"

that when Marc asked him whether he had known that it was washable all along, he said that he hadn't, although he knew perfectly well that it was. How, he asks, could he have started what they are calling the "trial period" of their friendship with such a "disappointing admission"? "On the other hand," he continues, "was it right to start with a lie?"

Is it wrong to lie in order to cement a friendship, Serge asks himself? "Let's be reasonable. Why am I so absurdly virtuous?" he muses. Remember that Serge had never told Marc that he liked Paula: what he had actually said was that she was "a perfect match" for him. That wasn't an out-right lie—it is more like the ambiguous statements that can function as tests of friendship, depending on whether they are taken in a positive or in a negative sense. At the time, Marc took it as an unqualified compliment since Serge was his friend, and he assumed that Serge thought highly of him. True, if Serge liked Marc, saying that Paula was a perfect match for him would indicate he liked her, too. But did Serge like Paula at the time? We know from his complaints about her manner of reacting to cigarettes that at some point he found her deeply annoying, perhaps even from the very beginning. But, if Serge didn't like her, saying that she was a perfect match for Marc would indicate that he liked him no more than he liked her. Or was he perhaps just evading the issue, choosing to overlook one of Marc's weaknesses for the sake of their friendship? The play does not decide between these alternatives. It leaves us to worry about them as we might well worry about our own friendships also, and with the same uncertain results. What it does suggest is that friendship is a much more complicated and ambiguous relationship than the naive view, derived ultimately from Aristotle, that friends (being good people) have nothing to hide from one another. Perhaps Kant was right when he warned us never to tell even our closest friends everything about us because, if we do, they are bound to find us detestable.

The play ends on an even more ambiguous note. It gives the last word to Marc, just as it gave him the first. What he says now recalls what he said at the beginning, but with a significant difference. At first, he had seen nothing in that "white painting with white lines": now he sees a whole world within it. Here is what he says:

> Under the white clouds, the snow is falling.
>> You can't see the white clouds, or the snow.
>> Or the cold, or the white glow of the earth.
>> A solitary man glides downhill on his skis.
>> The snow is falling.
>> It falls until the man disappears back into the landscape.
>> My friend, Serge, who's one of my oldest friends, has bought a painting.
>> It's a canvas about five foot by four.
>> It represents a man who moves across a space and disappears.

ART IS REMARKABLE BECAUSE IT DEMONSTRATES HOW incidents that may be insignificant in themselves can sometimes, under certain circumstances, go to the very heart of one's view of oneself and others, especially among friends. In itself, buying an abstract painting, even if it's very expensive, is normally not enough to threaten a complex and long-standing relationship. But what is it to say that an event is insignificant "in itself"? These are the questions to which we must now turn.

Intuitively, what something is "in itself" seems to be what it is independently of its relations to anything else in the world. Serge has simply bought an abstract white

painting: "in itself," his action is independent of its antecedents in his life and character—his reasons for buying
it or for coming to value abstract art, for example—and
its consequences—its role, say, in the breakdown of his
friendship with Marc. Antecedents and consequences are,
as we say, part of an action's "significance," and significance depends on the context within which the action is
set, on its relations with other actions and events.

The distinction between an action itself and its significance is parallel to the contrast we draw between what the
action *is* and what it *means*, which allows us to say that we
may know what the action is without knowing what it
means. Serge and his two friends seem to confront such a
situation in the play. They all agree on what Serge has
done—he has bought a more or less white painting for a
lot of money—but they have vastly different views of what
that means. For Marc, it signifies Serge's new snobbish-
ness and his betrayal of their friendship; for him, its significance is far-ranging and deeply disturbing. "You don't
understand the seriousness of this, do you?" he asks Yvan.
But Yvan replies, evasively, "Er, no," and simply changes
the subject when Marc continues to press him: "Would
you like a cashew nut?"

The distinction between what something is and what it
means seems as clear as it can possibly be. Yvan, always in
character, tries to avoid a confrontation and deflect Marc's
criticisms of Serge: as long as Serge can afford the picture,
which makes him happy without harming anyone else,
what is there to worry about? That makes it tempting to

say that Yvan thinks that Serge's action has no significance beyond itself, but the difference between him and Marc is not that Marc takes Serge's decision to mean something while Yvan doesn't. As far as Yvan is concerned, buying the painting confirms that Serge is a sophisticated art lover who enjoys owning the sort of abstract art that his friends—Yvan himself above all—have trouble appreciating. Marc first tried—and failed—to interpret the painting as a joke and explain it as an expression of Serge's sense of humor. That would have allowed him to see it as an expression of a character trait with which he was already familiar and require no change in his attitude toward his friend: their relationship could continue as it was. Yvan, though, succeeds where Marc failed. He takes the painting as yet another manifestation of Serge's involvement with modern art, with which he was already familiar and at peace, and therefore has no reason to be surprised or to readjust his attitude. Serge's decision is meaningful and significant for both Marc and Yvan, unlike a tic or something that merely happened to Serge, like his getting caught in a rainstorm. The difference between them is that the painting shows nothing *new* about Serge to Yvan, nothing that requires him to revise his understanding of his character, whereas Marc believes that it reveals something radically new about him, something that requires a distressing reinterpretation of Serge's personality. Both think that what Serge did was significant; they only disagree about what exactly it signifies and how far-ranging that is. For both, though, Serge's decision can't be understood "in itself." It can only be understood in connection with other things they know, or need to come to know, about him.

Not only that. What the two friends believe that the painting reveals about Serge also reveals something about themselves—and that is true of friendship in general. Who our friends are and what they mean to us depends not only on their character but also on ours. When Yvan claims that the painting hasn't harmed anyone, Marc shouts that it has—it has harmed *him*: it hurts him to see Serge "let himself be ripped off and lose every ounce of discernment" by the snobs whose circle he has entered. Marc discerns a double error of judgment in what Serge has done: admiring the painting, an intellectual failing, and yielding to the authority of snobs, an ethical one. He is so deeply hurt because he had taken himself to be the authority that Serge most respects, and he fears that the painting and "all it implies" have usurped his position. Early on, Serge describes him as "quite breathtakingly arrogant," which is perhaps further confirmed when Marc dismisses Yvan, before he has yet come on stage, as "a very tolerant bloke . . . very tolerant because he couldn't care less." That is not only arrogant but also cunning: it prepares the ground for disregarding Yvan's response to the painting if it turns out not to match his own. What we find to like or dislike in our friends, and why we love them, is due not only to who they are—"Because it was he"—but also to who we are as well—"Because it was I": this is still Montaigne's territory.

What friends do always means something to them—usually something more than it means to a third person: it reveals something about the character of both. In that respect, it is not different from any human action. Even conventional behavior, say, discussing a restaurant's wine list with a waiter, indicates something about me. To the waiter, it may indicate that I am someone who likes and knows something about wine; to someone else, it may indicate a weakness for impressing others with my sophistication. (Both can be right.) Every one of our actions is meaningful and expresses something about our character. Some of our actions express generic features of ours: greeting a colleague at the office expresses a modicum of sociability, which I share with many others. Others express more specific, idiosyncratic, even unique aspects of our personality. Some of our features may be indifferent, others admirable, still others compromising; some may be new, casting new light on our character, others are already manifest, confirming what others already know about us; some do and others do not make it necessary to reevaluate what we take ourselves or others to be. But they all depend as much on the features of those who observe our actions as they do on our own nature and character.

The distinction between the action itself and its significance, what the action is and what it means, appears natural because two people may seem to be performing the same action—changing a tire in a crowded school yard, say—that in one case expresses friendship and in the other a way to make a living. Similarly, the action of a single individual—for example, buying an abstract white painting—may reveal either good taste or the desire to belong to a particular social class. Sometimes, one of these interpretations (or some other one still) is correct and the others wrong; sometimes, several are correct at the same time; sometimes, an action is truly ambiguous and can be interpreted in distinct and incompatible ways. Here, then, is a question for the theater: How is an action to be represented so that it can give rise to two or more alternative, even incompatible, interpretations and make them all, at least to a certain extent, plausible?

Art faces that question directly and forces it upon us because much of the interest of the play derives from the fact that it is not clear who among the three friends is right about the significance of Serge's buying the painting and who is not. For Serge, it is just an expression of his appreciation of the work. For Marc, it represents the erosion of his authority over Serge. And what does Yvan's changing attitude toward the painting signify? At the start, it is lukewarm at best: "I didn't like the painting . . . but I didn't actually hate it." But as he becomes familiar with it, he comes to agree with Serge that it is not purely white—he finds in it "various colors . . . yellow . . . grey, some slightly ochrish lines"—and a little later, he confesses, "The more I see it, the more I like it, honestly." Marc takes it that Yvan is just being cowardly and wants to avoid a confrontation with Serge. But Yvan's change of mind might have been an act of kindness, an effort to protect Serge from Marc's carping complaints. Or, again, his sympathy for Serge may have gradually enabled him to see the painting through Serge's eyes and truly come to appreciate it in its own right. Any one of these alternatives is plausible, and any production of the play must somehow allow them to emerge and seem plausible to its audience. The friends' attitudes toward the painting can't be simply arbitrary—that would be a complete dramatic failure.

A successful production of *Art* must present Serge's action so that its audience is made to see that it is capable of giving rise to the different interpretations the friends, each with his own degree of certainty, give to it. But the play, I believe, does not finally endorse the attitude of any one of the friends over the others', nor does it reveal who among them has the proper understanding of their friendship. We don't even know whether, by the end of the play, their friendship has been genuinely restored or whether it has become mere pretense. We don't know whether Serge lies to Marc about the ink in order to show that he doesn't really care for the painting after all and protect their friendship or simply in order to distract them from their fight and their dark self-revelations. We never even learn Serge's real motive in buying the painting. Indeterminacy is essential to this play. Each friend understands the others not only because of who and what they are but also because of who and what he is himself. And each one is who and what he is in part because of who and what each of the others is: their friendship has affected them deeply. Yvan's psychiatrist, whose convoluted words Yvan has had to write down in order to remember, may have gotten it right: "If I'm who I am because of who I am and you're who you are because of who you are, then I'm who I am and you're who you are. If, on the other hand, I'm who I am because you're who you are, and if you're who you are because I'm who I am, then I'm not who I am and you're not who you are." We are who we are in large part through our interactions with our friends, and who we are with one friend is not who we are with another.

IS THE WHITE PAINTING OF *ART* REALLY WHITE? THE stage directions tell us simply that it is "white . . . with fine white diagonal scars" but white comes in many guises. Is it a pure white (whatever that is), white like a piece of white paper (and what exactly is that?), white like commercial paints, which are always mixed with some different hue or other, white as the cover of the play's published text depicts it (which is actually a light beige) with gashes across its surface, like one of Lucio Fontana's ripped canvases (Figure 11), or white like Robert Ryman's paintings (Figure 12), which, looked at closely, reveal a shimmering array of the most diverse colors (that are, unfortunately, not visible on the printed page of a book)? The play does not decide, and the painting, which measures four feet by five feet, is small enough to prevent the audience from making a final judgment.

Nothing illustrates the indeterminacy of the painting's nature and color better than Marc's reactions. At the play's beginning, as we have seen, he sees mostly white in the

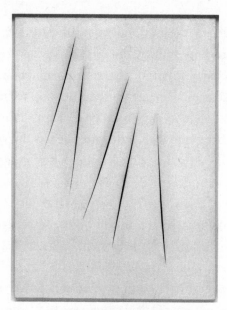

FIGURE 11. LUCIO FONTANA,
Concetto Spaziale, Attese (1965)

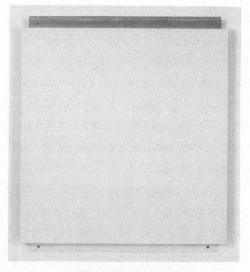

FIGURE 12. ROBERT RYMAN,
Attendant (1984)

painting: "My friend Serge has bought a painting. It's a canvas about five foot by four: white. The background is white and if you screw up your eyes, you can make out some fine diagonal lines." Throughout the action, he insists that the various colors Serge and Yvan claim to discern in it are not there. But at the end, after he has drawn and erased the little skier, he still sees the painting as a traditional representational work.

Although he probably doesn't know it, Marc's closing words locate him within a long tradition in the history of art. That tradition begins with Alphonse Allais (1854–1905), the great French humorist who anticipated some of the twentieth century's most controversial and provocative artistic gestures. In 1897, Allais composed his *Funeral March for the Obsequies of a Deaf Man*, the score of which is completely blank (Figure 13), well in advance of Erwin Schulhoff's silent *In Futurum* (1919) (Figure 14), which consists entirely of rests, and John Cage's *4′33″* (1952), which is still widely considered the first piece of its kind. More directly connected to our own concerns is the set of monochrome paintings Allais produced between 1883 and 1897, over twenty years before Kazimir Malevich's *Suprematist Composition: White on White* (1918) could even be imagined (Figure 15).

Allais's titles, in stark contrast to Malevich's minimalism, were prodigiously descriptive: so, for instance, his uniformly lime-green painting was entitled *Some Pimps, Known as Green Backs, on Their Bellies in the Grass, Drinking Absinthe*, while his white painting, which was considerably purer in

173

FIGURE 13. ALPHONSE ALLAIS,
Funeral March for the Obsequies of a Deaf Man (1897)

FIGURE 14. ERWIN SCHULHOFF,
In Futurum (1919)

color than the Malevich, was also much more complex in representational content than Marc's skier-version of Serge's painting. It is entitled *Anemic Girls on Their Way to Their First Communion in a Snowstorm* (Figure 16).

Like Allais, Marc belongs not only to an artistic tradition but also to a philosophical tradition whose main contemporary exponent is the philosopher Arthur Danto, who has proposed a theory of art inspired by Søren Kierkegaard: "The result of my life," Kierkegaard wrote, "is simply nothing, a mood, a single color. My result is like the painting of the artist who was to paint a picture of the Israelites crossing the Red Sea. To this end, he painted the whole wall red, explaining that the Israelites had already crossed over, and that the Egyptians were drowned."

FIGURE 15. KAZIMIR MALEVICH,
Suprematist Composition: White on White (1918)

PREMIÈRE COMMUNION DE JEUNES FILLES CHLOROTIQUES
PAR UN TEMPS DE NEIGE

FIGURE 16. ALPHONSE ALLAIS,
Anemic Girls on Their Way to
Their First Communion in a Snowstorm (1883)

What makes something a work of art, according to
Danto, is never the way it looks because many objects that
look exactly like works of art fail, for all that, to be works
of art themselves: they remain everyday or (as Danto pre-
fers) "mere real" objects. Danto's favorite examples are
Marcel Duchamp's *Fountain* and Andy Warhol's *Brillo
Boxes*. Countless urinals manufactured by the Mott Company of Philadelphia look just like the one Marcel Duchamp laid on its side, signed "R. Mutt," and exhibited at
the New York Armory show in 1917, but none of them is a
work of art. Similarly, Andy Warhol's *Brillo Boxes*, though
made of painted plywood, are indistinguishable in appearance from the containers we find in supermarkets, yet
only they, and not the containers, are works of art. Danto's
view is that there are no limits on what a work of art must

look like: it may look like anything in the world. What makes art out of a mere object is not the way it looks but an interpretation that accompanies it and turns it into something with a meaning. Kierkegaard's account of the red wall is intended to turn such an object into a work of art, while Marc's account of the white painting transforms one work of art into another—or, rather, it shows that one and the same mere object can constitute, depending on what meaning we attribute to it, two vastly different works of art.

Danto would reject Marc's final view of the painting because the only interpretation to which he grants that kind of authority is the interpretation of the artist who created the work of art in the first place. But privileging the artist in this manner—a view that is deeply controversial—is not part of the world of *Art*. Serge appears merely pompous and snotty when he scoffs at Marc's suggestion that he might want to frame his painting: "You say the artist as if . . . as if he's some unattainable being . . . some sort of god," Marc responds. In the end, *Art* does not take a stand on that issue, either. It does not allow us to decide whether Marc's interpretation of Serge's painting is or is not legitimate: Is the painting a purely abstract work with no discernible content, or is it, rather, the complex representational work of the invisible skier that Marc describes as the play closes? We don't know. We can only tell that the painting has generated two radically different interpretations, each accounting perfectly well for the way it looks.

The indeterminacy of the white painting can itself be viewed as an emblem of the matter of friendship—of the words and actions whose significance and importance are one thing to two friends, another to a third friend who listens to them, and yet another to people who are not part of their relationship. Spending 200,000 francs on a white painting is immensely important and a matter of pride to Serge because what it means to him is that he now owns a work he admires and it allows him to enter a world to which, so far, he has only aspired. It is also immensely important to Marc, but only because its meaning appalls him: it reveals a side of Serge that disturbs him to no end and forces him think differently about much that he had taken for granted about Serge, himself, and their friendship. Huntington, the dealer who sold the painting to Serge, presumably thinks of the whole affair as a successful transaction in which he has no further interest. To the audience, finally, Serge's decision has to be like the painting itself, capable of tolerating the two friends' different interpretations with their different implications for his friendship with Marc, and Marc's two different interpretations of the painting itself. A production of *Art* must make it clear that, like the painting's significance, the significance of much that the play's three characters say and do depends not simply on what they take it to be but also on the person who is interpreting their behavior at the time and on their relationship to each other.

How, then, as we asked earlier, can words and actions that may reasonably seem to carry several meanings with varying importance be represented? When Serge tells Marc that "the artist" would not want his painting framed, a good actor will speak his line so that the audience can see that it is possible, though not necessary, to find it snotty and pompous. The tone must tolerate Marc's hearing it as a reference to the artist "as some sort of god" but it must also allow Serge the ability to deny it. Similarly, after years of friendship, Marc and Serge seem to be used to Yvan's habitual evasions and his constant attempts to mediate between them. Still, Marc finds his tone of voice, his "finicky, subservient voice of reason" intolerable. For that reason, Yvan's appeals must be capable of sounding both honest and furtive, motivated both by his concern for their friendship and by his fear of confrontation. If he seems merely honest, the other two will be guilty of crudely misunderstanding him as their relationship deteriorates; if he appears simply furtive, they must have misunderstood him as crudely during the fifteen years they had been friends. These ambiguities must be preserved because they are essential to the play's representation of friendship.

They are also essential to friendship itself, and not only when it is, like the relationship depicted in *Art*, in danger of falling apart. While Tom was changing my car's tire in the school yard, some of the people there were merely facing an inconvenience, others an amusing eccentric, or a shocking display of disregard for the proprieties, or even a generous and charitable act—and all of them were right: I, though, was seeing friendship in action. In Tom's behavior I saw much that I knew about him already and, in addition, one way of fulfilling the promise that has kept our friendship alive for so many years. That promise was fulfilled in the new aspect of Tom that emerged through his action—novel, surprising, but also perfectly in character. It was a promise that existed only for the two of us because it depended not just on what happened that morning but also on our whole history together—a history that no one else could share. "You'd have to know him," as we commonly say, and even then you could never see him exactly as I did. For that, you'd need to know him as only I know him.

Friendship is an embodied relationship, and its depictions require embodiment as well: they must include the looks, the gestures, the tones of voice, and the bodily dispositions that are essential to textured communication and on which so much of our understanding of our intimates is based. But no description of looks, gestures, and tones of voice can ever be complete, and so no description can communicate whether these belong to an act of friendship or not. Many aspects of the behavior of friends are irreducibly visual, and that is another reason that friendship is a difficult subject for narrative, to which description is essential. But, as we have also seen, it is inherently temporal, and that makes friendship a subject unsuitable to painting. Looks, gestures, tones of voice, and bodily dispositions are the stuff of drama, which is, accordingly, the medium in which friendship is best represented—represented, that is, as a subject in its own right: friendship, not art, is what *Art* is about. And yet, by drawing a parallel between the indeterminacy of the white painting and the indeterminacy of the friends' behavior, *Art* makes another important point about both. It shows that in a crucial respect, they are on a par.

It is difficult to believe that being struck by the beauty of a person or a work of art is a merely subjective reaction, which others are completely free to accept, reject, or ignore without a second thought. We feel there is a serious difference between our taste for flavors or colors—things about which we say that "It's purely a matter of taste"— and our reaction to what we consider not just tasty or pleasant but actually beautiful. Especially when it comes to works of art, we take our views and our reasons for them too seriously to think that they have no significance for anyone but ourselves. Yet although we give reasons and arguments for our aesthetical views, we also know that nothing we can say could ever, on its own, convince others that our judgment is right. Not only do they have to experience the object we admire for themselves in order to decide whether it strikes them the same way, but they may dismiss it for the very same reasons we praise it. And so we swing back and forth between the horns of this dilemma: on the one hand, aesthetic judgments are susceptible to argument like objective judgments of fact but, on the other, they are impervious to it like subjective expressions of taste.

Immanuel Kant called the dilemma produced by aesthetic judgment "the antinomy of taste" and his *Critique of the Power of Judgment* is the most ambitious and ingenious effort to resolve the conflict that generates it. For Kant, our sense that something is beautiful is produced not by that object's features but by a particular feeling of pleasure that object occasions in us. Being a reaction to a subjective state of ours and not to the objective world, aesthetic judgment is therefore, like everything subjective, unresponsive to reasons in the way of ordinary judgments, which address how things are in the world. At the same time, that pleasure, which he called "disinterested" in order to distinguish it from simple liking and moral approval, is not, like the pleasant taste of ice cream, produced by some idiosyncratic inclinations of ours but by a harmonious interaction ("the free play") of two cognitive capacities—imagination and understanding—that are common to every human being. Because these capacities are common to all, our aesthetic judgment makes a claim not just on ourselves but on everyone else as well. So, on the one hand, its subjectivity prevents it from depending on reasons in the way of our judgments of fact. We find things beautiful, Kant believes, because they produce a certain kind of pleasure in us, and they can only produce that pleasure if we experience them directly. On the other hand, we expect everyone who shares the capacities whose harmony, according to Kant, produces that pleasure—every human being—to experience a pleasure like ours. We therefore "ascribe" that pleasure to them: we expect that if they were to experience the object we find beautiful, they, too, would be moved as we are. And although a persisting disagreement may indicate that the feelings of one (or both) of us are unjustified, there is no full-proof method for determining who is right and who is not.

Like every brilliant idea, this one is full of serious difficulties. But what interests me here is the fact that Kant's resolution of the antinomy took the terms in which the original dilemma had been posed for granted. He assumed that a judgment of taste can only be either subjective, and so binding on no one other than the person whose judgment it is, or objective, and therefore binding on everyone without exception. He then combined these two: insofar as the judgment of beauty is based on pleasure, which is a feeling, it must be subjective; but because that pleasure is produced by the activity of capacities that we share with everyone else, it is also more than that and for that reason is universally valid. Aesthetic judgment, as he put it, possesses "subjective universality." But the assumption that a judgment can hold either for one or for all without anything in between is disputable. And the space between these two extremes is where friendship is located.

Aesthetic judgment, just as Kant thought, does occupy an intermediate position between the subjective and the objective, but not, as he proposed, by combining both in a single whole. It expresses more than a purely idiosyncratic preference but it does not ascribe agreement to every human being. The judgment of beauty is neither purely private nor thoroughly public: it is a *personal* judgment, and persons are inherently social entities, grounded in many distinct but overlapping communities. When I judge that something is beautiful, I hope that others—but only *some* others—will join me in a community centered around that object and I issue an invitation to them to do so. I want to find people who will share my enthusiasm, and I hope that some of them will already be among my friends, while others may become my friends as our paths cross in our pursuits. But the invitation is not open to everyone— better said, I don't *expect* everyone to accept it and in many, perhaps most, cases I won't blame them if they don't. In fact, I would be devastated if everyone accepted even one of my aesthetic judgments. Something on which, for whatever reason, everybody agrees is no longer, as aesthetic preferences are supposed to be, a matter of taste. For the same reason, I would be equally devastated if even one person accepted every one of my judgments.

By juxtaposing aesthetic judgment and friendship as it does, *Art* highlights two distinct relations between them. First, it shows how deeply one can *affect* the other: the depiction of a friendship that is about to disintegrate because the friends discover that their aesthetic views are so violently opposed suggests that aesthetic harmony can confirm our old friendships and lead us into, or proceed from, new ones. Or, of course, it can destroy them. Serge's decision to buy the painting is obviously influenced, as Marc realizes, by the new friends he has made: "There comes a day when your creature has dinner with the Desprez-Couderts and, to confirm his new status, goes off and buys a white painting." But nothing is wrong with that in principle: it is only that Marc doesn't like these people.

Second, and perhaps more important, the play shows that our reactions to art can *model* our friendships. Most centrally, of course, we love both art and our friends, and in the same way. We love some people but not others, just as we love some artworks but not others, and we treat everything we love differently from the way we treat everything else. If I love *these* works, I will necessarily dislike or be indifferent to some others: it is not only impossible but also undesirable to love every artwork. Just so, if I am a friend of *these* people, I can't *be* a friend of those others: it is impossible to be friends with everybody. And we may well not want to be: all rhetoric aside, universal friendship is no more desirable than universal beauty. Both signal the end of individuality. Just like our taste in art, our circle of friends is a crucial expression of our character, and character both establishes who we are and distinguishes us from others. And when the aesthetic judgments of two friends conflict as seriously as they do in *Art*, they also reveal deep character differences between them, and their aesthetic dispute carries over immediately into their attitude toward each other, leaches into everything they say and do, and threatens their relationship.

What we find beautiful is, like our friends, what we love, and where each one of us is likely to find what to love always reflects, and helps determine, who we are. But who each one of us is depends crucially on our differences from one another. For that reason, the place of both beauty and friendship in our lives is far removed from the universal claims of morality—claims that depend on our commonalities with one another and aim to bind us together. The values of love are instead to be found in the space that separates us from those to whom we are bound only by such common ties. That space consists of our differences from everyone else, even those who are closest and perhaps most similar to us. We can't choose whether or not to be different from one another. We can only try to shape our differences, and so ourselves, in ways that are novel, important, and worthy of admiration. Or again, we can remain satisfied with leaving them as we find them, conventional and tired. But no one has an obligation to take the first route and to avoid the second. That is a matter of ability and choice. Aesthetics and friendship are both, as we will see, among the most important mechanisms of individuality available to us.

Chapter 6

THE GOOD OF FRIENDSHIP

THE BENEFITS OF FRIENDSHIP ARE MANY. THE LOVE
friendship provokes gives depth and color to life; the loyalty it inspires erodes the barriers of selfishness. It provides companionship and a safety net when we are in
various kinds of trouble; it offers sympathy for our misfortunes, discretion for our secrets, encouragement for our
efforts. All that is true, and it has been pointed out and
discussed again and again. Aristotle, who thought that
friendship was either itself a virtue or a relationship limited to the virtuous, and the long philosophical tradition
that follows him have found in friendship an unalloyed
good.

Yet like every form of love, friendship begets joy and
contentment but it also leads to affliction and misery—
the dull aches of abandonment, the sharp stabs of betrayal,
the agonizing dilemmas of loyalty: "If I had to choose between betraying my country and betraying my friend, I
hope I should have the guts to betray my country," E. M.
Forster once wrote, recalling that Dante cast Brutus and

Cassius in the lowest circle of Hell because in assassinating Caesar, they had forsaken not their country but their friend.

Friendship is not, of course, a singular, easily characterized thing. We have seen that it takes countless forms. Painting has shown us that friendship cannot be defined by behavior because friends can do just about anything together. Narrative literature reminded us that the many things that friends do together are most often mundane and trivial, despite the extraordinary behavior of Achilles and other epic figures. From Montaigne and the parallel between friendship and metaphor we learned that as long as friendship is alive, it is inexhaustible and not fully explicable. Yasmina Reza's *Art*, and drama more generally, has driven home the point that friendship is expressed not just in the motives with which friends undertake their actions but also in their bodily dispositions and the tones of voice with which their motives and attitudes are expressed.

And that is not all. Among the most remarkable features of friendship is that even a good friendship, valuable as it is, can involve base, even abhorrent behavior: friendship transformed Achilles into a raging beast, and Pylades helped Orestes murder his own mother. And sometimes immoral behavior can actually provoke our admiration: that's what we feel for Silien, the hero of Jean-Pierre Melville's stunning film, *Le Doulos* (1962), a gangster who lies, cheats, beats, kills, and eventually dies tragically in what turns out to have been all along a vain effort to save his only friend in the world. Most tellingly, immorality may sometimes be part and parcel of a good friendship, and that means that friendship's positive aspects may lie elsewhere, not in the moral domain but in another area of life. We will have to ask what that area might be if we are to understand the complex role that friendship plays in our lives. And to answer that question we will begin by turning to another film, *Thelma and Louise* (1991), whose uncomfortable, well, moral is that friendship and immorality are often found together.

TWO WORKING-CLASS WOMEN FROM A SMALL OKLAHOMA town are getting ready to spend a weekend in a friend's cabin. Thelma (Geena Davis) is a housewife whose housekeeping is as slapdash as her character is flighty. Racked by self-doubt and cowed by Darryl, the vulgar, stupid classmate she married as soon as they graduated from high school, she is even afraid to let him know that she is going away (she has never left home without him before). Louise (Susan Sarandon) is a waitress at a local coffee shop, always, as the stage directions to the script specify, "meticulously groomed, even at the end of her shift." She is cool, supremely well-organized—a few shots of her apartment tell the story—and fully self-possessed. She is the grown-up in their relationship. Her only weakness seems to be her boyfriend, a musician who is always on the road and doesn't take their relationship seriously enough.

On their way to the cabin, Thelma, already half drunk on her new freedom, insists that they stop at a bar where, to Louise's annoyed disapproval, she has several cocktails, flirts with an obviously wrong type of man, and finds herself on the verge of being raped by him in the bar's parking lot. Louise, who has come out to find her, stops the man by threatening him with a gun that Thelma had haphazardly thrown, among all sorts of other things, into her luggage. As the women are leaving, though, the man's vulgar haranguing enrages Louise: she whirls around and shoots him dead.

The killing is completely gratuitous since neither woman was any longer in danger. (Louise, as we learn later, had been the victim of rape some years earlier.) Louise refuses to turn herself in: she proposes to escape to Mexico, and Thelma, panicked and without resources of her own, decides to go along. Childishly unable to recognize the seriousness of their situation, she keeps thinking of their flight as a lark, a vacation from the awful Darryl. At the same time, though, she begins to show signs of an awakening self-confidence. After the murder, for example, she calls Darryl, who, unaware of what she and Louise have done, tries to bully her into returning home. Instead of capitulating, Thelma waves him aside: "Darryl, please . . . You're my husband, not my father, Darryl." Her words, though, are not quite her own: they are the words with which Louise had been berating her for her timidity a little earlier: "You mean you haven't asked him yet? For Christ's sake, Thelma, is he your husband or your father?"

During their adventure's early stages, Thelma's flightiness is a constant source of trouble. Feeling free for the first time in her life, she begs her friend, again and again, to give a lift to J. D. (Brad Pitt), a handsome drifter who keeps crossing their path. Louise finally relents, and Thelma spends the night with him in a roadside motel. Two things happen during their time together. First, J. D. reveals that he is a professional robber and acts out for Thelma exactly how he goes about his business: "My gosh," she exclaims, "you sure are gentlemanly about it," and J. D. replies, "I've always believed that if done right, armed robbery doesn't have to be a totally unpleasant experience." Second, her night with him is a revelation: "I finally understand what all the fuss is about. This is just a whole 'nother ball game! . . . For once in my life I ha[d] a sexual experience that isn't completely disgusting."

That is what Thelma tells Louise at breakfast the next morning, while J. D. is still in her room—along, it turns out, with Louise's entire life savings, which of course he steals, leaving them penniless. The loss proves too much for Louise, who falls apart, unable to cope with this new misfortune. But Thelma's sexual awakening seems to have consolidated her earlier, faltering steps toward self-confidence. This time, she relies not on what she has learned from Louise but on what J. D. had showed her the night before. She makes Louise give her the gun, enters a roadside market and, in J. D.'s gentlemanly style ("Alright, ladies and gentlemen, let's see who'll win the prize for keepin' their cool. Everybody lie down on the floor. If nobody loses their head, then nobody loses their head"), and robs the store of the money they need to get to Mexico.

Her friend and her lover have provided her with the material she needs to come into her own.

In the meantime, J. D. is arrested and reveals the women's destination to the police. And though Louise, appalled by the fact that they have added a robbery to their troubles, begins to have second thoughts about her plan, Thelma, who gradually comes to see things differently, urges her on. When a policeman stops them on the highway, it is Thelma, not Louise, who takes the initiative. She coolly asks Louise to shoot the policeman's radio with his gun, uses her own gun to shoot two holes in the trunk of his car ("air holes," she explains), and very politely asks him to get into the trunk, which she then slams shut. A little later, she dismisses Louise's second thoughts about the parking-lot murder:

> That guy was hurtin' me. And if you hadn't come out when you did, he'd a hurt me a lot worse. And probably nothin' woulda happened to him. 'Cause everybody did see me dancin' with him all night. And they woulda made out like I asked for it. And my life woulda been ruined a whole lot worse than it is now. At least now I'm havin' fun. And I'm not sorry the son of a bitch is dead. I'm only sorry that it was you that did it and not me. And if I haven't, I wanna take this time to thank you, Louise. Thank you for savin' my ass.

Thelma has begun to fend for herself. When they telephone Darryl once again, it is she who understands immediately that the police are tracing the call and Louise who naively stays on the phone long enough for them to establish their location.

A certain quietness—resignation, or perhaps peace—now descends upon them, but only for a short while. On the road, they keep running into a truck driver who taunts them with obscenities; the third time that happens, they invite him to stop and join them. He expected an orgy: what he gets instead is a bevy of bullets that turns his tanker into a giant fireball. Throughout this episode, the two women act as one: a kind of equality has been established between them.

The quietness returns. They drive through a beautiful stretch of land—which, reminiscent as it is of John Ford's Monument Valley, turns them into modern, car-driving descendants of Ford's traditional horse-riding outlaws. As they are driving, Thelma keeps looking at the landscape receding in the car's side mirror as if it were her own past. When they finally realize that they won't be able to escape from the police, Thelma confesses, "No matter what happens, I'm glad I came with you. . . . You're a good friend," and Louise replies, "You too, sweetie, you're the best." They both depend on each other now, and they know it.

A whole army of police cars and a helicopter finally trap them at the rim of the Grand Canyon (Figure 17). As the police are getting ready to shoot, Thelma asks, "Now what?" and Louise replies, "We are not giving up, Thelma." Their dialogue continues:

FIGURE 17. IMAGE FROM
Thelma and Louise (1991)

THELMA: Then let's not get caught.

LOUISE: What are you talkin' about?

THELMA: (indicating the Grand Canyon) Go.

LOUISE: Go? (Thelma is smiling at her.)

THELMA: Go. (They look at each other, look back at the
wall of police cars, and then look back at each other.
They smile.)

Their very last words repeat what they had already told
each other earlier: "You're a good friend"; "You too,
sweetie, you're the best." Louise then floors the gas pedal,
and the car springs forward in a cloud of dust, sails over
the cliff, freezing in midair in a sort of apotheosis, and the
film ends to the sound of B. B. King's song "Better Not
Look Down":

Better not look down, if you want to keep on flying
Put the hammer down, keep it full speed ahead
Better not look back, or you might just wind up crying
You can keep it moving, if you don't look down.

Thelma and Louise doesn't simply suggest that questionable ways of acting can sometimes be part of a good friendship: that is obvious enough. It shows something much more disturbing. By forcing the two friends to abandon their hometown, the would-have-been rapist's murder allows them to escape from their dead-end lives, from a dismal future whose shape Louise sees again and again in the blank, sad, and incurious faces of the old people sitting idly by the roadside in the nowhere-towns they drive through. Thelma's original act of rebellion—her furtive decision to spend the weekend with Louise without Darryl's approval—gradually enables her to establish her own manner of doing things, and when Louise, buffeted by adversity, begins to lose her almost neurotic self-composure, Thelma leaves both her husband's violent authority and her friend's patronizing protectiveness behind. Louise, for her part, refuses to continue to let her boyfriend dictate the terms of their relationship and sends him away: she learns how not to yield to a man without rancor and how to yield to a woman without sacrificing her independence. They both take responsibility for their future together, and they finally face it as two equal and sovereign individuals. Why is that disturbing? Because their friendship is a good, not despite the fact that it leads them to kill, rob, intimidate, and destroy but *because* of it.

They don't just do bad things; they become admirable on account of doing them—or, rather, on account of what these things reveal about them and their new take on the world and each other.

THAT A GOOD FRIENDSHIP CAN DEPEND ON IMMORALITY suggests very strongly that, whatever its value, friendship cannot be a moral virtue. Different moral virtues might occasionally conflict with one another, but no moral virtue can express itself in immoral behavior. Justice, for example, is never manifested through lies or crimes. We attribute the atrocities that are all too often committed in the name of justice to a wrong conception of what justice is, not to justice itself. And although virtue comes in degrees and some people may not be very just, what little justice they have is still genuine. If they fail to act justly, it is because they were unable to exercise the virtue they have: it is never their virtue itself, such as it is, that prompts them to immorality. Anything other than a true or genuine virtue is not a virtue at all.

Friendship, like virtue, also comes in degrees. Its range, of course is overwhelmingly broad. Politicians, for example, regularly describe themselves as, and sometimes are, friends of each other, although they may detest what the other stands for. Facebook can make "friends" of people who will never in their life meet each other in person and generally learn only of each other's good moments in life. Some friends meet only at sports games, others only at the opera. Some are, or have been, student and teacher; others are, or have been, married to each other, and so on. Within this great variety, some relationships stand out. These are not unrelated to Aristotle's *philia* of the virtuous, although the nonvirtuous are not excluded from them; to St. Aelred of Rievaulx's spiritual friendships, although they don't need to depend on a religious commitment; and to what contemporary philosophers call "character," "companion," or "end" friendships, although they are not to be contrasted with "utility," "pleasure," or "instrumental" friendships, which are not friendships at all. There is, though, a perfectly good word for such relationships: they are our *close* friendships. And just as friendship comes in degrees, so does closeness itself: the closer the friendship, the more widely it permeates the lives of the people who share it and the more deeply it affects them; the more distant, the less of our life it occupies and the weaker its influence. So, what holds of close friendships, on which we are mainly concentrating, holds of all, though to a more limited extent.

A "true" friend may be, among our genuine friends, the one on whom we can depend most securely, the one who will sacrifice the most on our behalf: a true friend is the best of friends. But although a bad friend may not be a friend at all, a genuine friendship can still have catastrophic results—not only for other people but even for the friends themselves. Several popular books warn against bad friends and the harm they can do, and a great many more detail the benefits of good friendships. But we haven't paid nearly enough attention to friends who genuinely love and want to do well by each other and yet, through their friendship itself, are either led into immorality or into other values and activities that are harmful to them, whether they know it or not. We can never be sure that friendship, however genuine, guarantees that we will end up better off than we were before we met, whatever we thought at first.

Bouvard and Pécuchet, whom we already encountered, are genuine friends. Their friendship, though, by leading them to one abortive attempt after another to understand and control the world, also destroys whatever dignity they might have had when they were making their living separately, copying other people's ideas. It is an equally genuine friendship that leads Lefty (Al Pacino) to vouch for Donnie Brasco (Johnny Depp), an FBI undercover agent, to his criminal colleagues and causes Brasco to end up more like them than like his earlier, honest self. And it is often true affection, and not heartless manipulation, that prompts one teenager to convince a friend to turn to destructive drugs. Friendship only involves the *desire* to benefit our friends—Aristotle's goodwill. And although Aristotle himself was convinced that friends can only improve one another, goodwill is not enough to bring that about on its own. For Aristotle, friendship involves benefits because only the virtuous can be friends and, being virtuous, they know exactly what is and what isn't truly good. Without an objective account of the good like Aristotle's, we can't go from the desire to do well by our friends to our actually doing so. Genuine friendship depends more on our intentions, feelings, and attitudes than on the results of our behavior.

But while friendship, like moral virtue, comes in degrees, it is, unlike moral virtue, two-faced. Even close friendships are often much less edifying than the rhetoric that surrounds the institution would have them be. As we have seen, the bulk of our interactions with our friends are, at least at first sight, trivial and inconsequential. We spend considerably less time offering our life in exchange for theirs, sacrificing our happiness so that they can live with the love of their life, or generously helping them out of bankruptcy than we do exchanging news and gossip; discussing books, movies, and love affairs; going places; or just being together—conversation and everyday activity, mostly casual, are what friendship lives on. That's probably what led the Greek philosopher Epicurus (341–270 BC) to say that what matters in friendship is not so much what our friends actually do for us as the sense that they would come to our aid if we ever needed them. But the sense, however strong, that our friends won't let us down when we are in difficulties is too weak a benefit to justify his praising friendship as wisdom's greatest blessing or Aristotle's claim that human beings can't live without friends— that to live alone, as he put it, one has to be either a god or a beast. Aristotle, of course, said that about all *philia*, which includes every relationship of mutual dependence, and his point is obvious: we can't live without others on whom we depend one way or another. But what he said is true of friendship in particular as well—it is very hard to imagine that one could lead a good life bereft of friends.

If we think that true or perfect friendship must be a totally faultless relationship, then La Rochefoucauld was right and his pessimistic evaluation—"However rare true love may be, it is less so than friendship"—was perfectly apt. A realistic view must take the double nature of friendship into account. Ideally, we need to explain why we think that friendship is a great good despite its conflicts with morality, the pain it causes, and the dangers it harbors.

ONE OF THE DANGERS OF FRIENDSHIP—A DANGER THAT is often the other face of one of its virtues—is the possibility of loss. But here is a curious fact: C. S. Lewis described friendship as a relationship that is "almost wholly free from jealousy." Surprisingly—since he wrote so well for children—he seems not to have kept in mind how desperately hurt children and adolescents can be when they are abandoned by their friends. By thinking, like Aristotle, only of an ideal version of adult friendship, free of problems and shortcomings, he seems to have forgotten that the friendships of children, who tend to abandon old friends and make new ones often and without much thought, provoke sufferings and jealousies as intense as any relationships we are ever likely to have. Adults also abandon old friends, and that can sometimes be as painful but, on the whole, they do so less frequently, often because their relationships fray and atrophy gradually, and seldom with such acrimony. And, especially after the age of forty or so, adults make new friends more slowly and less enthusiastically. The usual explanation is that family and professional obligations increase with age and leave little time for making new friends while old friends move away and distance makes it difficult to keep in touch. But there is more to it than that.

Losing a good friend hurts much more deeply than the disappointment of losing a playmate, a school-yard ally, a sports or theater companion, a tennis partner, a secret sharer, or a helping hand in times of adversity. Friendship provides many such benefits and their loss can be painful, but mourning the end of a friendship is not mourning the loss of its benefits. It is mourning the loss of oneself.

An example may help explain what I mean. A friend of mine used to play tennis regularly with two of her own friends until they began to offer excuses and beg off whenever she tried to arrange a game. My friend, who assumed that they didn't want to play with her because they no longer liked her, was devastated. One day, she finally confessed both her suspicions and her anguish to them. Her friends, deeply relieved, confessed in turn that they had been avoiding her simply because she could no longer match their level of play. They hadn't told her in order to spare her feelings, not realizing how much worse that had made her feel, and apologized for the pain they caused her. And though the criticism, true as it was, stung her, their friendship remained intact, if perhaps, at least for a while, just a little strained.

Losing something a friend provides, however unpleasant it may be, is nothing like losing a friend. Sometimes, of course, the two are the same. When, years ago, a friend of mine canceled our regular weekly dinner because he

couldn't "deal with it any longer," I was deeply hurt because I realized that I had lost more than just a dinner
companion. My grief was brought about by a rejection not
merely of what we had done together but, overwhelmingly, of who I was. The end of that friendship signified
that what my friend had come to dislike or hate or, worst
of all, become indifferent to was *me*.

That explains why such things happen more often
among children and adolescents than among adults. Children are always trying to establish who they are: they are
constantly rejecting who they have been and trying to become something new instead. Whenever they begin to
develop in a new direction, which is often, they abandon
at least those of their older friendships that provided
them with possibilities for change based only on who they
had been at the time; and they find new friends who, they
feel, fit better with what they currently want to be and to
become.

We are, after all, more changeable when we are young
than we are later in life. The formation of the self begins at
birth. Open at first to a myriad possibilities, it gradually
narrows down, and the narrower it gets, the more difficult
it becomes to envisage an alternative to it. As we grow
older, we become more settled into who we are. A new
friendship always brings with it the prospect of serious
and unpredictable change, which, the more our character
and personality are set, the less willing or able we are to
confront. That, not the additional obligations that age
brings with it, is the main reason it becomes more difficult
to make new friends. The pain of abandonment is the

other face of the exhilaration of the sense that we are becoming something new, which every new friendship promises to us. Our friendships are indissolubly connected with who we are. As an old Greek proverb has it, "Show me your friends, and I'll show you yourself."

The distress of losing a friend is connected with something that Lewis in this instance correctly observed: friends "discover that they have in common some insight or interest or even taste *which the others do not share* . . . every real Friendship is a sort of secession, even a rebellion . . . Friendship must exclude." Friendship is selective and partial: "If I say, 'These are my friends,' I imply, 'Those are not.'" That sort of exclusion is essential to every friendship, although it is most evident in the relationships of early life. When I become your friend, our relationship makes us different from "the others" and so determines, to a great extent, who we *both* actually are. So when a friend abandons me, she rejects not only me but also what *she* has become through our relationship: she repudiates my part in what she is. The end of a friendship is a kind of death for us both: it is really something to mourn.

Philosophical discussions of friendship address it invariably as a relationship that brings people together, as if every bringing together is not also a pulling apart. As it joins us to each other, a friendship also separates us from everyone else. Lewis's word, "rebellion," is just right, for in many cases it is through our friends and through them only that we find the space, the means, and the strength to refuse to become what the world around us would have us be, indifferent to what that might mean for us. Without necessarily endorsing the more sweeping part of his claim, we can agree with Michel Foucault: "Maybe the target nowadays is not to discover what we are but to refuse what we are . . . We have to promote new forms of subjectivity through the refusal of the kind of individuality that has been imposed on us for several centuries." Friendship provides a context for working through such refusals, developing in ways that are distinct from the ways of "the others," and becoming, as we put it, ourselves.

In such cases, friendship can be a bulwark against inertia and conformity. In others, it can also impose them: that's one reason for its double face. When a friendship develops into a clan or a coterie, it requires not just difference from those outside but also unquestioning conformity to those within. But some degree of conformity is necessary in every friendship, and it is not always a bad thing (just as the refusal to conform is not always a good one). Conformity is the other face of discipline, which begins in a conscious effort to act in a certain way because we accept a rule, explicit or not, that says we must. And through discipline we train ourselves to internalize some of those rules, to follow them not because we are compelled to do so but because they have become part of our own way of seeing and acting in the world—part, literally, of a new self.

But there is a limit to how new that self can be. Our lives are firmly embedded in a social, cultural, and historical context. Everything that we do, like everything that we are, is bound to be in some way similar to every action and every life that occurs in the same context. Our similarities to others are important, not to be overlooked, and help constitute who each one of us is. But so are the ways in which we differ from one another. In one sense, of course, everyone is different from everyone else. Who we are depends on a combination of genetic background and personal history that is absolutely unrepeatable: we can't possibly share it with anyone else in the world. But in themselves, and unless we use them to accomplish something important, such differences, which we possess simply by being alive, are nothing to be proud of, nothing to admire, despite the insistence of elementary American education that every child is, as the unfortunate expression has it, "unique" and for that reason worth celebrating. As encouragement, that may have some uses; as statement of fact, it is a miserable failure. It is not a reason for celebration—not because it's wrong but because it can't possibly fail to be right. But the truth is that not every difference counts.

The differences that count are those that literally make a difference, differences that distinguish us from others in interesting, valuable, or admirable ways, or even in ways that are base and contemptible. It is here that pride and joy, but also regret and disappointment, have their place. And it is here that friends make a difference that counts. Through them, and throughout life, we develop characteristics and capacities that emerge only because of our interaction: a new friend means a new way of approaching both oneself and others—a new way of approaching life itself. Despite its dangers and pains, friendship can still be a good because, again, it is a mechanism of individuality, and we become who we are in great part because of the friends we have.

TO SAY, AS I HAVE BEEN SAYING, THAT MOST OF WHAT friends do together is commonplace and insignificant is not exactly wrong. It's like saying that Tom's behavior in the school yard was eccentric, which is also not exactly wrong. We would do no better if we described Tom as decisive, practical, and blithely indifferent to convention, for that would not communicate that Tom expressed his decisiveness in just *that* particular manner and revealed something startlingly new about himself and the sort of decisiveness of which he was capable. Our interactions with our friends often lead us into novel and unanticipated directions. That is one of friendship's glories, as it is also the other face of one of its starkest dangers.

We have already seen that we often can't predict what our friends will do or, for that matter, what we will accomplish together. Friendship leads in new and surprising directions and, for that reason, our understanding of each other and ourselves is, and will always be, provisional, contestable, and incomplete. What exactly we do is not settled once and for all: it can change as unpredictable actions and their equally unexpected consequences require us to revise what we had taken our earlier behavior to be. That's not to say that we are, or need be, confused or uncertain about the nature of our actions. As long as we establish where they begin and end, their nature is determinate and we can know it as well as we know anything in the world. But where exactly our actions begin and end is not independent of other things that we do or that happen to us, and sometimes these can change both the beginning and the end of our actions and therefore also their nature and significance. Nietzsche was keenly aware of this relativity: "Cause and effect [he could as well have written 'beginning and end'], such a duality probably never exists; in truth we are confronted by a continuum out of which we isolate a couple of pieces, just as we perceive motion only as isolated points and then infer it without actually seeing it." From this, he seems to have concluded that the ideas of cause and effect represent "an arbitrary division and dismemberment." But that is wrong: that we specify beginnings and ends in light of our interests doesn't make them arbitrary—only revisable. Here, for example, is the narrator of Ian McEwan's *Enduring Love* relating a horrible accident that had an indelible long-term effect on his life:

> I have already marked my beginning, the explosion of consequences, with the touch of a wine bottle and a shout of distress. But this pinprick is as notional as a point in Euclidean geometry, and though it seems right, I could have proposed the moment Clarissa and I planned to picnic after I collected her from the airport, or when we decided on our route, or the field in which to have our lunch and the time we chose to have it. There are always antecedent causes. A beginning is an artifice, and what recommends one over another is how much

sense it makes of what follows. The cool touch of glass on skin and James Gadd's cry—these synchronous moments fix a transition, a divergence from the expected.

In one sense, of course, what's done is done: there is no element I can excise from the story of my life, no event that can be removed from it. But excision isn't the only way of dealing with the past: further activity can turn a past event into material for something else and change what it was (or, once we have described it in different and perhaps better terms, what it seemed to be) at the time. Montaigne, who knew that, confessed, "I do not correct my first imaginings by my second—well, yes, perhaps a word or so, but only to vary, not to delete"; "I add but I do not correct." But by adding to what was already and, in one sense, unalterably there, Montaigne manages to turn an earlier thought or action into something no longer of his past but of his present. He did so, in fact, with his nonexplanation of his friendship with La Boétie. In the first version of his essay, he wrote: "If you press me to tell why I loved him, I feel that this cannot be expressed"— which is true and commonplace. In the Bordeaux Manuscript, he added: "except by answering: Because it was he, because it was I" (Figure 18). Does the addition refute or amplify the original thought? It certainly makes it other.

As Montaigne's example shows, this applies not only to the actions of others but also to our own. What I have already done may lead me in new and unanticipated directions, which reveal themselves only as I go on and

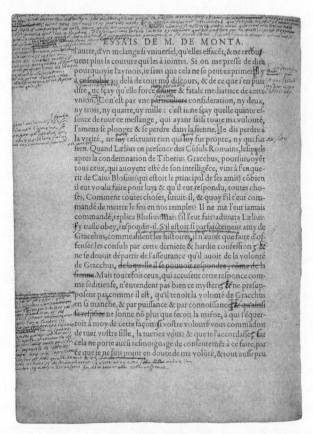

FIGURE 18. MONTAIGNE,
The Bordeaux Manuscript (*Essais, Exemplaire de Bordeaux*),
page 71 (1588). The addition is at the top of the right margin.

which, once followed, may affect how I understand the
actions that led to them. A new step may require a new
interpretation of what has already occurred, and events
that occur after the end we have assigned to some activity
may create a new and different context within which the

activity has a different beginning, a different nature, and a different end. All told, I understand myself as provisionally as I understand my friends.

And that is another reason friendship is dangerous: apart from those activities through which friends are useful to one another—activities that generally have anticipated and foreseen results—our interactions that depend on our loving one another don't have a predetermined end. There is no telling where they will lead: we only know that when they have already brought us to it.

What I do, of course, isn't subject to my own interpretation only. Others can and usually do have a hand in it as well, which is one reason we are told to choose our friends with caution: they influence what we do and how we understand it, how we understand ourselves, and what we are likely to become. Friends are not the only ones who do so—parents, teachers, colleagues, and many others all play a part in this lifelong process of self-formation. But friends have, by and large, a more intimate understanding of our character, and they can affect deeper and more important aspects of our selves. Our interactions are also freer: they are seldom governed by the specific purposes that characterize our instrumental relationships.

Now we can begin to see that the commonplace and insignificant activities of friendships are, in the end, neither commonplace nor insignificant. During our seemingly idle conversations and pointless activities, within the safety zone that mutual trust creates, we confront desires, ideas, hopes—aspects of what we are—that we hide from others and sometimes even from ourselves. And we try out ways of being—still perhaps inarticulate, perhaps embarrassing if revealed to a larger group, sometimes of dubious benefit—some of which we pursue and some of which we discard. Friendship has its own mortars and pestles, its own alembics and retorts: it comes closer to transmuting the self than any alchemist ever came to transmuting his metals. Like alchemy, friendship often delivers nothing but dross; unlike it, however, it sometimes arrives at gold. Whether for better or worse, what we become is very much our friends' doing, and the less settled we are in ourselves, the greater their contribution and the more pervasive their influence.

We often say that when we are young we try to find out who we really are. It would be more accurate to say that we try to become something we are not (or not yet), without knowing exactly what that is or how to go about it: the what and the how are here inseparable. When people feel that they have finally become something that they want (or, sadly, don't want) to be, it feels natural to say that that's what they really are and always have been. But it isn't. What we "really" are is not a hidden, unchanging nature that is within us from the beginning, sometimes unearthed and brought to light. It is something that we become—the result, but not the overall purpose, of countless activities and the vagaries of life. It was neither in Thelma's nor in Louise's nature when we first meet them to be capable of becoming their own person: they became capable of it as they came into their own in the particular circumstances they found themselves in, and it was their friendship and the situations they confronted that led them to develop the features that allowed them to declare their independence. They did not discover their "real" self—they created it.

Friends have a privileged role in this lifelong process of self-construction, not because they are good people, moral, wise, or generous, but because we love them. We often blame the poverty of language for our failure ever to fully express our love, for the flat and feeble results of our best efforts to explain it. But language has nothing to do with it. We fail because we love our friends not just for what we know them to be but also for what we feel both they and we will become through our relationship. As we've seen, our love for our friends is entwined with the sense that we haven't yet exhausted what's good in them—that's why every serious effort to account for our love must end with an "and so on." But we might add here that our love for our friends is also entwined with a sense that we haven't yet exhausted what's good in *ourselves*. "Friends bring out the best in one another": not just what we believe is best in us already but something that we'll come to recognize as a good only when we have acquired it, in which our best self will be expressed; what this adage forgets, though, is that friends, despite their good intentions, can also sometimes bring out our worst self as well. Whatever else we expect from our friendships, we also expect them to lead us to need and desire new things: that, they always do, though it isn't always to the good. This constant possibility of error and failure—friendship's contribution to the making of a new self—is the cause of both the best and the worst in it.

Friendship, like every form of love, points ineluctably to the future. As long as the future remains open, the beginnings and ends—the very nature—of what we do or have done together, are variable. But once we feel that we know what there is to know about a person, once our interaction promises nothing new, freezes what has already happened, and becomes routine, we have already become indifferent to them: our friendship is effectively over. We may honor it on account of the role it has played in our life so far, but it is no longer a source of excitement, pleasure, or passion. It has become inert.

Plato knew that love and knowledge go hand in hand: *erôs*, in the *Symposium*, is always pulling us further into the objects we love. It fills us with the certainty that they have more to offer than we have seen so far and is a constant incitement to try to understand what that is. For Plato, the effort to follow the lead of love was an ascent from a single beautiful individual to the abstract nature of perfect beauty and virtue, from sexuality to friendship. We can agree with him that friendship draws us further, though not, as his metaphysics held, into pursuing the abstract and universal but into the effort to know both friends and ourselves more concretely. We can also agree that this effort has an end, though not when it reaches perfection—which for Plato was the Form of beauty itself—but only when the friendship is over. A friendship that no longer provides for the possibility of change is a past friendship, its value limited to its role in our history.

This effort to know our friends and ourselves is not passive: "The person one loves at first is not the person one loves at last and love is not an end but a process through which one person attempts to know another." It doesn't leave untouched something that was already there. The knowledge it brings with it changes us in unforeseen and unforeseeable directions. As the hero of Tim Lott's *White City Blue* says: "Life is a habit. You do something, then you do it again, then again, and before you know it, that's what you are, and that's who you are, and you can't imagine being anything or anyone else." Only love and friendship, which suddenly enter his life, make it possible for him to imagine that he might still become something or someone else.

THE ARTS, WHICH PROVIDED US WITH SEVERAL EXAMPLES of friendship, also—and more important—share some central features with it, and illustrate how its virtues are not independent of its vices. Our friends, like the works of art we love, stand out among others of their kind, who recede into the background against which we notice and appreciate them. How exactly they both differ from their background and from one another attracts and intrigues us: it sparks the urge to understand exactly what they—friends or works of art—are and what makes them lovable. We want to come to know them as intimately as we can, and no feature of theirs is in principle irrelevant to what they are: "The minutest portion of a great composition is helpful to the whole," not only in art but in friendship as well.

To know something intimately is to know it in detail, to understand what "makes it tick"; it is to know, to some extent, what makes it the particular person or thing it is, and to be aware of the subtle ways in which it differs from others that are still very much like it: "The promise of intimacy is the promise of being vouchsafed a glimpse of your soul while offering up mine in return; despite the fact that the full blown promise is illusory." That promise is illusory because, as we have seen, what counts as the self is always incomplete, and, even more, doesn't remain the same as it enters into different relationships. But to understand what a friend or a favorite work is we need to compare them to the objects that form the background against which we perceive them. We know our friends in part by seeing how they differ from the other people we know.

And so, as love draws us deeper into each other it also draws us more broadly into the world: the protagonists of John Williams's *Stoner*, "like all lovers, . . . spoke much of themselves, as if they might thereby understand the world which made them possible." Friends do the same. *Erôs* and friendship are species of love, and the desire for intimacy applies equally to them both: erotic love adds the intimacy of bodies to friendship's intimacy of souls. Like lovers, friends speak much about themselves because they want to reveal as much of themselves as possible (or perhaps as much of themselves, if we keep Kant's warning in mind, as appropriate), for the more friends know about themselves and each other, the more of themselves they make available for appreciation or change. And as we come to know ourselves and each other better, if all goes well, we may also come to love what we have become as well as the friend who has helped make us what we find ourselves to be. But we also may not: it is here that love is at its most dangerous, for if all doesn't go well, we may end up loving a calamity.

Thelma and Louise showed us that friendship may lead not only to practical harm but into immorality as well. For many people, philosophers included, that would trump whatever other value a friendship might have because they think that moral values are overriding and always take precedence over every other kind. But although moral values—impartial and reflecting our commonalities—are important (though not necessarily for the reasons morality gives for promoting them), they are not the only values that determine whether a life is or is not worthwhile. If we call all the values that are important to life "ethical," moral values are one—but only one—of its important species. There are also the values of love and friendship, which belong to a realm closely enough connected with the arts that we might want to call them "aesthetic." Aesthetic (or, less controversially, nonmoral) values draw us toward our differences from one another, they foreground and celebrate them, and make different people and different objects attractive and important to each one of us. For the fact is that individuality is itself a value. We honor and admire people who are importantly and engagingly different from the rest of the world.

But, like all nonmoral values, individuality, along with beauty, charm, elegance, character, and style, is two-faced. "Important and engaging" differences are not always admirable—or, even if they are, they can sometimes be overridden either by their immorality or their destructiveness: great villains are individuals no less than great heroes. And just as our friends' defects can be part of what makes them the individuals we love, the other nonmoral values, too, can embody both admirable and questionable features. Beauty is the most obvious example. In Renaissance pornographic paintings, like Titian's *Venus of Urbino*, in Leni Riefenstahl's celebration of Nazism in her film *Triumph of the Will*, or in Robert Mapplethorpe's homoerotic and sadomasochistic *X Portfolio*, beauty and morality stand opposed and yet the aesthetic value of these and many other works like them is undeniable. When individuality and morality collide, it is never clear in advance which side should finally win out. In the end, how moral I am may be important to who I am, but it is only one part of it and not always the part that counts the most.

IN THE PROCESS OF COMING TO KNOW AND FORM THEIR friends and being in turn known and formed by them, some people may develop virtues of their own and become attractive individuals themselves—though not necessarily, and not often, in a moral sense. This has been one of my experiences with friendship, just as it has also been one of my experiences, again, with the arts.

To love a work of art is not simply to gaze at it with rapt attention, listen to it in pure delight, or read it in one enchanted evening—and then go our merry way. It is a much more complicated affair. To say, for example, that I find C. P. Cavafy's poetry as exquisite, fine, and delicate as the "artificial flowers" that delight him in one of his own works is to say, in part, that I return to Cavafy's work, with which I have spent some of my life's brighter moments, again and again. I have a sense that there is still much I don't understand about these poems and that coming to know them better will add more bright moments to my life. These poems are literally a part of my life. And not only because I read them often. They also took me to Alexandria, where I walked the streets many of them recall. I became familiar with the poet's own life, and his idiosyncratic publishing habits. I learned about his friendship with E. M. Forster and his homosexuality, which determines some crucial features of his work. I looked for parallels between Cavafy and Robert Browning as well as with *The Greek Anthology*, a vast collection of ancient poems from which he often drew inspiration. I sought people who had met him and others who were also taken with him. I thought hard about his ability to provoke strong feelings without the images, metaphors, or the lofty vocabulary of traditional poetry, his habit of focusing on those parts of Greek history and geography that had been left untouched by the official accounts of the nation. His poems are an essential part of me, and I am who I am partly through interacting, reading, and writing about them: I can't imagine myself apart from them.

I asked, for example, why Cavafy had even bothered to write the following poem:

"That's the One"

Unknown in Antioch, a stranger from Edessa produces
   a stream,
a torrent of writing. And, finally—there—it's all done.
The last hymn is complete. That is the consummation

of his work—eighty-three poems in all. But so much
   writing
has exhausted the poet—all that versification,
the strain of following the rules of Greek formation;
his life has now turned flat, dull, totally unexciting.

But one thought all at once removes his desolation:
The wondrous phrase, "That's the one,"
the phrase that Lucian heard once, in a dream.

Lucian, the great Syrian author of the second century AD, once dreamed that if he became a writer, people everywhere would recognize him and point him out. The unknown poet in Antioch, though, is not likely ever to hear that wondrous phrase. So why did Cavafy bother to write a poem about such an unknown author, a "fake" about whom he once remarked, "Art was not for him a need, a love, but only a means to an end. His writing, instead of giving him the joy, the delight of creating new, unknown sounds was a toil, versifying, an imposed task"? And what in the poem supports his negative judgment?

The answer is indicated by my rather forced translation, which preserves the poem's original rhyme-scheme
(abc/dccd/cba), an almost artificially formal, pyramidal
structure whose apex (represented here by "cc") is formed
by the words "versification" and "Greek formation." Their
central position in the poem and the fact that each one of
its lines matches the number of syllables in its rhyming
counterparts suggest that versification and good Greek
are the unknown poet's main concern. But Cavafy suggests that by means of composing a poem that is itself a
sample of the poetry it appears at first to say nothing
about. The poet remains "unknown." But in writing about
him, Cavafy redeems the shopworn commonplace that
poetry requires inspiration: he has produced an inspired
poem, which creates, in the most technically accomplished
way, the merely technically accomplished work it disdains.
Cavafy didn't expect his readers to take his word for this
poet's shortcomings: he *gives* us the kind of poem he
scorns. But in giving it, he also gives a voice to the unknown poet: we now have one of his poems, made for him
by Cavafy; his struggle has not been completely in vain;
his efforts have been rewarded: He *is* the one. But who
exactly is the one? The unknown poet or Cavafy himself?

Cavafy's poems—products of exceedingly prolonged
and vastly complex actions—attract me because I feel they
intimate something that nothing else in the world is capable of intimating (although, of course, I cannot say exactly what that is). If they didn't, why would I love *Cavafy's*
poetry and not some other poet's work? To the extent that
I can articulate my sense and find something these poems,

and only these poems, accomplish and to the extent that what I find is in fact admirable, Cavafy turns out to be an individual, importantly distinct from others engaged in similar work. And if what I find in him is something distinctly *his* own that others haven't found, then, to that extent, I see his poetry in a way that is distinctly *my* own as well, and different, in some serious way, from the way all others see it. Whether I have succeeded in doing so, however, and the extent to which that has made me more of an individual are not just for me to decide.

Exactly the same thing might happen to you if, impressed by my account of Tom, you were to make the effort to meet him and the two of you eventually became friends. You would try to understand why he acts as he does, you will connect his actions to one another by connecting them with others (just as, to understand "That's the One," I read it in light of Cavafy's several other poems about poems unread, unfinished, even unwritten). If you were to become Tom's friend, his actions would appear connected to one another and expressive of his character. And you would probably see in him something others, myself included, wouldn't. If you came to love him, then through your own interactions you would see him as an individual, distinct in some important ways from everyone else. To the extent that you did, you would be an individual yourself.

EACH ONE OF OUR FRIENDSHIPS—SOME MORE, SOME less—contributes an element of individuality to our character. Each one leads us in a particular direction that no other can duplicate. That, of course, may result in a shat-tered self moving in different directions without rhyme or reason, unity, or coherence. But such a shattered self is what we are all faced with at first—an accidental self, made up of haphazard elements, picked up at different times, in different contexts, from different people, from various books, pictures, and music, from diverse social, political, and cultural environments. Individuality requires the organization of these elements into a whole within which they are no longer haphazard—a coherent whole to which each makes a distinct contribution. But coherence is not enough. The whole these elements compose must also be distinctive. It must have a *style* that express one's distinctive character. And that, as Nietzsche knew, is

> a great and rare art! It is practiced by those who survey all the strengths and weaknesses of their nature and then fit them into an artistic plan until every one of them ap-pears as art and reason and even weaknesses delight the eye . . . In the end, when the work is finished, it becomes evident how the constraint of a single taste governed ev-erything large and small. Whether this taste was good or bad is less important that one might suppose, if only it was a single taste!

In this passage, Nietzsche seems to think that this is some-thing one accomplishes on one's own. Perhaps that is possi-ble for some people—perhaps (though I doubt it) it was possible for Nietzsche himself. But it is a task that most of us can only accomplish with the help of others—and these others, over the course of our life, are primarily our friends. In this role, friendship exhibits every feature we have traditionally attributed to it. One of them is the sense that we can always rely on our friends, not necessarily to save us from public embarrassment, bankruptcy, or death, but at least in most of the ordinary, everyday situations in which we find ourselves. We rely on them, even in our most casual conversations, to give us a space where we can express ourselves openly, where we can try different ways of being—different means of reducing our haphazardness—without embarrassment or shame. And that brings the sharing of secrets into the picture. We rely on our friends to listen attentively and sympathetically, though not uncritically, to us when we speak freely—often more freely than we speak to ourselves—and reveal aspects of ourselves of which we may be suspicious, unsure, or even ignorant and which, once revealed, can be cultivated or eradicated, as the case may be. These may or may not be "private information" as one account of the importance of secrets in friendship would have it. They may be things I tell other people as well—but when I tell my friends, both of us treat them as material that can help or hinder the formation of our character and personality. Our friends also have an idea of what we are or should be—an idea that, given our friendship, we are apt to take seriously. That is what we see of ourselves in them: not, as Aristotle may have thought, our virtuous similarities but a picture, an interpretation of who we are to them that we can use—not uncritically—to guide our self-formation.

Friendship, then, is tied to individuality in two distinct ways. We find something individual in each one of our friends and both of us become, to that extent, individuals. But friends also provide the ground on which we can turn all the disparate elements of ourselves, including "lesser" individualities (our liking this poet, our attitude toward another friend, our taste in clothes or books or pictures— different things for every one of us), into a more coherent and, in the ideal case, a more engaging and characteristic whole. As I've said, our idle conversations and common-place interactions with our friends are in the end neither idle nor commonplace. Our friends' words and actions, however insignificant, are expressions of their character that are visible to us though not to others, and we re-spond to them not as isolated incidents but as parts of a longer process, which our reactions mold and shape: what friends say and do together ramifies through their entire being. That's why, as Stanley Cavell wrote, what friends do together is less important than the fact that they do it together and that no time they spend together is ever time wasted.

And, of course, not always to the good. Nonmoral values—beauty, love, friendship, character, elegance, charm, trust, even intelligence—have a double aspect that their moral counterparts seem to lack. They can lead in either good or bad directions. A beautiful lover can cause me to behave in the most humiliating manner, a charming person can take brazen advantage of me, a good friend can draw me into shameless immorality.

Despite their double face, however, nonmoral values are and remain values—features without which life would be pointless, without variation, intricacy, intimacy, or joy. They provide a justification of friendship that is independent of both its benefits and its moral or immoral features, and despite the pains, disappointments, and dangers it brings with it. Such values are not reliable guides to success, goodness, or happiness. But then what is? Our lives are uncertain, subject to the workings of a world over which, individually and collectively, we have the most minimal power. Some ancients thought that friendship binds the whole universe together. We are more modest. Friendship does no more than bind a few people together: the people who can say to each other, "I love you because it is you, because it is I." But, friendship finally makes us ask, who here is the you and who the I?

Illustrations

Acknowledgments

THE IDEA FOR THIS BOOK EMERGED FROM A GRADUATE seminar Thomas Laqueur and I offered at Princeton University in 2003 with the generous support of the Mellon Foundation, which I am happy to acknowledge, once again, here. The book itself is based on the Gifford Lectures, which I delivered at the University of Edinburgh in 2007. I am grateful for this honor to the Gifford Lectureship Committee, for selecting me to the University's Institute for Advanced Studies, for providing me with a congenial place to work while I was in Edinburgh, and, especially, to Mrs. Isabel Roberts, secretary to the Gifford Lectureship Committee, for addressing every aspect of preparing and delivering the lectures with patience, resourcefulness, and goodwill.

Alison Mackeen encouraged me to complete an earlier version of this book. Dan Gerstle's help in clarifying my material has been invaluable, and his contribution to its final form has been absolutely crucial. I am deeply grateful to him. I am also grateful to Marcus Gibson for the persistence and good will with which he secured the rights of reproducing the images included here.

Too many audiences, friends, and colleagues have heard intermediate versions of this material for me to be able to thank them by name here. I am grateful to them all. But, once again, I must single out Thomas Laqueur, who has stood by this book since I first started working on it and by me, in all sorts of ways, ever since our friendship began during our heady college days.

Notes

INTRODUCTION

3 **our interactions are now easier:** The competitiveness that exists even between the closest friends—in her case, two young women growing up in Naples—is very much part of Elena Ferrante's *My Brilliant Friend*, trans. Ann Goldstein (New York: Europa Editions, 2012). Friendships between women more generally are the subject of Marilyn Yalom's book, written with Theresa Donovan Brown, *The Social Sex: A History of Female Friendship* (New York: HarperCollins, 2015). Yalom and Brown claim that their many fascinating case studies led them to identify four basic "ingredients" in women's friendships: affection, self-revelation, physical contact, and interdependence (pp. 344–346). In my opinion, as we will see in this book, all these are also ingredients in male friendships—with the possible exception of "physical contact." This last seems to me less common among American men than, say, among men in Southern Europe and the Middle East. Still, the ideology of friendship has consistently drawn a sharp dividing line between men and women. Aristotle thought that in a relationship between a man and a woman, the woman is necessarily inferior to the man (*Nicomachean Ethics*, VIII.7, 1158b11–14), and he doesn't discuss friendship between women at all. A modern version of this sort of inequality is apparent in the following passage, which, although from the early twentieth century, is egregious enough to quote here: "The fatal facility of women's friendships, their copious outpourings of grief to each other, their sharing of wounds and sufferings, their half-pleased interest in misfortune—all this seems a lesser order than the robust friendship of men who console each other in a much more subtle, even intuitive way—by a constant

pervading sympathy which is felt rather than expressed," Randolph S. Bourne, "The Excitement of Friendship," *Atlantic Monthly*, December 1912: 795–799, on p. 799. In other respects, though, this essay is an excellent discussion of some of the features of friendship that will occupy us in this book.

4   **"As the sun is to the firmament"**: Robert Burton, *The Anatomy of Melancholy* (New York: New York Review of Books Classics, 2001), p. 864.

5   **"O, friend, my bosom said"**: Ralph Waldo Emerson, *Essays and Letters*, ed. Joel Porte (New York: The Library of America, 1983), p. 339.

5   **"Why are we to be divided"**: Erna Olafson Hellerstein, Leslie Parker Hume, and Karen M. Offen, eds., *Victorian Women: A Documentary Account of Women's Lives in Nineteenth-Century England* (Stanford, CA: Stanford University Press, 1981), p. 89; quoted in Yalom and Brown, *The Social Sex*, p. 159.

5   **Aristotle, whose ideas about *philia***: Aristotle examines *philia* in Books VIII and IX of his *Nicomachean Ethics*. We will discuss his views, especially the connections between *philia* and friendship, in Chapter 1.

5   ***Philia* was for Aristotle**: Aristotle, *Nicomachean Ethics*, VIII.1, 1155a5–6.

6   **"We have as many sides"**: Bourne, "The Excitement of Friendship," p. 798.

CHAPTER 1 "A FRIEND IS ANOTHER SELF"

11   **to live without friends**: Aristotle, *Nicomachean Ethics*, trans. and ed. Roger Crisp (Cambridge: Cambridge University Press, 2000), VIII.1, 1155a3–5. The translations I use below are mine, although they follow the general lines of Crisp's approach.

11   **friends as a kind of mirror**: This is a tradition that goes back to *Nicomachean Ethics*, IX.9, 1170b6–7 and elsewhere.

11   **the essence of friendship**: Emerson holds this view, though he believes that what he calls "tenderness" is also crucial: "A friend is a person with whom I may be sincere. Before him I may think aloud," "Friendship," in *Essays and Letters*, p. 347. More recently, Laurence Thomas has made a similar case in "Friendship," *Synthese* 72 (1987): 217–236.

11 **our philosophy of friendship:** It's true that Plato composed a dialogue, the *Lysis*, that addresses questions connected with friendship. But it is quite inconclusive and its influence has been minor.

12 **His influence has been immense:** Aristotle devotes Books VIII and IX of the *Nicomachean Ethics* to *philia*. He also devotes part of his *Magna Moralia* and one book of the *Eudemian Ethics* to it as well, but his treatment, which is interesting in its own right, has not been nearly as widely read: see Corinne Gartner, "Aristotle's Eudemian Account of Friendship," PhD diss., Princeton University, 2011. For Cicero, see *De Amicitia*, trans. Frank Copley, in *On Old Age and On Friendship* (Ann Arbor: University of Michigan Press, 1967), reprinted in Michael Pakaluk, *Other Selves: Philosophers on Friendship* (Indianapolis: Hackett, 1991), and for the Latin text, see W. A. Falconer, *Cicero: On Old Age, On Friendship, On Divination* (Cambridge, MA: Harvard University Press, 1923).

12 **"With me I see not who partakes":** John Milton, *Paradise Lost*, 3rd ed., ed. Gordon Teskey (New York: W. W. Norton, 2004), Book VIII, ll. 363–366, p. 67.

12 **"A perfect solitude is":** David Hume, *A Treatise on Human Nature*, ed. L. A. Selby-Bigge (Oxford: Clarendon Press, 1888), p. 363.

12 **"a select and sacred relation":** Emerson, "Friendship," in *Essays and Letters*, p. 346.

13 **Some of us . . . are attracted:** For example, *Nicomachean Ethics*, VIII.3, 1156a6 ff. (*NE* in references below; cf. *Eudemian Ethics*, VIII.2, 1236a15 ff.).

13 **third kind of *philia*:** The Greek word *philia*, as we shall see, applies to an immense range of human attitudes and relationships but it is almost invariably translated as "friendship"—and so, not to prejudge any questions, I will leave it untranslated. An excellent discussion of the range of *philia* (which, in my opinion, he is too quick to identify with friendship) can be found in David Konstan, *Friendship in the Classical World* (Cambridge: Cambridge University Press, 1997).

13 **"friendship cannot exist at all":** Cicero, *De Amicitia*, 22, in Pakaluk, *Other Selves,* p. 100; Latin text in Falconer, *Cicero,* p. 132.

14 **the discussion of friendship constitutes:** If we assume that *philia* and *amicitia* are the Greek and Latin equivalents of friendship, then Aristotle, who devoted two whole books of the *Nicomachean Ethics*—a full one-fifth of the work—and his ancient followers seem

to have lavished much closer attention to friendship in their ethical thought than modern philosophy, which has by and large overlooked it for reasons we shall touch upon later. More recently, though, philosophers have returned to Aristotle, and friendship has reemerged as a subject of serious, though far from universal, interest.

14 **most profoundly isolated:** Friedrich Nietzsche, *Ecce Homo*, in *Basic Writings of Nietzsche*, trans. Walter Kaufmann (New York: Random House, 1968), p. 677.

14 **only good people can be friends:** For Aristotle, virtue (or excellence: *aretê*) includes several features that have no place among the virtues of today—especially not among the moral virtues, which have been the main concern of philosophy in modernity. The list of virtues Aristotle gives in *NE* II.7 includes courage, temperance, truthfulness, justice, and wisdom but also generosity (openness with small sums of money), magnificence (openness with large sums), greatness of soul (the proper pursuit of great honors), *philotimia* (literally the pursuit of honor, limited here to its less significant instances), an even temper, wit, friendliness, the correct experience of shame, and the proper dose of indignation.

14 **bad people can never be friends:** We will soon see whether and how these issues are relevant to the two lesser types of relationship that Aristotle classifies as *philia*.

14 **modern philosophy has acknowledged:** Friendship is "an arena for morally good . . . behavior and sentiments . . . acts of friendship are morally good insofar as they involve acting from regard for another person for his own sake . . . the deeper and stronger the concern for the friend . . . the greater the degree of moral worth," Lawrence Blum, "Friendship as a Moral Phenomenon," in Neera Kapur Badhwar, ed., *Friendship: A Philosophical Reader* (Ithaca, NY: Cornell University Press, 1993), pp. 192–210, on p. 194.

15 **It can exist between individuals:** These classifications of various "unequals" are Aristotle's own.

16 **comes down to three fundamental objects:** *NE*, VIII.2, 1155b17–26.

16 **Only another person can care for me:** This, of course, begs the question whether humans can be friends with animals. The issue is very complex, and it has received renewed importance by research on relationships between animals of different species. A short survey of recent work on the subject can be found in Erica Goode, "Learning from Animal Friendships," *New York Times*, January 26,

2015. Such issues, and many others relating to them, are discussed in Marc Bekoff, ed., *Encyclopedia of Human-Animal Relationships* [4 vols.]: *A Global Exploration of Our Connections with Animals* (Westport, CT: Greenwood Publishing Group, 2007).

16 **if you and I are *philoi*:** The term *philos* (of which *philoi* is the plural) is usually translated as "friend" (when it is used as a substantive) or "dear" (when it functions as an adjective) despite the obvious differences between *philia* and friendship we will note as we proceed. In discussing Aristotle, I will leave it, and all its cognates, untranslated.

16 **when I bear you good will:** As we have seen, Aristotle's virtues are not nearly exhausted by the virtues of morality as we understand them today, although the translation of the Greek term *arête* as "virtue" has encouraged its moral construal; that is part of the reason friendship has been considered a moral good by those who have tried to reintroduce it to philosophical discussion under Aristotle's influence.

17 **bound to each other by *philia*:** *NE*, VIII.2, 1155b17–1156a5. Aristotle adds another condition on *philia*—that we are both aware of how the other feels about us—that is not important for our purposes.

17 **pursuit of pleasure or benefit:** Ibid., VIII.3, 1156b20–21.

17 **"Such *philia* is rare":** Ibid., VIII.3, 1156b24–25.

17 **"and those like him":** Ibid., VI.5, 1140b8–9.

18 **"wish each other good things":** Ibid., VIII.3, 1156a9–10. The Greek expression for "insofar as they love each other" is *tautêi hêi philousin*, a construction common in Aristotle's thought, to which we will return. "Those who care" is a translation of *philountes* and "love" a lame translation of *philousin*. Both Greek words are forms of the verb *philein*, which like *philêsis*, covers a large range of feelings, from tepid to very strong.

18 **"Those who care for each other":** Ibid., VIII.3, 1156a10–19. Although Aristotle does not use the expression "for the friend's sake" in this passage, he doesn't seem to want to withhold it from the lesser *philiai*. In his general statements regarding good will (e.g., Ibid., III.2, 1155b31–32), he applies all three expressions to each kind without qualification.

19 ***philoi* wish each other well "insofar as":** For the other's sake: *ekeinou heneka* (e.g., Ibid., VIII.2, 1155b31, 1156b10); insofar as the other is virtuous, pleasant, or beneficial: *hêi* (e.g., 1156a10, 11, 16); on account of being virtuous, pleasant, or beneficial: *dia* (e.g., 1156a5,

1156a10, 15). See also 1155b28–29, where wanting what is good for the *philos* is given as a necessary feature of *philia* (only to be apparently denied later on). John Cooper's interpretation of these expressions rests on an ingenious distinction between the prepositions *heneka* and *dia*. He takes the *dia* construction to be retrospective, meaning something like "in recognition of" and expressing the grounds on which each particular *philia* has been based so far. By contrast, he reads the *heneka* construction (Aristotle's most common way of designating the final cause, the purpose for which things occur as they do) prospectively, as expressing the direct object of the well-wishing: "The pleasure-friend will now be said to wish well to his friend for his friend's own sake, in consequence of recognizing him as someone who is and has been an enjoyable companion, and the advantage-friend wishes his friends well for his friend's own sake, in consequence of recognizing him as someone who regularly benefits him and has done so in the past" ("Aristotle on the Forms of Friendship," in *Reason and Emotion* [Princeton: Princeton University Press, 1999], pp. 312–335, at 323). The interpretation I propose does not require that distinction, which, moreover, does not meet the objection I make in the main text.

19   **imperfect *philia* is not focused on:** *NE*, VIII.3, 1156a10–20.

20   **"Those who are *philoi*":** Ibid., VIII.4, 1157a15–16.

20   **erotic *philoi* separate "as soon as":** Ibid., IX.1, 1064a8–11. Aristotle seems to claim something similar at 1157b25–34, where he distinguishes virtue-*philoi* from others because "they wish good things for those they care for [not for themselves but] for their sake, because of a state they are in and not a feeling they have."

21   **if we are joined through virtue:** Aristotle is careful to emphasize that the *philia* of the virtuous, since it is perfect and complete, always brings with it both benefit and pleasure, e.g., at Ibid.,VIII.3, 1156b12–15. He does not offer a separate argument for that idea here, which seems to me plainly true, but he does, in connection with pleasure, at Ibid., I.8, 1099a11–16.

22   **anything that serves virtue:** Ibid., IV.1, 1120a23–24.

22   **I wish all my *philoi* well:** According to A.W.H. Adkins, in "'Friendship' and 'Self-Sufficiency' in Homer and Aristotle," *The Classical Quarterly*, n.s., vol. 13 (1963): 30–45, that is a difference without a difference. He argues that all *philia* is ultimately selfish: both pleasure- and benefit-*philoi* "feel affection of a selfish kind on

account of their own *agathon* [good]; but this is true of *philia kat'*
aretên [virtue-*philia*] as well" (p. 43). He claims that Aristotle is
forced into "contortions" that "show the gravity of the problems
which faced the Greek moral philosopher in his efforts to create a
civic morality out of the primitive and intractable materials which
lay to hand" (p. 45).

22   **A virtuous character:** *NE*, VIII.3, 1156b11–12.

22   **"friendship is eternal":** Aelred of Rievaulx, *Spiritual Friendship*,
       trans. Mary Eugenia Laker (Kalamazoo, MI: Cistercian Publica-
       tions, 1977), I.21, p. 55. More on Aelred in Chapter 2.

22   **may sometimes come to an end:** *NE*, IX.3, 1165b17–31.

23   **all along masked selfishness:** Some further ideas on this topic can
       be found in Chapter 5.

23   **nobility (*to kalon*):** *NE*, IX.8, 1169a18-b2.

24   **friends, we believe, are:** The sense of this expression is the subject
       of Chapter 4.

24   **based on benefit:** And that is not all. Aristotle devotes much of
       Books VIII and IX of the *Nicomachean Ethics* to a long and detailed
       specification of what *philoi* owe one another that would be com-
       pletely out of place in a modern treatise on moral philosophy.
       When, for example, should a benefit-*philos* pay another when the
       latter delivers some goods to him? In some cases, Aristotle answers,
       immediately (that is a "completely mercenary" relationship; in oth-
       ers, when the relationship is "liberal," when he becomes able to do
       so, *NE*, VIII.13, 1162b20–31). Surely a relationship that is based on
       explicit contractual arrangements and presupposes no trust be-
       tween its parties can't have anything to do with friendship. This
       part of the work reads not as an ethical treatise but as an introduc-
       tion to contract law.

       That benefit-*philia* is a kind of exchange rather than a friend-
       ship is also shown by Aristotle's wanting to determine the value of
       the goods one *philos* provides another in order to establish how
       much is owed in return. Is the standard "the benefit that accrues to
       the recipient . . . or instead . . . the good turn done by the benefac-
       tor"? (The answer, at *NE*, VIII.12, 1163a8–23, is that for benefit- and
       pleasure-*philia*, the standard is the value that accrues to the recipi-
       ent, but in virtue-*philia* it is the value of what the provider supplies.
       When, again, two *philoi* are unequal in some respect that prevents
       one from making an exact repayment to the other, "the superior

person should get more honor, and the needy person more profit, since honor is the reward of virtue and beneficence, while profit [assists in times of] need" [*NE*, VIII.14, 1163b1–5].) And although in general one should first repay one's debts before doing favors for one's *philos*, the rule is not without exceptions. Imagine, for example, that a *philos* once ransomed you from the pirates who had abducted you: are you now obliged to ransom your *philos*, who was recently abducted himself, in return? Or suppose that your *philos* needs his money for some other reason while your father has been abducted: should you discharge your debt or ransom your father first? "It would seem," Aristotle writes in a judicious mood, "that you should ransom your father, even in preference to yourself." Yet another exception to the rule occurs when making a gift to a third party appears "nobler *or more necessary*" than discharging a debt (*NE*, IX.2, 1164b33–1165a5). On the mutual obligations assumed by those connected through *philia*, see Mary Whitlock Blundell, *Helping Friends and Harming Enemies: A Study in Sophocles and Greek Ethics* (Cambridge: Cambridge University Press, 1989), pp. 42–49. Aristotle's discussion of the benefit-*philia* (generally, though inaccurately, called "civic friendship") that, according to him, holds every city together and unites its citizens also has little or nothing to do with friendship in our contemporary sense.

24 **or pleasure:** Pleasure-*philia* might have been more likely to be a kind of friendship, since friends are clearly supposed to enjoy each other's company. And so it might, had Aristotle limited himself to the narrow range of examples his commentators appeal to: drinking companions, squash partners, amusing acquaintances, or temperate pleasures like the sight of "a vigorous colt prancing about a field on a fine spring morning, or the look of delight on a child's face as he rides on a swing." See Michael Pakaluk, *Aristotle's Nicomachean Ethics: An Introduction* (Cambridge: Cambridge University Press, 2005), p. 266. But Aristotle's own examples are much more often cases of erotic and sexual passion—primarily paederastic, sometimes matrimonial—than the witty conversations so common among his interpreters.

Aristotle's straightforward inclusion of *erôs* under *philia* contrasts sharply with the contemporary commonplace that sex conflicts with friendship and can be the cause of harmful self-deception. In addition, if a man expects the boy he pursues erotically to give him pleasure while the boy expects the man to be useful to him and help him assume the duties of an adult citizen, as was the official Athenian custom, the likely outcome of their disagreement is the end of their relationship (*NE*, IX.9, 1164a7–10). Here, too, then, all that we find is an instrumental relationship. But instrumental relationships, which are focused on what we want to get out of them, are not friendships.

24 *philia* **does not correspond:** It is commonly said that Aristotle's long discussion of *philia* shows that friendship was much more important to the Greeks than it is to us. But that's not right. Aristotle here turns from the internal, psychological structure of the virtuous individual, which is the subject of the rest of the *Nicomachean Ethics*, to a serious examination of interpersonal relationships. It is only here, in Books VIII and IX, that Aristotle assumes an interpersonal point of view and addresses "what we owe to each other" and also, to a certain extent, some of the issues that have been the primary concern of modern moral philosophy. The phrase "what we owe to each other" comes from T. M. Scanlon's *What We Owe to Each Other* (Cambridge, MA: Harvard University Press, 2000).

24 **virtue-*philia* brings with it:** *NE*, VIII.4, 1156b17–21.

24 **troubles that friends can cause:** John Cooper's gentler "character friendship," which, unlike Aristotle's perfect *philia*, "is not the exclusive preserve of moral heroes," can much more easily accommodate such imperfections; see "Aristotle on the Forms of Friendship," pp. 317 ff.

25 **impossible to have the perfect sort:** Aristotle discusses this issue in chaps. 4–6 of Book VIII. An interesting story is connected with Aristotle's claim that one can only have a few friends. Both Montaigne and Nietzsche refer to an otherwise unknown (and, for Aristotle, quite unusual) text: "Oh, my friends; there is no friend!"(*ô philoi, oudeis philos*)—a statement that Jacques Derrida, who is not unaware of the history of the phrase, uses extensively in *The Politics of Friendship* (New York: Verso, 1997; see pp. 224–225, nn. 1, 10). Montaigne and Nietzsche derive the text from Diogenes Laertius' *Lives of the Eminent Philosophers*, 5.21.8, which, in its present editions, actually quotes Aristotle as saying, *hôi philoi oudeis philos* ("He who has [many] friends has no friend"). In his article "Friendship" (*Contretemps* 5 [2004]: 2–7), Giorgio Agamben traces this latter, most reasonable reading of Diogenes' text to Isaac Casaubon's 1616

edition of Diogenes. The grammatical difference between the two versions is slight—Casaubon simply changed the breathing and added a subscript to the initial omega of the phrase—and so attributed to Aristotle a reasonable view that conforms to the spirit of the *Nicomachean* and, more or less, to the letter of the *Eudemian Ethics*: *outheis philos hôi polloi philoi* ("There is no friend for someone who has many friends," 1245b21). Montaigne's text, of course, predated Casaubon's edition, but Nietzsche, who had written on Diogenes, should have known better: see *Beiträge zur Quellenkunde und Kritik des Laertius Diogenes* (Basel, 1870).

25   **who has done what for whom:** *NE*, IX.1, 1164a34-b3.

25   **"incurably" vicious:** Ibid., IX.3, 1165b13–22. At another point, Aristotle's dry prose, "The defining features that are found in *philiai* toward one's neighbors (*hoi pelas*) would seem to be derived from the features of *philia* toward oneself" (*NE*, IX.4, 1166a1–2), is an uncanny anticipation—of no more, I think, than the language—of the Christian command to "love your neighbor (*ho plesion*) as yourself" (Matthew 19:16–19). Only the virtuous can have such an attitude: Aristotle holds the bizarre view that the vicious, whose souls are in constant conflict and who are always regretting their deeds, hate their life and bear no *philia* toward themselves since (they know that) nothing about them can be the object of *philêsis*; the vicious hate themselves. And so, most likely, do the many, who are all base: although Aristotle considers the possibility that they may be satisfied with themselves, thinking that they are decent people, he finally decides that they too lack anything that may attract *philêsis* and cannot be *philoi* to themselves (*NE*, IX.4, 1166b2–26).

25   **"a friend is another self":** *NE*, IX.4, 1166a30–32.

25   **in a qualified sense, their wives:** Ibid., VIII.12, 1162a16–27.

26   **"best and dearest friend":** *Philtatos philōn, Iphigenia in Tauris*, trans. Witter Bynner, in *Euripides II: Four Tragedies* (Chicago: University of Chicago Press, 1956), l. 708.

26   **"captain of this misadventure":** *Iphigenia in Tauris*, ll. 599–600. Pylades' loyalty is manifested in his own refusal to allow Orestes to die alone: "If you meet knife and flame, then so do I" (l. 685).

27   **"usually fight over":** *NE*, IX.8, 1169a21.

27   **Pylades' loyalty really is a virtue:** Plato, who was an enemy of the theater, would have argued that no feature depicted in tragedy could ever be a genuine virtue.

27 **"friendship is a moral good":** Neera Kapur Badhwar, "Why It Is Wrong to Always Be Guided by the Best: Consequentialism and Friendship," *Ethics* 101 (1991): 483–504, at 504. Badhwar is not alone in considering relationships based on pleasure or benefit as "instrumental friendships" (which, I will claim in Chapter 4, is a contradiction in terms) in her "Introduction: The Nature and Significance of Friendship" to her valuable anthology, *Friendship: A Philosophical Reader* [Ithaca, NY: Cornell University Press, 1993], p. 3). She also distinguishes between "end love," which is involved in "end" (perfect) friendship, and "means love" (another contradiction in terms), which characterizes friendship's lesser kinds ("Friends as Ends in Themselves," *Philosophy and Phenomenological Research* 48 [1987]: 1–23).

28 **"for themselves":** *NE*, VIII.4, 1156b8–9.

28 **virtues that you already possess:** Although Aristotle knows well that people's character changes and that friends affect one another, he says almost nothing about how virtuous one must be in order to enter into a virtue-*philia* and about whether, how, and to what extent such a relationship can make its participants more virtuous than they already are.

28 **"Why is a certain peculiarity":** Gustave Flaubert, *Bouvard and Pécuchet*, trans. Mark Polizzotti (Urbana, IL: Dalkey Archive Press, 2005), p. 9.

30 **vanishingly small segment:** That is also true of Aristotelian civic *philia*, which ends at the walls of the *polis*. Aristotle does not have the Christian notion of universal love or the Enlightenment idea of universal respect, which we shall be discussing in what follows.

30 **love one's neighbor as oneself:** Mark 12:28–31. The principle that Mark attributes to Jesus here is a radical generalization of Leviticus 19:18, "You shall not take vengeance or bear any grudge against the children of your people, but you shall love your neighbor as yourself: I am the LORD," *The New Oxford Annotated Bible with the Apocrypha*, rev. standard version, ed. Herbert G. May and Bruce M. Metzger (New York: Oxford University Press, 1977), slightly altered. As "the children of your people" makes clear, "your neighbor" is literally the person who lives near you and not everyone, as it is in the Gospels.

30 **repugnant to the doctrine . . . of Christianity:** Several features of early Christianity were, in turn, influenced by Stoicism, especially

in its late, Roman variety, which promoted the idea of cosmopolitanism—that is, being a citizen of the world at large and not primarily a member of a more specific group; see Runar M. Thorsteinsson, *Roman Christianity and Roman Stoicism: A Comparative Study of Ancient Morality* (Oxford: Oxford University Press, 2010). Thorsteinsson, however, attributes a less ecumenical attitude to the early Christians than he does to the Stoics. Where the Stoics' cosmopolitanism was meant to include the whole world, Christian ethical concern was, at least early on, more focused on other Christians; see chap. 10, "Ethical Scope Compared."

31 **Saints Perpetua and Felicitas:** See John Boswell, *Christianity, Social Tolerance, and Homosexuality* (Chicago: University of Chicago Press, 1980), p. 135.

31 **"Through all chances":** Poem 11, translated by Helen Waddell in *Mediaeval Latin Lyrics* (New York: Holt, Reinhard, 1948), p. 37. For more on Paulinus, see Dennis Trout, *Paulinus of Nola: Life, Letters, and Poems* (Berkeley: University of California Press, 1999). Some, like Rictor Norton, ed., *My Dear Boy: Gay Love Letters Through the Centuries* (San Francisco: Leyland Publications, 1997), take Paulinus' feelings for Ausonius to be sexual; others, like Boswell, *Christianity, Social Tolerance, and Homosexuality*, pp. 133–134, do not. Peter Brown, *The Body and Society: Men, Women, and Sexual Renunciation in Early Christianity* (New York: Columbia University Press, 2008), pp. 403, 409, emphasizes the continence of Paulinus' marriage, which made a big impression on Augustine.

32 **"We could talk and laugh together":** Saint Augustine, *Confessions*, trans. R. S. Pine-Coffin (Harmondsworth: Penguin Books, 1961), IV.8, p. 79.

33 **only object of true love:** See William Riordan O'Connor, "The Uti/Frui Distinction in Augustine's Ethics," *Augustinian Studies* 14 (1983): 45–62. It is, in fact, Augustine, under the influence of Neoplatonism, and not Plato himself, who holds the otherworldly view that has been wrongly considered to be Plato's own: that the right way to love our friends is not to love *them* but what there is of God in them. In Plato's terms—had Plato held that view—the real object of love is the Form of Beauty, which is the ultimate object of love in the *Symposium*, or the Form of Goodness, which plays that role in the *Republic*. Beauty and Goodness are very intimately connected with each other for Plato, and features of both became part of the concept of the god of Christianity.

33 **"What madness"**: Saint Augustine, *Confessions*, IV, pp. 78–80. The view of *De Doctrina Christiana* is more complex; it is well discussed by Robert M. Adams in "The Problem of Total Devotion," in Badhwar, ed., *Friendship: A Philosophical Reader*, pp. 108–132.

33 **"the next human being"**: Søren Kierkegaard, *Works of Love*, trans. Howard and Edna Hong (Princeton: Princeton University Press, 1998), pp. 34–98. An excerpt from sec. II.B of that work is included in Michael J. Pakaluk, *Other Selves: Philosophers on Friendship* (Indianapolis: Hackett, 1991), pp. 235–247.

33 **"Love of one's neighbor"**: Kierkegaard, *Works of Love*, p. 67.

33 **Kierkegaard saw, correctly, that friendship:** John Lippit, in *Kierkegaard and the Problem of Self-Love* (Cambridge: Cambridge University Press, 2013), esp. chap. 2, argues that Kierkegaard's disdain for friendship rests on his overemphasizing the Aristotelian view that friends must be similar to one another. He claims that with a different understanding of friendship, much that Kierkegaard admires in Christian love can be found in, or at least prepared for, in friendship. I am grateful to Anthony Rudd for letting me know about this book.

34 **"Nothing more sacred"**: Aelred of Rievaulx, *Spiritual Friendship*, II.9, 10.

34 **"mutual harmony in affairs human"**: Ibid., I.11, p. 53.

34 **"The carnal springs from"**: Ibid., I.38: *dicatur itaque amicitia alia carnalis, alia mundialis, alia spiritalis*. By "vice," Aelred has pleasure, particularly sexual pleasure, in mind. In this, he is actually closer to Aristotle, who clearly thought of paederastic relationships under the rubric of *philia*, than Aristotle's modern followers, who generally confine themselves to much tamer pleasures.

35 **"after the Fall"**: Ibid., I.58–59, pp. 63–64.

35 **"the eternal enjoyment by which"**: Aelred of Rievaulx, *The Mirror of Charity*, trans. Elizabeth Connor OCSO (Kalamazoo, MI: Cistercian Publications, 1990), III.39.108, p. 297.

35 **Aelred's trusting and generous nature:** See, for example, Walter Daniel, *The Life of Aelred of Rievaulx*, trans. F. M. Powicke (Kalamazoo, MI: Cistercian Publications, 1994). Daniel was Aelred's pupil and knew him over many years.

36 **"friendship for the useful"**: St. Thomas Aquinas, *Summa Theologica*, ST II–II.25.1. On the differences between Aquinas and Aristotle, see Daniel Schwartz, *Aquinas on Friendship* (New York: Oxford University Press, 2007).

CHAPTER 2   "A SORT OF SECESSION"

38   **Clinton escaped yet another bout:** Some of the details of the case appear in Douglas Martin, "Marc Rich, Financier and Famous Fugitive, Dies at 78," *New York Times,* June 26, 2013. See also Justin Peters, "How Eric Holder Facilitated the Most Unjust Presidential Pardon in American History," at www.slate.com/blogs/crime /2013/07/02/marc_rich_presidential_pardon_how_eric_holder _facilitated_the_most_unjust.html. For Rich's own account of the pardon, see Daniel Ammann, *The King of Oil: The Secret Lives of Marc Rich* (New York: St. Martin's Press, 2009), esp. chap. 18, "The Pardon," pp. 239–263.

38   **president's tendency to reward familiarity:** "The President's Stealth Nominee," *New York Times,* editorial, October 4, 2005.

38   **Bush withdrew his nomination:** Michael A. Fletcher and Charles Babington, "Miers, Under Fire from Right, Withdrawn as Court Nominee," *Washington Post,* October 28, 2005.

38   **"loved the Earl of Buckingham":** *Documentos Inéditos para la Historia de España,* vol. 1, pp. 101–102, cited by Roger Lockyer, *Buckingham: The Life and Political Career of George Villiers, First Duke of Buckingham* (London: Longman, 1981), p. 43.

39   **Buckingham's income:** Details in Lockyer, *Buckingham,* and also in his "Villiers, George, first duke of Buckingham (1592–1628)," *Oxford Dictionary of National Biography* (Oxford University Press, September 2004); online ed., January 2008, at www.oxforddnb.com /view/article/28293, accessed February 22, 2008.

39   **Buckingham's relationship to James:** See Alan Bray, *The Friend* (Chicago: University of Chicago Press, 2003), pp. 96–104.

39   **likened both to Piers Gaveston:** See Danielle Clarke, "'The Sovereign's Vice Begets the Subject's Error': The Duke of Buckingham, 'Sodomy' and Narratives of Edward II, 1622–28," in Tom Betteridge, ed., *Sodomy in Early Modern Europe* (Manchester: Manchester University Press, 2001), pp. 46–63.

39   **"If he Spencer":** The quotation comes from the *Camden Miscellany,* 20, CS, 3rd ser., 83, 1953, 33, cited by Lockyer, "Villiers, George, first duke of Buckingham."

40   **"In this lost world":** David Wootton, "Francis Bacon: Your Flexible Friend," in J. H. Elliot and L.W.B. Brockliss, eds., *The World of the Favourite* (New Haven, CT: Yale University Press, 1998), pp. 184–204, at 185.

40 **"relatives by blood and marriage"**: Keith Thomas, *The Ends of Life: Roads to Fulfillment in Early Modern England* (Oxford: Oxford University Press, 2009), pp. 190–191; see p. 339, n. 18, for various references.

40 **"friends were valued because"**: Ibid., p. 191.

41 **"Even if the good is the same"**: Aristotle, *Nicomachean Ethics*, I.2, 1094b7–10, trans. Roger Crisp (Cambridge: Cambridge University Press, 2000, slightly modified; cf. VI.8, 1142a8–10). The connection between friendship and public life emerges repeatedly throughout friendship's history: women's friendships, for example, had a profound influence on the politics of nineteenth-century France; see Sarah Horowitz, "States of Intimacy: Friendship and the Remaking of French Elites, 1815–1848," PhD diss., University of California at Berkeley, 2008.

42 **"activity of the practical virtues"**: Aristotle, *Nicomachean Ethics*, X.8, 1077b6–7.

42 **Cicero, too, connected friendship and war:** Cicero, *De Amicitia*, xxii.84. Glory is clearly military, but so is *honor: honos*, to which the word is closely related, and *virtus* were celebrated as the gods of soldierly valor and its just rewards in several temples in ancient Rome. See Nicholas Purcell, "Honos," in *The Oxford Classical Dictionary*, ed. Simon Hornblower and Antony Spawforth (Oxford: Oxford University Press, 2009).

42 **"to weet / The deare affection"**: Edmund Spenser, *The Faerie Queene*, ed. Thomas P. Roche Jr. (New Haven, CT: Yale University Press, 1981), Book IV, Canto IX, Stanza 1.

43 **"first three books of the *Faerie Queene*"**: Charles G. Smith, "Spenser's Theory of Friendship," *PMLA* 49 (1934): 490–500; the passage occurs on p. 490. I first became aware of this way of reading Spenser when I attended one of the lectures of my Princeton colleague, Jeffrey Dolven. Paul Alpers was kind enough to share some of his knowledge of Spenser while I was revising the manuscript of this book.

43 **"Concord she cleeped"**: Spenser, *The Faerie Queene*, IV. X. 34–35.

43 **For Spenser, as for several ancient thinkers:** Aristotle attributes such a view to Euripides and to the philosophers Heraclitus and Empedocles (*NE*, VIII.1).

43 **"encompasses the harmonious order"**: William Allan Oram, *Edmund Spenser* (New York: Twayne Publishers, 1997), p. 218; see also

John Erskine, "The Virtue of Friendship in the *Faerie Queene*," *PMLA* 45 (1915): 831–850, at 835.

44 **Aristotle had rejected the relevance:** At the very beginning of his discussion of *philia* in the *Nicomachean Ethics*, when Aristotle attributes such a view to Euripides, Heraclitus, and Empedocles, he relegates the subject to physics and not to his present concern with ethics.

44 **"an aristocratic and upper-middle-class audience":** Stephen Greenblatt, *Renaissance Self-Fashioning: From More to Shakespeare* (Chicago: University of Chicago Press, 1980), p. 222.

44 **"Of Friendship" is an effort:** Michel de Montaigne, *The Complete Works of Montaigne*, trans. Donald Frame (Stanford: Stanford University Press, 1958), I.28.

44 **as we might naturally have expected:** I say "naturally," but, as Arnaldo Momigliano has shown in *The Development of Greek Biography* (Cambridge, MA: Harvard University Press, 1993), the distinction between "the work" and "the life," which was introduced by Xenophon in his *Life of Agesilaus* in the fourth century BC, is a historical construction. It is not without serious problems, some of which I have discussed in *The Art of Living* (Berkeley: University of California Press, 1998), chap. 6, as well as in "Writer, Text, Work, Author," in A. J. Cascardi, ed., *Literature and the Question of Philosophy* (Baltimore: Johns Hopkins University Press, 1987), pp. 267–291.

45 ***Essays*, which mention him quite sparsely:** The *Essays* contain twelve references to La Boétie in addition to those we find in "Of Friendship." Of these, five are short quotations (*The Complete Works*, I.10, I.14, II.12, twice in III.13). From the others we learn that he and Montaigne had different views on the suffering of the dying (II.6, "Of Practice," p. 270); that he was the greatest man Montaigne ever knew, closer to possessing all the virtues than anyone of his time, "a full soul, handsome from every point of view" (II.17, "Of Presumption," p. 500); that he received bad medical care during his final illness (III.4, "Of Diversion," p. 588); that people would have completely destroyed his reputation had Montaigne not defended him (III.9, "Of Vanity," p. 752); and that he was ugly, though only superficially so: he had "a very beautiful" soul (III.12, "Of Physiognomy, p. 810).

45 **"has no other model than itself":** Montaigne, "Of Friendship," p. 141.

46   **to give his friend the "place":** More on this "place" in Chapter 4.

46   **"I know his soul":** Montaigne, "Of Friendship," pp. 140, 141.

46   **"a hazy mirror":** Montaigne, III.13, "Of Experience," p. 1088.

47   **"by contrast rather than by example":** Montaigne, III.8, "Of the Art of Discussion," p. 922.

47   **"free and voluntary":** Montaigne, "Of Friendship," p. 139. A more generous attitude is expressed by Nietzsche: "Here and there on earth we may encounter a kind of continuation of love in which this possessive craving of two people for each other gives way to a new desire and lust for possession—a shared higher thirst for an ideal above them. But who knows such love? Who has experienced it? Its right name is friendship" (*The Gay Science*, trans. Walter Kaufmann (New York: Random House, 1974), sec. 14).

48   **"abhorrence of instrumentality in personal relations":** Allan Silver, "Friendship in Commercial Society: Eighteenth-Century Scottish Theory and Modern Sociology," *American Journal of Sociology* 95 (1990): 1474–1504, at 1479.

48   **Adam Smith:** Smith, of course, is perhaps best known for *The Wealth of Nations* (1776), which is the foundation of modern economics.

48   **"the natural objects of [one's] warmest affections":** Adam Smith, *The Theory of Moral Sentiments*, ed. D. D. Raphael and A. L. Macfie (Indianapolis: Liberty Press, 1982), pp. 219, 222.

48   **"casual inter-personal physical and verbal violence":** Lawrence Stone, *Family, Sex and Marriage in England, 1500–1800* (New York: Harper, 1983), p. 77.

49   **friendships among both men and women:** Bray, *The Friend*.

50   **devoting oneself seriously:** Aristotle remarks that since people have different and often conflicting needs and desires, being a close friend of many is likely to force one to participate in the pleasure of one friend and the distress of another at the same time, *Nicomachean Ethics*, IX.10, 1171a4–8.

50   **A direct connection doesn't always:** In Book III of *The Faerie Queene*, Britomart falls in love with Artegal after seeing him in a magic mirror; a portrait would also have been enough, provided some causal connection between them was established.

50   **Friendship—unlike charity:** How could Christian love, then, take everyone as an object? It is reasonable to think that the essence of charity doesn't lie in the actual experience of love for unknown

people but in the willingness to treat whoever it is who needs us as we would treat ourselves. That is still something that friendship is incapable of.

51 **friends recognize in one another:** In the essay that first drew the attention of contemporary philosophers to the importance of friendship, Elizabeth Telfer described the affection of friends for each other as a desire for another's welfare and happiness as a particular individual: "This desire," she wrote, "is thus to be distinguished both from the sense of duty and from benevolence. For these motives prompt us to seek others' good in general, whereas we want to say that those who feel affection feel a concern for another which they do not feel for everyone" (Elizabeth Telfer, "Friendship," *Proceedings of the Aristotelian Society* 71 [1970–1971]: 223–241, at 234). The affection of friends is "not for each individual, but for this individual rather than others" (p. 225).

51 **"have in common some insight":** C. S. Lewis, *The Four Loves* (Orlando, FL: Harcourt, 1988), pp. 65, 80. See, for a more detailed discussion of that issue, Marilyn Friedman, *What Are Friends For?: Feminist Perspectives on Personal Relationships and Moral Theory* (Ithaca, NY: Cornell University Press, 1993) and Jacques Derrida, *The Politics of Friendship*, trans. George Collins (London: Verso, 1997), pp. 231–255.

51 **reemerged among philosophers of different stripes:** The starting point for this approach appeals to Aristotle's connection between *philia* and politics in the hope that it can be used to reinsert friendship into the public domain. "Friendship appears to be the bond of the Polis," writes Jürgen Gebhardt, quoting the *Nicomachean Ethics* in his "Friendship, Trust, and Political Order," in *Friendship and Politics: Essays in Political Thought*, ed. John von Heyking and Richard Avramenko (Notre Dame, IN: University of Notre Dame Press, 2008), p. 338; the Aristotelian passage quoted is *Nicomachean Ethics*, VIII.11, 1161a23–24. This anthology provides a good entry point to the vast literature on this subject, which it is not my purpose to examine in detail here. But Aristotle, as we saw, thinks of civic *philia* as a relationship of mutual benefit, not as a bond between the virtuous (how could he, contemptuous of "the many" as he was?), and certainly not as friendship in today's terms. The only kind of *philia* that comes close to what we might consider friendship to be, Aristotle and the tradition that follows him say, is extremely rare and

much more discriminating than the *philia* that bound the 30,000 male citizens of ancient Athens together. And even if we could convince ourselves that the fractious Athenians did all feel genuine friendship for one another, the complexity of modern society and the vastness of contemporary nations compared to the Greek city-state would make it impossible to imagine that contemporary political structures could sustain such a relationship.

52 **Jacques Derrida points out that:** Derrida, *The Politics of Friendship.*

52 **traditional account of "the friend":** See, in particular, Derrida's discussion of Carl Schmitt in ibid., chap. 5.

52 **what such a politics would look like:** See Mariana Valverde, "The Personal Is the Political: Justice and Gender in Deconstruction," *Economy and Society* 28 (1999): 300–311, esp. p. 308.

52 **Carol Gilligan's widely influential book:** Carol Gilligan, *In a Different Voice* (Cambridge, MA: Harvard University Press, 1982). This book, along with Gilligan's subsequent work, has received tremendous attention on the part of psychologists and philosophers. The secondary bibliography is enormous, and I cannot claim to do it any justice here. Good starting points for philosophical approaches to the issues are Annette Baier, "What Do Women Want in a Moral Theory?" *Nous* 19 (1985): 53–63 and "Trust and Antitrust," *Ethics* 96 (1986): 231–260; Friedman, *What Are Friends For?*; Eva Feder Kittay, *Love's Labor: Essays on Women, Equality and Dependency* (New York: Routledge, 1999); Nel Noddings, *Caring: A Feminine Approach to Ethics and Moral Education*, 2nd ed. (Berkeley: University of California Press, 2003). More recently, Virginia Held's *The Ethics of Care: Personal, Political, and Global* (Oxford: Oxford University Press, 2006) is a comprehensive discussion and contains what is in fact an extensive bibliography.

53 **"dominant theories" of morality:** The term, which applies to consequentialism and Kantianism in morality and liberalism in politics, is used by Held, *The Ethics of Care*, p. 13 and *passim.*

53 **"an ethics of care":** A recent discussion of some of its central issues, which includes a review of several approaches, can be found in Sybil A. Schwarzenbach, *On Civic Friendship: Including Women in the State* (New York: Columbia University Press, 2009), especially chap. 7. Schwarzenbach makes a strong case for a civic organization based on friendship conceived along Aristotelian lines, insisting that civic *philia* is genuine friendship: "Although Aristotle at points

classifies political friendship between citizens as a form akin to 'advantage friendship' . . . civic friendships nonetheless retain the three necessary aspects of all friendship . . . that is, although this form of friendship is based upon the general experience or expectation of 'mutual benefit,' is still a *real* friendship. Like all relationships deserving the name, political friendship must involve mutual good will and trust . . . a reciprocal wishing fellow citizens well for their own sake, as well as a practical doing of things for them" (p. 53). If the argument I gave in Chapter 1 is correct, however, political *philia* does not qualify as friendship at all.

53 **matter to us more than the rest:** In a slightly different context, both Bernard Williams, in *Moral Luck* (Cambridge: Cambridge University Press, 1982) and *Ethics and the Limits of Philosophy* (Cambridge, MA: Harvard University Press, 1986), and Harry Frankfurt, in *The Importance of What We Care About* (Cambridge: Cambridge University Press, 1988), have turned their attention not just to the people but also to the various projects that we care about and that play such a serious role in our lives. Neither Frankfurt nor Williams is optimistic about the compatibility of care and impartiality.

53 **"Every person starts out":** Held, *The Ethics of Care*, pp. 12–13; cf. pp. 43–44.

54 **"communitarian" political theorists and philosophers:** Important works on communitarian theory are Alasdair MacIntyre, *After Virtue* (Notre Dame, IL: Notre Dame University Press, 1981); Michael Sandel, *Liberalism and the Limits of Justice* (Cambridge: Cambridge University Press, 1982); Michael Walzer, *Spheres of Justice* (Oxford: Blackwell, 1983); and Charles Taylor, *The Sources of the Self: The Making of the Modern Identity* (Cambridge, MA: Harvard University Press, 1989).

55 **age, family background, sex, race, and ethnicity:** Ethnicity actually seems to be turning into something more like a matter of choice for young people in America today, at least because so many of them are the product of "mixed" marriages. The same seems to be true of gender and, perhaps to a lesser extent, of race, well discussed by K. Anthony Appiah in *In My Father's House: Africa in the Philosophy of Culture* (Oxford: Oxford University Press, 1993).

55 **Others are "achieved":** The terms *ascribed* and *achieved* were first introduced by Ralph Linton, *The Study of Man* (New York: Appleton-Century-Crofts, 1936), pp. 115–131. Since then they have

been used, in a variety of related senses, in many of the social sciences. Some of the problems they generate are well discussed by Irving S. Foladare, "A Clarification of 'Ascribed Status' and 'Achieved Status,'" *Sociological Quarterly* 10 (1969): 53–61. We must be careful here to notice that, as the previous note also suggests, a relationship that is achieved for one person may be in fact ascribed for another. Many men born in the mountains of West Virginia, for example, may have no real choice about becoming coal miners.

55 **taking private friendship as a model:** Virginia Held is right that care is not to be limited to very close personal relationships but needs to enter the public realm of justice, just as considerations of justice are essential to the private sphere (*The Ethics of Care*, pp. 134–135). But I find it impossible to say with her that care is more basic than impartiality.

55 **impartiality has to take priority:** Even if we understand impartiality, with Marilyn Friedman, as the effort to "eliminat[e], from moral thinking, the substantive manifestations of particular nameable biases" (*What Are Friends For?* p. 34).

55 **Others may be beyond our control:** The topic is discussed by Sarah Stroud, "Epistemic Partiality in Friendship," *Ethics* 116 (2006): 498–524 and Simon Keller, *The Limits of Loyalty* (Cambridge: Cambridge University Press, 2007), pp. 24–51; Keller gives a general account of the phenomenon of partiality in *Partiality* (Princeton: Princeton University Press, 2013). Stroud provides references to some of the extensive psychological research of the subject.

56 **it can "provide social support":** Friedman, *What Are Friends For?* p. 248. See also, for an application of this principle to homosexuals, Andrew Sullivan, *Love Undetectable: Notes on Friendship, Sex, and Survival* (New York: Alfred A. Knopf, 1998).

57 **"a mockery of God":** Søren Kierkegaard, *Works of Love*, trans. Howard and Edna Hong (Princeton: Princeton University Press, 1998), p. 37.

57 **"Romanticism" and "the exaltation of Sentiment":** Lewis, *The Four Loves*, pp. 58–59.

57 **Modern moral thought centered its attention:** See John M. Cooper, "Aristotle on the Forms of Friendship," in *Reason and Emotion* (Princeton: Princeton University Press, 1999), pp. 312–335, at 312.

58 **The moral treatise that will convince:** Bernard Williams is the main contemporary skeptic on this issue; see, among others, his

Ethics and The Limits of Philosophy. See also Richard Rorty, "Human Rights, Rationality, and Sentimentality" in Stephen Shute and Susan Hurley, eds., *On Human Rights: Oxford Amnesty Lectures* (New York: Basic Books, 1994), pp. 111–134. It is unfortunately also true that even the very vocabulary of human rights can be used to justify the kinds of treatment that it explicitly seeks to abolish: the Rights of Man are available only to those who, on each occasion, are taken to satisfy the essentially contestable account of who is and who is not Man. At the same time, though, that vocabulary opens the way to extending those rights to new categories of people: the very notion of the Rights of Man was instrumental in securing such rights, to the extent that we have done so thus far, for women.

58   **all moral behavior must be impartial:** This bald statement requires serious qualification. Moral philosophy contains more variations— for example, virtue theory and intuitionism—and one approach, particularism, claims that the moral point of view is not impartial. But it is the very general lines of this outlook that are important to me now. For some of the complexities of the issues, see Troy Jollimore, "Impartiality," *The Stanford Encyclopedia of Philosophy* (Fall 2008 edition), ed. Edward N. Zalta, at plato.stanford.edu/archives/fall2008/entries/impartiality. For efforts to make morality more sensitive to particular situations, see Jonathan Dancy, *Ethics Without Principles* (Oxford: Oxford University Press, 2006), and Lawrence A. Blum, *Friendship, Altruism, and Morality* (London: Routledge and Kegan Paul, 1980) and *Moral Perception and Particularity* (New York: Cambridge University Press, 1994). See also John Kekes, "Morality and Impartiality," *American Philosophical Quarterly* 18 (1981): 295–303; Annette Baier, "The Moral Perils of Intimacy," in *Pragmatism's Freud: The Moral Disposition of Psychoanalysis,* ed. Joseph H. Smith and William Kerrigan (Baltimore: Johns Hopkins University Press, 1986), pp. 93–101; and Lynne McFall, "Integrity," *Ethics* 98 (1987): 5–20.

59   **both Kantian and consequentialist philosophers:** See, for example, Troy Jollimore, *Friendship and Agent-Relative Morality* (New York: Garland Publishing, 2001), for a Kantian approach and, for a consequentialist alternative, Peter Railton, "Alienation, Consequentialism, and the Demands of Morality," *Philosophy and Public Affairs* 13 (1984): 134–171.

60   **"For most people, the relevance":** Harry G. Frankfurt, *Necessity, Volition, and Love* (Cambridge: Cambridge University Press, 1998), p. x. The issues involved are raised in more detail, and with a

different conclusion than Frankfurt's, in Craig Taylor, *Moralism* (Montreal: McGill-Queens University Press, 2012).

60   **"Friendship (as the ancients saw)":** Lewis, *The Four Loves*, p. 80.

61   **"A circle of Friends can":** Ibid., p. 82.

61   **but actually *require* attitudes or actions:** That possibility underlies what the late historian Alan Bray highlighted as its "uncertain ethics" in its early modern (and, we may add, in its contemporary) form: "Friendship required fidelity, but what if that fidelity required one to act *un*ethically? . . . A potential for wrong as well as a potential for right; there lay the ethical problem"; see Bray, *The Friend*, pp. 312, 125.

61   **When morality and preferential relationships:** Bernard Williams, "Persons, Character and Morality," in *Moral Luck* (Cambridge: Cambridge University Press, 1981), pp. 1–19, at 17. But see also Harry Frankfurt's discussion of Williams in *The Reasons of Love* (Princeton: Princeton University Press, 2006), pp. 35–37. Williams believes that the thought "This is my friend" is one's reason for saving one's friend and not some further thought, for example, "In a situation of this sort it is permissible to save my friend": the latter, he said, is "one thought too many." Frankfurt claims instead that even the thought "This is my friend" is one thought too many: the only reason needed is that I love my friend, which gives me, on its own, a reason to save my friend rather than the stranger.

62   **"A friend helps you move house":** Dean Cocking and Jeannette Kennett, "Friendship and Moral Danger," *Journal of Philosophy* 97 (2000): 278–296, p. 279. See also their "Friendship and the Self," *Ethics* 108 (1998): 502–527.

62   **"mere collusion and cynical self-advancement":** Bray, *The Friend*, p. 125.

62   **the relationship between Kim Philby:** An excellent account of their story, which doesn't decide the case clearly one way or the other, is given by Ben Macintyre, *A Spy Among Friends: Kim Philby and the Great Betrayal* (New York: Crown Publishers, 2014).

62   **"I have always operated on two levels":** Ibid., p. 284.

62   **"I understand you":** Ibid., p. 259.

63   **impossible to think of Philby as a *good* friend:** Philby's deception of Elliott (and everyone else in his circle, including James Jesus Angleton, the CIA chief of counterintelligence) is an immensely greater and more sinister version of a deception we will discuss in Chapter 4.

CHAPTER 3   A STRUCTURE OF THE SOUL

66   **"My own death, I'll meet it freely"**: *Homer: The Iliad*, trans. Robert
Fagles, introduction and notes by Bernard Knox (New York: Viking Penguin, 1990), Book 18.25, 94–95; 254–255, Book 22.431; Book
24.550–810.

67   **"soul was knit with"**: 1 Samuel 18–20, *The New Oxford Annotated
Bible with the Apocrypha* (New York: Oxford University Press, 1973).

67   **when Phintias, sentenced to death:** The story is preserved by Aris-
toxenus Musicus, fr. 31, 17–40.

67   **"Now that you are dead"**: *The Song of Roland*, trans. Glyn Burgess
(London: Penguin, 1990), ll.151, 153.

68   **ancient Sumerian epic of Gilgamesh:** J. B. Pritchard, ed., *Ancient
Near Eastern Texts Relating to the Old Testament*, 3rd ed. (Princeton:
Princeton University Press, 1969).

68   **Harmodius and Aristogeiton:** Thucydides, *The History of the Pelo-
ponnesian War*, trans. Rex Warner (London: Penguin Books, 1972),
1.20, 6.53ff; Herodotus, *The Histories*, rev. ed. trans. John M. Marin-
cola and Aubrey de Selincourt (London: Penguin Books, 2003),
5.55–65.

68   **Amis and Amile:** When Amis is struck with leprosy, the archangel
Gabriel reveals that he will be cured if Amile kills his children and
bathes Amis in their blood. Amile complies but, fortunately, his
children are restored to life just as Amis is cured. See Eugene Ma-
son, *Amis and Amile* (New York: Kessinger, 2004). A more detailed
account of these and other stories about friendship can be found
in A. C. Grayling, *Friendship* (New Haven, CT: Yale University
Press, 2013), pp. 123–166.

68   **their heroes are *literally* heroes:** This is partly what Voltaire must
have had in mind when he remarked, with some exaggeration: "The
temple of friendship has long been a household word, but it is well
known that the place has been little frequented . . . Orestes,
Pylades, Pirithous, Achates, and the tender Nisus, they were all
genuine friends and great heroes; but alas they existed only in
fable." See his *Philosophical Dictionary*, quoted in D. J. Enright and
David Rawlinson, *The Oxford Book of Friendship* (Oxford: Oxford
University Press, 1991), p. 21.

68   **When their relationship is hierarchical:** Gilgamesh does not in
fact die in the course of the epic. Instead he becomes reconciled to

abandoning the pursuit of immortality or eternal fame and immerses himself in the everyday activities of a mortal life. That is a triumph of a different sort.

68 **they may die together:** The same is true of Saints Perpetua and Felicitas, as we saw in Chapter 2—saints, of course, are the heroes of Christianity.

68 **"a specific cultural formation":** David Halperin, "Heroes and Their Pals," in his *One Hundred Years of Homosexuality and Other Essays on Greek Love* (New York: Routledge, 1990), pp. 75–87. Halperin discusses *Gilgamesh*, the *Iliad*, and the Books of Samuel. I believe, though, that his general idea applies to a larger class of narratives, which includes the other stories I mention here. My discussion is indebted to this essay.

70 **Pontormo composed a portrait of two men:** Giorgio Vasari, *The Lives of the Most Excellent Painters, Sculptors, and Architects*, trans. Gaston de C. De Vere, ed. Philip Jacks (New York: Random House, 2006), p. 317.

71 **"Pontormo's own circle of friends":** Carl Brandon Strehlke, *Pontormo, Bronzino, and the Medici: The Transformation of the Renaissance Portrait in Florence* (Philadelphia: Philadelphia Museum of Art and Pennsylvania State University Press, 2005), p. 66. On the basis of a similarity to the subject of a portrait by Andrea Del Sarto, which may be of Paolo da Testarossa, the man on the right in Pontormo's painting has sometimes been identified as that well-known Florentine merchant; see p. 64 with n. 3.

72 **"the person who corresponds to":** Elizabeth Cropper, "Pontormo and Bronzino in Philadelphia: A Double Portrait," in Strehlke, *Pontormo, Bronzino, and the Medici*, pp. 1–33, at 14.

72 **According to the first interpretation:** Many of these questions are asked by Cropper, "Pontormo and Bronzino," and elaborated in her "The Beauty of Woman: Problems in the Rhetoric of Renaissance Portraiture," in *Rewriting the Renaissance: The Discourses of Sexual Difference in Early Modern Europe*, ed. M. W. Ferguson, M. Quilligan, and N. J. Vickers (Chicago: University of Chicago Press, 1986), pp. 175–190, as well as in Elizabeth Cropper and Charles Dempsey, *Nicolas Poussin: Friendship and the Love of Painting* (Princeton: Princeton University Press, 1996).

74 **Without their titles:** Imagine, for example, that we gave them the following titles: "The Surprise" (Fig. 4), and "Consoling the

Widower" (Fig. 5). Groups to whom I presented with such titles were perfectly willing to accept them as descriptive of their content.

76   **"We picture lovers face to face":** C. S. Lewis, *The Four Loves* (Orlando, FL: Harcourt, 1988), p. 66.

77   **The visual features of painting:** Bernard Faucon's work is a combination of photography and mixed media: the effect is that of a painting. In any case, what applies to painting in this context applies to photography as well.

79   **Plato was the first to notice:** Plato, *Laches*, in *Plato: Collected Works*, ed. John M. Cooper (Indianapolis: Hackett Publishing, 1997), p. 676.

79   **And so is friendship:** Ironically enough, friendship seems to have given Plato a great deal of trouble. The dialogue *Lysis*, with which philosophical speculation on the subject began, ends with the admission that it has proved impossible to say what a friend is. On whether "friendship" is an adequate rendering of the Greek term *philia*, see Chapter 1.

80   **depends on the motives with which:** An excellent discussion of the role of motivation in friendship is given by Michael Stocker, "Values and Purposes: The Limits of Teleology and the Ends of Friendship," *Journal of Philosophy* 78 (1981): 747–765, and reprinted in Neera Kapur Badhwar, ed., *Friendship: A Philosophical Reader* (Ithaca, NY: Cornell University Press, 1993), pp. 245–263.

80   **"Are you dying for him?":** Charles Dickens, *A Tale of Two Cities* (Garden City, NY: Doubleday, 1964), p. 332. Interestingly, in the film version of the novel (1935), Carton's answer to the seamstress's question is changed into "He is my friend": the myth is still powerful.

82   **the behavior of two people fits:** Although friendship can join more than two people to each other, my focus throughout this book is on relationships between two people.

82   **"At our first meeting":** Michel de Montaigne, "Of Friendship," trans. Donald M. Frame, *The Complete Works of Montaigne: Essays, Travel Journal, Letters* (Stanford: Stanford University Press, 1958), I.28, p. 139.

82   **"Every beginning / Is only a sequel":** Wislawa Szymborska, *Poems New and Collected*, trans. Stanislaw Baranczak and Clare Cavanagh (San Diego: Harcourt, 2000), p. 245.

82   **"the precipitancy of our mutual understanding":** Montaigne, "Of Friendship," p. 139. We should also note that the feelings that over-

whelm Montaigne, however strong, may dissipate when two people meet again.

82 **"time and familiarity":** Aristotle, *Nicomachean Ethics*, trans. and ed. Roger Crisp (Cambridge: Cambridge University Press, 2000), VIII.3, 1156b25–32, translation slightly modified.

83 **Time is of the essence:** Aristotle, *Nicomachean Ethics*, VIII.5, 1157b10–19.

83 **"Mr. Bingley," Jane Austen writes:** Jane Austen, *Pride and Prejudice* (Oxford: Oxford University Press, 1923), p. 10. Whether their friendship is successfully represented is, of course, a separate question.

83 **important to literature written by women:** Jane Austen is paradigmatic here. Still, in her effort to show that friendships among women are more important to her novels than even her best readers allow, Deborah Knuth ("'We Fainted Alternately on a Sofa': Female Friendship in Jane Austen's *Juvenilia*," *Persuasions* 9 [1987]: 64–71) needs to appeal to her early, unfinished works and finally concedes that "the subject of the later novels seems unequivocally 'love' rather than 'friendship'" (p. 71).

84 **none of them is *about* friendship:** I am fully aware that my claim here is deeply controversial. A much more positive approach to the importance of literature for friendship and their structural interconnections is taken by Gregory Jusdanis in *A Tremendous Thing: Friendship from the Iliad to the Internet* (Ithaca, NY: Cornell University Press, 2014).

84 **Horace, praying for Virgil's safe journey:** Horace, *Odes*, I.3.

84 **"Precious friends hid in death's dateless night":** Helen Vendler, *The Art of Shakespeare's Sonnets* (Cambridge, MA: Harvard University Press, 1999).

85 **"Half my life I left behind":** Alfred Lord Tennyson, *In Memoriam*, 2nd ed., ed. Erik Gray (New York: W. W. Norton, 2004), LVI, p. 82.

85 **Ann Patchett recounts her friendship:** Ann Patchett, *Truth and Beauty* (New York: HarperCollins, 2004).

85 **from a heroin overdose:** Abraham Verghese's engaging novel, *The Tennis Partner* (New York: HarperCollins, 1998), also involves a friend who is tortured and eventually killed by addiction, and, narrated in the first person as it is, is formally similar to a memoir. It contains some brilliant observations, but it is not, in the end, capacious enough to be what I have called work of the first rank.

85   In *Huckleberry Finn*, **Huck and Jim:** Mark Twain, *The Adventures of Huckleberry Finn* (Colorado Springs, CO: Piccadilly Books, 2010).

86   **As for Joyce's Leopold Bloom:** James Joyce, *Ulysses* (New York: Milestone Books, n.d.).

86   **"In estimating the value":** William Hazlitt, *Characteristics: In the Manner of Rochefoucauld's Maxims*, 2nd ed. (London: J. Templeman, 1837), p. 77; also quoted in D. J. Enright and David Rawlinson, *The Oxford Book of Friendship* (Oxford: Oxford University Press, 1991), p. 10.

86   **"more active, more scorching":** Montaigne, "Of Friendship," p. 137.

87   **friendship, in modern times:** And not in modern times only: Achilles' desperate mourning for Patroclus' death and his inhumanly bloodthirsty revenge prompted classical Athens to see their relationship as a love affair; that is at least what Plato reports in his *Symposium*; see *Symposium* 179e-180a. The sexual interpretation of the relationship between Achilles and Patroclus may have originated in Aeschylus' lost *Achilleis*; see Stella Miller, "Eros and the Arms of Achilles," *American Journal of Archaeology* 90 (1986): 159–170. Montaigne himself, when he describes his relationship with La Boétie, adds strong fuel to the moderate warmth of friendship and acknowledges the force that, "having seized my whole will, led it to plunge and lose itself in his; which, having seized his whole will, led it to plunge and lose itself in mine." In these words, several of his readers have heard the stirrings of lust, tempered perhaps by his need to give voice to "an egalitarian, sexual relationship between men, a concept that his discussion suggests was not available to him, even as he may seem to desire it and strive eloquently to describe it" (Marc D. Schachter, "'That Friendship Which Possesses the Soul': Montaigne Loves La Boétie," *Journal of Homosexuality* 41 [2001]: 5–21, on p. 13).

87   **"They called each other by their Christian":** Jane Austen, *Northanger Abbey* (New York: New American Library, 1965), pp. 28–29.

88   **"what this pair does together":** Stanley Cavell, *Pursuits of Happiness: The Hollywood Comedy of Remarriage* (Cambridge, MA: Harvard University Press, 1981), p. 88.

89   **"full nature, like that river":** George Eliot, *Middlemarch*, ed. Gregory Maertz (Peterborough, Ontario: Broadview Press, 2004), p. 640.

90   **"spit . . . the gall that chokes me":** See René Descharmes, "Autour de *Bouvard et Pécuchet*," in his *Études documentaires et critiques*

(Paris, 1921), quoted by Raymond Queneau in the preface to Mark Polizzotti's translation of the novel (Champaign, IL: Dalkey Archive Press, 2005), p. xxii.

91 **"their personal tastes were complementary"**: Gustave Flaubert, *Bouvard and Pécuchet*, p. 9.

91 **we are as often drawn to our friends:** This was first pointed out by Plato in his *Lysis* (214e–216b), in John M. Cooper and D. S. Hutchinson, eds., *Plato: Complete Works* (Indianapolis: Hackett Publishing Company, 1997), pp. 695–699.

91 **"How can one explain why"**: Flaubert, *Bouvard and Pécuchet*, p. 9.

92 **only friends—very close friends:** Ibid., pp. 279–281.

92 **"boring it's not"**: Translator's introduction to *Bouvard and Pécuchet*, p. xiii, where the two excerpts from Flaubert's letters—the first to Léonie Brainne and the second to Émile Zola—also appear.

92 **"It is aesthetically stubborn":** Julian Barnes, "Flaubert, C'est Moi," *New York Review of Books* 53 (9), May 25, 2006.

93 **"a huge part of its comic effect"**: Translator's introduction to *Bouvard and Pécuchet*, p. xiii.

93 **not exactly a novel but a picaresque:** A picaresque is an account of the adventures of a character, often a rogue (which is what *picaro* means in Spanish). The adventures often have the same structure, and the central character behaves very much in the same way throughout. There is much less variation in plot and character development than in the canonical novel.

93 **Sancho and Quixote remain indissolubly:** In that respect, they are similar to the heroes of the epic, and they are related hierarchically, more as "boon companions" than equal friends.

94 **protagonists of the modern detective-story series:** Such pairs are also a staple of television police shows. They all originate in Jack Webb's *Dragnet*, which first appeared on radio and was later transferred to television and film, in several versions. Could the name of Jack Webb's character, Joe Friday, applied to the dominant character and not to his associate, have something to do with Daniel Defoe's *Robinson Crusoe*?

95 **"One day a servant called [Deslauriers]"**: Gustave Flaubert, *Sentimental Education*, trans. Robert Baldick, rev. ed. (London: Penguin Books, 2004), p. 17.

95 **remains a serious and genuine friendship:** As Sandra Lynch writes in her wide-ranging *Philosophy and Friendship* (Edinburgh: Edinburgh University Press, 2005), "It is important to recognize

that those we might consider to be thoroughly bad characters appear capable of friendship" (p. 113).

96   **"reconciled once again by that irresistible element"**: Flaubert, *Sentimental Education*, p. 457.

97   **"They told one another the story"**: Ibid., pp. 459–460.

CHAPTER 4   "AND SO ON"

101   **"*How many friends have you got*"**: Tim Lott, *White City Blue* (London: Penguin Books, 2000), p. 41.

101   **"*Oh, loads*"**: Ibid., pp. 45–46.

103   **fewer friendships than there were "instincts"**: L. L. Bernard, "Hereditary and Environmental Factors in Human Behavior," *Monist* 37 (1927): 161–182: "I examined nearly six hundred volumes by over five hundred authors and discovered approximately six thousand separate classes of more or less complex instincts, as distinguished from reflexes, under nearly fifteen thousand different forms. And when I stopped, because of fatigue and the limitations of time and money, new additions to my collection were coming in strong" (pp. 166–167).

103   **"Despite the very large literature"**: Ray Pahl, *On Friendship* (Cambridge: Polity Press, 2000), chap. 4, esp. p. 142.

104   **"This is my, um, *friend*"**: Lott, *White City Blue*, p. 80.

104   **If *x* loves *y*:** Gabriele Taylor, "Love," *Proceedings of the Aristotelian Society* 76 (1976): 147–164, p. 157. Cited, along with several other similar formulations, by J. David Velleman, "Love as a Moral Emotion," *Ethics* 109 (1999): 338–374, at 352.

104   **True enough, as far as it goes:** Indeed, if we take the desire to do good as the central feature of love and friendship, we risk pushing friendship, and affection more generally, into a kind of unrelenting preoccupation with being helpful—a preoccupation that, as one philosopher puts it, can turn friendship into "an interfering, ingratiating nightmare" (see Velleman, "Love as a Moral Emotion," p. 353). It is exactly that kind of solicitude that destroys the life of Lola, the protagonist of William Inge's *Come Back, Little Sheba*, who has become such an "interfering, ingratiating nightmare" that her beloved dog, which gives the play its title, has vanished even before the play begins, as if it knew that nothing short of disappearing could spare it from her unrelenting, oppressive concern.

I should say that I am ignoring various complications here. For example, we don't have to believe that "all men kill the thing they love" to suspect that love, especially when it is unrequited, can sometimes create the desire to harm, even to kill, rather than to benefit.

104 **"are not attracted to each other":** Aristotle, *Nicomachean Ethics*, 1157a15–16. The issue is complex. See my "Aristotelian *Philia*, Modern Friendship?" *Oxford Studies in Ancient Philosophy* 39 (2010): 213–247.

105 **"In the best friendships":** Neera Kapur Badhwar, "Friends as Ends in Themselves," *Philosophy and Phenomenological Research* 48 (1987): 1–23, p. 2. See also Laurence Thomas, "Friendship," *Encyclopedia of Applied Ethics* (Washington, DC: Academic Press, 1998), vol. 2, p. 323: "No one is oblivious to the difference between, at one end, friends who are mere acquaintances or who interact socially from time to time—casual friends, let us say—and, at the other end, friends who constitute a deep friendship—that is, individuals who are the best of friends." It is not accidental, I think, that while Badhwar includes love in her account of "the best friendships," she avoids referring to it when she comes to friendship's "lesser kinds." By contrast, Sybil A. Schwarzenbach (*On Civic Friendship: Including Women in the State* [New York: Columbia University Press, 2009], p. 44) writes that in those lesser forms of friendship "one loves the other friend . . . as someone who generally brings advantage to me or who is typically fun to be around." But, first, Aristotle seems to think that the advantage and the pleasure involved here are neither "general" nor "typical" but specific: otherwise, it would not be necessary to dissolve a relationship when someone does something that is not to my advantage since I may benefit from the relationship in the future; second, we have seen that "fun" is much too weak for the pleasures Aristotle has in mind; and, third, to say that I love you as my friend because of what I can obtain from you seems to be a contradiction in terms.

106 **"The religion of my doctor":** Michel de Montaigne, "Of Friendship," *The Complete Works of Montaigne: Essays, Travel Journals, Letters*, ed. and trans. Donald C. Frame (Stanford: Stanford University Press, 1958), I.28, p. 142.

107 **any equally qualified barber:** This is an oversimplification. Several other factors are relevant to the decision to adopt a particular

barber (or any other provider of services) but these, too—like cost or distance from my house—are abstract and could be equally well or better satisfied by several individuals.

107 **"The delivery man, the money-lender"**: Georg Simmel, *The Philosophy of Money*, trans. Tom Bottomore and David Frisby (London: Routledge and Kegan Paul, 1978), pp. 295–303 (originally published in 1900). The quotation is from p. 297. As the previous note may have suggested, I am not at all sure that what makes the difference between an impersonal and a personal relationship is, as Simmel implies, the number of features of the other we take into account in our interactions. What exactly does make the difference is what this chapter tries to determine.

108 **But some impersonal relationships can gradually:** To avoid misunderstandings, I should say that I am using the terms "impersonal" and "instrumental," even when I qualify them by a term like "purely," for relationships that include the minimum decency to which I refer in my text, hoping to conform to the (somewhat) Kantian ideal of treating as many people as possible not merely as means but also as ends. When our relationship is personal in the sense I am using the term here, my concern for your (nonprofessional) interests will not be the same as my concern for everyone else's.

110 **"Among our valued friends is there not"**: George Eliot, *Middlemarch* (Boston: Houghton Mifflin, 1908), vol. 1, chap. 15, pp. 214–215.

111 **"Yes, I love you, I do"**: "Liquid Heat," *The L Word*, season 5, episode 9, Showtime Networks, aired March 2, 2008.

112 **"love, and wish each other well"**: Badhwar, "Friends as Ends in Themselves," p. 2.

113 **"Instrumental friendship"**: Someone who knows both of us might say that I am your friend because you can help me advance my career. But, far from explaining why I am your friend, that would suggest that I am not really your friend at all, that I am merely taking advantage of you. For the same reason, I can't say such a thing myself because to tell you that I like you because you can help me advance my career is to reveal that I don't like *you* but only what I can get from you. Of course, I may have been what is sometimes called a "false" friend without ever admitting this, even to myself—and countless relationships are considered friendships when they are in fact just covert ways of exploitation. It is also possible that although I honestly believe I am your friend and love you

not for what you can do for me but for who you are, I may come to
recognize my true feelings belatedly, when, to my shame, I lose all
interest in you once I have exhausted the benefit of our association.
Such a discovery can be very painful and harmful to our self-image:
we often fight hard to push it away from consciousness. I suspect,
though, that many of us have had precisely this experience at some
time or other—and, afterward, realized exactly what had attracted
us to that person in the first place: the particular benefit, whatever
it was, that we obtained through our relationship.

113   **"Iron sharpeneth iron":** Proverbs 27:17, in the King James version
of the Bible.

114   **"My brother, my brother":** Montaigne, letter to his father on the
death of La Boétie, in Frame, *Complete Works*, p. 1053.

114   **"was still breathing and speaking":** Ibid.; translation slightly
altered.

114   **"consubstantial with its author":** Montaigne, "Of Giving the Lie,"
Essays II.18, in Frame, *Complete Works*, p. 504.

114   **"I am myself the matter":** Montaigne, "To the Reader," in Frame,
Complete Works, p. 2.

115   **each of the *Essays'* readers:** See Frame, *Complete Works*, p. v.: "The
book reveals a man and . . . the man becomes a friend and often
another self . . . the reader takes the place of the dead friend." See
also Jean Starobinski, *Montaigne in Motion*, trans. Arthur Gold-
hammer (Chicago: University of Chicago Press, 1985), p. 31.

115   **the centerpiece of the whole work:** By the time the first edition of
the first volume finally appeared, Montaigne had already composed
a second. He then worked on a third volume, which appeared in
the *Essays'* second edition, published in 1588.

"Of Friendship" is the twenty-eighth of the fifty-seven essays
of which the first book of the *Essays* consists and, along with the
twenty-ninth, which is also devoted to La Boétie, its place is almost
at the volume's exact center. For a detailed and engaging treatment
of Montaigne's incorporation of La Boétie's *On Voluntary Servitude*
in his work, see François Rigolot, "Friendship and Voluntary Servitude: Plato, Ficino, and Montaigne," *Texas Studies in Literature and
Language* 47 (2005): 326–344. Interesting material is also found in
Zahi Zalloua, "Sameness and Difference: Portraying the Other in
Montaigne's *De l'amitié* (I.28)," *Montaigne Studies* 15 (2003): 177–
190 and Zalloua's book, *Montaigne and the Ethics of Skepticism*

(Charlottesville, VA: Rockwood Press, 2005), pp. 74–98. A detailed discussion of these issues can be found in Gérard Defaux, *Montaigne et le travail de l'amitié* (Orléans: Paradigme, 2001). Defaux connects La Boétie's request with Jesus's telling his disciples that he will soon leave them in order to prepare for them "a place" by the side of his Father (John 14: 1–3). Montaigne, if that is right, has relocated that "place" from the afterlife to (his own) life on earth. I am grateful to François Rigolot for bringing Defaux's book to my attention and for sharing his vast knowledge and understanding of Montaigne with me.

115 **"grotesques and monstrous bodies"**: Montaigne, "Of Friendship," in Frame, *Complete Works*, p. 135.

116 **La Boétie's treatise was published:** It was published in full in 1576, four years before the publication of the *Essays'* first volume in 1580.

116 **better to leave it out:** To minimize the political implications of La Boétie's book, he also wrote that "the subject was treated by him in his boyhood, only by way of an exercise," in Frame, *Complete Works*, p. 144.

116 **"listen a while to this boy":** See the notes on pp. 183 and 195 in Pierre Villey, *Montaigne: Les Essais*, Livre I (Paris: Presses Universitaires de France, 1965). Montaigne's practice of leaving the text of his essays more or less intact ("I only add," he wrote, "I don't correct") raises fascinating questions, which I address in Chapter 6.

116 **"I was already so formed":** Montaigne, "Of Friendship," in Frame, *Complete Works*, p. 143.

117 **"gayer and more lusty":** Ibid., p. 145.

117 **the poems appeared in both editions:** Montaigne, *Essays*, I.29, "Twenty-nine Sonnets of Étienne de la Boétie," in Frame, *Complete Works*, p. 145.

117 **"He loved him so because":** Here, too, he left his own text intact. He retained his short introduction, now introducing nothing, and explained his omission in a brusque coda: "These verses may be seen elsewhere."

118 **"the complete fusion of our wills":** Montaigne, "Of Friendship," in Frame, *Complete Works*, p. 141.

118 **"It is not one special consideration":** Ibid., p. 139.

119 **"If you press me to tell why":** Ibid.

119 **"*Because it was he*":** Ibid.

120 **"It is myself that I portray":** Montaigne, *Essays*, "Note to the Reader," in Frame, p. 2.

120 **The *Essays* are the very "place":** Compare Starobinski, *Montaigne in Motion*, p. 50: to keep La Boétie alive is not "merely to discharge an obligation to a lost friend. It is also a way . . . of allowing Montaigne to continue to see (in the fraternal image he carries in his memory) the light of the gaze that La Boétie directed at him, and the image of himself that La Boétie's gaze offered. The place that his dying friend wanted him to secure lies in his own consciousness."

120 **"In the friendship I speak of":** Montaigne, "Of Friendship," in Frame, *Complete Works*, p. 139.

121 **"has no model but itself":** Ibid.

121 **discussion of metaphor by . . . Stanley Cavell:** Cavell's discussion is embedded in his essay, "Aesthetic Problems of Modern Philosophy," in *Must We Mean What We Say?* (New York: Charles Scribner's Sons, 1969); all citations are from pp. 78–79. Unfortunately, what most of Cavell's readers seem to have taken from his essay is his particular example—Romeo's "Juliet is the sun"—which has been endlessly repeated, as if this elementary instance is all a philosopher need know about metaphor in order to produce a comprehensive theory of this extraordinarily complex phenomenon. This unfortunate situation is remedied in the work of David Hills, who bases his valuable discussions on a wilderness of metaphors; see in particular his discussion and extension of Cavell's work, "Problems of Paraphrase: Bottom's Dream," in *A Figure of Speech*, vol. 3 of *The Baltic International Yearbook of Cognition, Logic and Communication* (2007).

122 **"Those who wish good things to":** Cicero, *De Amicitia*, xxvi.100.

122 **"Romeo means that Juliet is the warmth":** Similes themselves do not belong to literal language, as is often thought: the respects in which Juliet and the sun are alike are bound to be themselves metaphorical; similes are not comparisons. See Nelson Goodman, *Languages of Art* (Indianapolis: Bobbs-Merrill, 1968), pp. 77–78.

123 **"A ship is like a lady's watch":** Rod Scher, ann., in Richard Henry Dana's *The Annotated Two Years Before the Mast* (Lanham, MD: Sheridan Press, 2013), p. 17.

123 **"The over-reading of metaphors":** The reference is to William Empson, *Seven Types of Ambiguity*, 2nd ed. (London: Chatto and Windus, 1947), p. 140. Although Cavell's statement is perfectly apposite, Empson in that passage seems to me to be concerned with the metaphor of pregnancy rather than the pregnancy of metaphor.

127 **neither similarities nor differences:** These difficulties were first introduced, discussed, and left unsolved in Plato's *Lysis* and form

part of the background against which Aristotle constructs his own, similarity-based account of friendship in both the *Nicomachean* and the *Eudemian Ethics.*

128 **"not one special consideration"**: Montaigne, "Of Friendship," in Frame, *Complete Works*, p. 139.

128 **"Shall I compare thee"**: William Shakespeare, *Sonnets*, XVIII. On the complexities of the poem, in particular, the gradual transformation of the permanent into the temporal, see Helen Vendler, *The Art of Shakespeare's Sonnets* (Cambridge, MA: Harvard University Press, 1997), pp. 119–122.

129 **"If you're ever in a jam"**: Cole Porter, "Friendship," from *Du Barry Was a Lady*, quoted in D. J. Enright and David Rawlinson, *The Oxford Book of Friendship* (Oxford: Oxford University Press, 1991), p. 27.

130 **"You know about a person"**: *The Writings of Henry Thoreau*, ed. Bradford Torrey and F. B. Sanforn (Boston: Houghton Mifflin, 1906), Vol. 17, *Journal*, Entry for February 20, 1859, p. 451

130 **We can never say everything**: That, I believe, is the import of his notion of the "free play" of the imagination and the understanding, which accounts, according to Kant, for the pleasure we feel in the presence of beauty. This idea is well developed by Paul Guyer in "The Harmony of the Faculties Revisited," in his *Values of Beauty* (New York: Cambridge University Press, 2005), pp. 77–109.

130 **"no rule in accordance with which"**: Immanuel Kant, *Critique of the Power of Judgment*, trans. Paul Guyer and Eric Matthews (Cambridge: Cambridge University Press, 2000), para. 8, p. 101. I develop Kant's idea in chap. 1 of *Only a Promise of Happiness: The Place of Beauty in a World of Art* (Princeton: Princeton University Press, 2007).

131 **"the individual, in . . . his or her individuality"**: That is an expression Gregory Vlastos used in order to describe what Plato should have realized love is directed at, instead of, as he thought, at the features of the individual in question (Gregory Vlastos, "The Individual as an Object of Love in Plato," in *Platonic Studies* [Princeton: Princeton University Press, 1981], 2nd ed., pp. 3–37, at 31, followed, among many others by Badhwar, "Friends as Ends in Themselves," p. 6). Vlastos believed that if we love our friends on account of any of their features, we love not *them* but their features instead, and he accused Plato of making just that mistake in his *Symposium* because

he held that "what we are to love in persons is the 'image' of the Idea in them." The "Idea" here is the Platonic Form of perfect beauty and goodness, whose pale reflections we see in those we love. But since, Vlastos continued, none of us is purely good or beautiful, to love you for your beauty and goodness can't be to love *you* as the individual you are, blemishes and all: "The individual, in the uniqueness and integrity of his or her individuality, will never be the object of our love." For the same reason, Plato is also accused of thinking that if you realize that someone else is more beautiful than the person you love, you will automatically transfer your feelings from one to the other, transferring your affect and loyalty from one individual person to all bodily beauty, the beauty of soul, the culture that produces beautiful souls, the knowledge that establishes the right sort of culture, and finally the Form of Beauty, which account for the beauty of every beautiful object, itself. Thus, for Plato, your beauty (or any other virtue you may have) is as detachable from who you are as your money or your house.

But that criticism is neither fair to Plato nor to the view that our friends' features are involved in our love for them (see my "Beauty of Body, Nobility of Soul: The Pursuit of Love in Plato's *Symposium*," in Dominic Scott, ed., *Maieusis: Essays in Ancient Philosophy in Honour of Myles Burnyeat* [Oxford: Oxford University Press, 2007], pp. 97–135.) To love you for your kindness is not to love your kindness *instead* of loving you—no more, I suppose, than to fire you for your incompetence is to fire your incompetence rather than you (see the argument of Simon Keller, "How Do I Love Thee?: Let Me Count the Properties," *American Philosophical Quarterly* 37 [2000]: 163–173).

133 **there is more to know here:** This is the central thesis of *Only a Promise of Happiness*. Whether a person or a work of art, whatever we love is always a step beyond our current understanding, inviting us to come to know it better and promising that we shall both be better off for it. Metaphor, as I use it here, is, so to speak, a synecdoche for every work of art.

133 **"not so much for one's own sake":** Immanuel Kant, *Lectures on Ethics*, trans. Peter Heath (Cambridge: Cambridge University Press, 1997), p. 188.

134 **"Love is not an end":** John Williams, *Stoner* (New York: New York Review of Books, 2006; orig. pub. 1963), p. 194.

135 **I can't approach it with anyone but you:** Of course, that doesn't mean that we can't have more than one friend. It only means that each one of our friends makes a distinct, individual contribution to our life.

138 **Charles Lamb said somewhere:** C. S. Lewis, *The Four Loves* (Orlando, FL: Harcourt, 1988), p. 61.

CHAPTER 5 "NO SENSE OF HUMOR"

142 **Yasmina Reza's play *Art*:** Yasmina Reza, *Art*, trans. Christopher Hampton (New York: Faber and Faber, 1994).

142 **Drama can also depict . . . repetitive situations:** I realize that I can't help but limit myself to the play's script (ditto for my discussion of *Thelma and Louise* in Chapter 6)—that is unavoidable. But much that I have to say will depend on my having seen two productions of the play and recalling (or proposing) different ways in which the characters can express themselves by look, posture, tone, or gesture. The representation of repetitive situations isn't affected by this inevitably textual approach.

142 **a particular painting:** The discussion that follows is indebted to Nöel Carroll's illuminating essay, *"Art* and Friendship," *Philosophy and Literature* 26 (2002): 199–206.

143 **"Isn't it pure gush to speak of":** Mary Mothersill, *A Theory of Beauty* (Oxford: Clarendon Press, 1984), p. 274.

144 **Interacting with works of art:** For more on the parallels between the love of people and the love of art, see *Only a Promise of Happiness: The Place of Beauty in a Work of Art* (Princeton: Princeton University Press, 2007), pp. 74–76, 124–126.

144 **"My friend Serge has bought a painting":** Reza, *Art*, p. 1.

144 **"Expensive?":** Ibid., p. 3.

145 **"You can't have a laugh with him":** Ibid., p. 10.

146 **"no warmth when he dismissed it":** Ibid., p. 4.

146 **"You have no substance":** Ibid., p. 35.

147 **"You can't tell if it's you":** Ibid., p. 47.

147 **"see much more in one another's actions":** In *Only a Promise of Happiness,* I argued that the real contrary of beauty or love is not ugliness or hate, respectively, but the failure to register. Beauty and ugliness, love and hate are considerably more continuous with one another—they all indicate intense involvement—than we generally

suppose. This failure to register results in indifference, which is a lack of concern for, or even awareness of, objects that provoke neither love nor hate, that appear neither beautiful nor ugly. The same is true, I believe, of friends and enemies, both of whom matter significantly—positively and negatively, respectively—in contrast to people with whom we are not emotionally involved.

148 **the purpose with which an action is undertaken:** Michael Stocker is a main proponent of the idea that motives as well as purposes are necessary for understanding the ethical character of much of our behavior. See, for example, his "Values and Purposes: The Limits of Teleology and the Ends of Friendship," in Neera Kapur Badhwar, *Friendship: A Philosophical Reader* (Ithaca, NY: Cornell University Press, 1993), pp. 245–263, in which he gives the view its most complete and detailed formulation; "The Schizophrenia of Modern Ethical Theories," *Journal of Philosophy* 73 (1976): 453–456; and "Duty and Friendship: Toward a Synthesis of Gilligan's Contrastive Ethical Concepts," in Eva Kittay and D. Meyers, eds., *Women and Moral Theory* (Totowa, NJ: Rowman and Allanheld, 1986), pp. 56–68. See also his *Plural and Conflicting Values* (Oxford: Oxford University Press, 1990), pp. 91–95. The main point is that not everything we do *with* our friends is also something we do *for* them.

148 **it must be done *out of* friendship:** Even the act of a friend need not be an act of friendship: I might help my friend in order to impress someone else. Such a lapse may show that I am not as good a friend as I would like to think, but it doesn't, on its own, undermine the whole of our relationship.

149 **act . . . without a second thought:** A second thought of this sort may remind readers of what Bernard Williams once called "a thought too many." Williams was criticizing the view that the moral justification of a man's decision, say, to save his wife rather than a stranger when both are about to drown, would appeal to a moral principle according to which in certain circumstances saving one's wife is (at least) morally permissible. That principle, he argued, is a thought too many: "It might have been hoped by some (for instance, by his wife) that his motivating thought, fully spelled out, would be the thought that it was his wife, not that it was his wife and that in situations of this kind it is permissible to save one's wife"; see "Persons, Character and Morality," in his *Moral Luck*

(Cambridge: Cambridge University Press, 1981), pp. 18–19. Harry Frankfurt, in turn, has claimed that even the one thought that it is the man's wife is too many: "Surely the normal thing is that he sees what's happening in the water, and he jumps in to save his wife. Without thinking at all. In the circumstances that the example describes, any thought whatever is one thought too many"; see his *The Reasons of Love* (Princeton: Princeton University Press, 2004), p. 36. I believe Frankfurt's view is closer to Williams's than he thinks, because "That's my wife who is drowning" is a "fully spelled out" expression of the man's motivating thought and not what went consciously through his mind. Susan Wolf has added significantly to this debate; see "'One Thought Too Many': Love, Morality, and the Ordering of Commitments," in her *The Variety of Values* (Oxford: Oxford University Press, 2015), pp. 143–162.

149 **"because it is the just thing to do":** That thought is necessary in order to determine whether we are acting justly *by our lights*, independently of having the right definition of justice, which would guarantee that our action is in fact just.

149 **would simply seem the natural thing to do:** See Bernard Williams, *Ethics and the Limits of Philosophy* (Cambridge, MA: Harvard University Press, 1985), pp. 9–11; Stocker, "Values and Purposes," pp. 256–258; and Julia Driver, "Virtues of Ignorance," *Journal of Philosophy* 86 (1989): 373–384. I suspect that Williams felt uncomfortable with the fact that, as we just said, both the just and the brave do what they do *because* it is the just or the brave thing to do, and changed the construction: "A just or fair person is one who chooses actions because they are just . . . But a courageous person does not typically choose acts *as* being courageous," p. 10. That is true enough. But it is equally true that a courageous person chooses acts *because* they are courageous. The difference is that the thought that they are courageous will not occur to the brave, whereas the thought that one's actions are just must occur to the just.

151 **Friendship differentiates us from the rest:** More on this in Chapter 6.

153 **"Crazy, or what?":** Reza, *Art*, pp. 15–16.

154 **"Read Seneca!":** This is an excellent example of the difference between narrative representation and dramatic action. The actor who plays Serge has a large number of different tones at his disposal, and the difference between the two versions of his statement is as

understandable on stage as the exclamation point in the text is inadequate to represent it.

154　**an escalation of hostilities:** Reza, *Art*, pp. 24–25.

155　**"Bit heavy, isn't it?":** Ibid., pp. 32–33.

156　**"I can't imagine you genuinely loving":** Ibid., p. 45.

156　**Either Serge, under the influence:** Ibid., p. 53.

157　**"asked me what I thought of Paula":** Ibid., p. 45.

158　**"I couldn't care less":** Ibid., pp. 51–52.

158　**"I had no idea whatsoever":** Ibid., p. 53.

159　**"Now when we talk we can't even":** Ibid.

159　**"Serge: So here we are":** Ibid., p. 54.

159　**"sheer neutral inertia has lured Marc":** Ibid., pp. 56–58.

159　**"I made you laugh":** Ibid., pp. 58–59.

159　**"Haven't you got any nibbles?":** Ibid., p. 59.

160　**Marc laughs along with him:** Ibid., p. 60.

160　**he draws a little skier:** The drawing is adapted from a videotaped production of the play by the Open Door Repertory Company, Oak Park, Illinois, 2009, at vimeo.com/6789494.

161　**"Let's be reasonable":** Reza, *Art*, pp. 62–63.

163　**"Under the white clouds":** Ibid., p. 63.

163　**bought an abstract white painting:** To avoid awkwardness, I will use the expressions "the painting," "buying the painting," and "deciding to buy the painting" interchangeably.

164　**what it *means*:** "Means," in this context, can be replaced by any one of a family of semantic terms, including "indicates," "reveals," "shows," "expresses," and several others.

164　**"You don't understand the seriousness":** Reza, *Art*, p. 9.

164　**distinction between what something is and:** Nevertheless, the distinction is deeply misleading and an obstacle to a better understanding of both friendship and human action more generally. I will have more to say about it in Chapter 6. Here, I want to take it for granted for the moment and stay with the disagreement between Marc and Yvan.

164　**as long as Serge can afford:** Reza, *Art*, pp. 9–10.

165　**Serge is "an exhibition freak":** Ibid., p. 9.

165　**Serge's decision is meaningful:** What counts as an event's meaning actually depends on the context in which it is examined and the questions we want to ask about it. In a medical context, buying the painting, especially if Serge was serious when he said that paying so much for it was "crazy," could be an instance of compulsive buying, and a symptom of (might mean that Serge suffers from) bipolar disorder. For one type of psychiatrist, that has no further meaning—bipolar disorder is an irregularity in brain structure or development. For another, the significance of choosing to buy the painting rather than, say, twenty pairs of shoes would be a further issue.

166   **be understood "in itself"**: It is important to note that something can be significant in the semantic sense I am using here without being important: to be significant is simply to signify *something*, however trivial or banal. To say that something is insignificant is not to say that it is unimportant but that it has no significance at all, like a tic or an event that merely happens to a person.

166   **"let himself be ripped off"**: Reza, *Art*, p. 10.

166   **the painting and "all it implies"**: Ibid., p. 3.

166   **"a very tolerant bloke"**: Ibid., p. 5.

167   **distinction between the action itself and its significance**: Complex philosophical issues are raised by these statements. G.E.M. Anscombe was the first to observe that a single intentional action can be correctly described in several ways. In her example, we can say of a particular man who is engaged in a certain activity that he is moving his arm up and down, operating a pump, replenishing the water supply, and poisoning the inhabitants of a particular house (he knows the water is poisoned). She discusses this in *Intention* (Ithaca, NY: Cornell University Press, 1966), pp. 37 ff. Anscombe takes it that one and the same action can bear these distinct descriptions, and her view seems to be the most widely accepted among philosophers. But two alternatives have been proposed. The first holds that the situation she describes involves four distinct actions and was introduced by Alvin Goldman in *A Theory of Human Action* (Englewood Cliffs, NJ: Prentice-Hall, 1970). Proponents of the second find here one action with several components; the view, I believe, first appeared in Irving Thalberg, *Perception, Emotion, and Action* (Oxford: Blackwell, 1997). In what follows, I assume that Anscombe's view is most nearly correct. I will offer some qualifications as I go along.

168   **a question for the theater**: The answer to this question can only be given by a successful performance of the play, not by a philosopher writing about it.

168   **"I didn't like the painting"**: Reza, *Art*, p. 17.

168 **"various colors . . . yellow":** Ibid., p. 35.

168 **"The more I see it":** Ibid., p. 42.

168 **Yvan is just being cowardly:** Ibid., p. 35.

170 **"If I'm who I am":** Ibid., pp. 41–42.

170 **"white . . . with fine white diagonal scars":** Ibid., p. 1.

172 **"a canvas about five foot by four: white":** Ibid.

172 **Allais's titles, in stark contrast to:** On Allais, see François Cara-dec, *Alphonse Allais* (Paris: Fayard, 1997) and, on some of the general issues involved in his works, John C. Welchman, *Invisible Colors: A Visual History of Titles* (New Haven, CT: Yale University Press, 1997), pp. 103–108.

174 **"The result of my life":** Søren Kierkegaard, *Either/Or*, ed. and trans. Howard V. Hong and Edna H. Hong (Princeton: Princeton University Press, 1987), part 1, p. 28.

176 **"You say the artist as if":** Reza, *Art*, p. 25.

178 **his "finicky, subservient voice of reason":** Ibid., p. 57.

180 **a merely subjective reaction:** The aesthetic issues addressed in the following pages are a central topic of *Only a Promise of Happiness.*

181 **a persisting disagreement may indicate:** Immanuel Kant, *Critique of the Power of Judgment*, trans. Paul Guyer and Eric Matthews (Cambridge: Cambridge University Press, 2000), paras. 55–57, pp. 213–221.

Here is an example of one critic praising a feature as a virtue and another denouncing it as a failure. The critics Janet Maslin and Roger Ebert, for example, agreed that the pace of Theo Angelopoulos's film *Ulysses' Gaze* (1995) is extraordinarily slow. But though for Maslin the film's "overall effect is genuinely entrancing, with a sense of tragic inevitability that gives meaning to the film's maddeningly attenuated rhythms," Ebert confessed that he "would not be able to look you in the eye if you went to see it, because how could I deny that it is a numbing bore? . . . [Angelopoulos] is so impressed with the gravity and importance of his theme that he wants to weed out any moviegoers seeking interest, grace, humor or involvement." See Janet Maslin, "Ulysses, Ozymandias and Lenin in the Balkans," *New York Times*, January 17, 1997, and Roger Ebert, "Ulysses' Gaze," *Chicago Sun-Times*, April 18, 1997.

183 **I would be equally devastated:** Detailed considerations for this view in *Only a Promise of Happiness*, chap. 3.

183 **"There comes a day":** Reza, *Art*, p. 54.

CHAPTER 6   THE GOOD OF FRIENDSHIP

187   **"If I had to choose between betraying":** E. M. Forster, "What I
Believe," in *Two Cheers for Democracy* (San Diego: Harcourt Brace,
1966), p. 68.

188   **can involve base, even abhorrent behavior:** I realize that these
examples are drawn from fiction. But only a work of art—not necessarily fictional—can have the richness of texture and detail that
are needed to show these two aspects of a friend's behavior. And
let's not forget that most of the examples of the best friendships in
our tradition are also drawn from fiction, beginning with the *Iliad*
itself.

189   *Thelma and Louise*: The film's screenplay, which won an Academy
Award for Callie Khouri, can be found at mypage.netlive.ch
/demandit/files/M_BFNO38KLSZ567NYSJ29/dms/modul_03
/ThelmaLouise.pdf. All references are to the screenplay as it appears on that site. The film was directed by Ridley Scott.

196   **Different moral virtues might occasionally conflict:** The subject
is vast and the literature on it extensive. Since it is not directly rele-
vant to the issues addressed here, I won't have anything more to say
about it. But see Michael Anthony Slote, *Goods and Virtues* (New
York: Oxford University Press, 1983), pp. 77–107; Marcia Baron,
"Admirable Immorality," *Ethics* 96 (1986): 557–566; Owen Flanagan,
"Admirable Immorality and Admirable Imperfection," *Journal of
Philosophy* 83 (1986): 41–60; Walter Sinnott-Armstrong, *Moral Dilemmas* (Oxford: Basil Blackwell, 1988); Troy Jollimore, "Admirable
Immorality," *American Philosophical Quarterly* 43 (2006): 159–170;
and especially Susan Wolf, "'One Thought Too Many': Love, Mo-
rality, and the Ordering of Commitment" and "The Importance of
Love," in her *The Variety of Values* (Oxford: Oxford University Press,
2015), pp. 143–152, 181–195.

196   **Politicians, for example, regularly describe themselves:** See
Ross K. Baker, *Friend and Foe in the U.S. Senate* (New York: Free
Press, 1980).

196   **Facebook can make "friends":** The scare quotes seem appropriate
here: this is as attenuated a sense of friendship as there can be. The
only direct personal contact between them may be just the original
request to be accepted as a "friend" and a positive response. From
then on, whatever information is available to one is available to

many. It is also a fact that by and large, Facebook friends don't communicate publicly most of the misfortunes they meet in life. And I doubt that responding to the news of a Facebook friend's birthday, wedding, or new job by clicking a button that says "Like" is enough to make such friends "share" one another's joys.

197 **books warn against bad friends:** Typical titles: Jan Yager, *When Friendship Hurts: How to Deal with Friends Who Betray, Abandon, or Wound You* (New York: Touchtone, 2002); Lorraine Smith-Hines, *Toxic Friends: A Practical Guide to Recognizing and Dealing with an Unhealthy Friendship* (West Bloomfield, MI: Foxglove Publications, 2010); Suzanne Degges-White and Judy Pochel Van Tieghem, *Toxic Friendships: Knowing the Rules and Dealing with the Friends Who Break Them* (New York: Rowman and Littlefield, 2015).

197 **detail the benefits of good friendships:** See, for example, Robert Garfield, *Breaking the Male Code: Unlocking the Power of Friendship* (New York: Gotham Publishing, 2015); Hugh Black, *The Art of Being a Good Friend: How to Bring Out the Best in Your Friends and in Yourself* (Bedford, NH: Sophia Institute Press, 1999); John Cuddeback, *Friendship: The Art of Happiness* (Las Vegas, NV: Epic Publishing, 2010).

198 **also destroys whatever dignity:** Gustave Flaubert, *Bouvard and Pécuchet*, trans. Mark Polizzotti (Urbana, IL: Dalkey Archive Press, 2005).

198 **genuine friendship that leads Lefty:** *Donnie Brasco* (1997), a film by Mike Newell.

199 **what our friends actually do for us:** Epicurus, *Vatican Sayings*, 34, in A. A. Long and D. N. Sedley, *The Hellenistic Philosophers*, vol. 1 (Cambridge: Cambridge University Press, 1981), p. 126.

199 **praising friendship as wisdom's greatest blessing:** Epicurus, *Key Doctrines*, 27, in Long and Sedley, *The Hellenistic Philosophers*, p. 126.

199 **to live alone, as he put it:** Nietzsche added their combination: "To live alone one must be a beast of a god, says Aristotle. Leaving out the third case: one must be both—a philosopher," *Twilight of the Idols*, trans. Walter Kaufmann, *The Portable Nietzsche* (New York: Viking Penguin, 1954), "Maxims and Arrows," 3. It may be worth remarking that both the traditional Greek gods (though not Aristotle's impersonal "Prime Mover") and, presumably, some of the beasts of the fourth century BC often depended on others for help and support in difficult situations.

199 **Aristotle, of course, said that:** Had he made that claim about the *philia* of the virtuous only, he would have made beasts of the rest of the world.

200 **"However rare true love may be":** François, duc de La Rochefoucauld, *Maxims*, trans. Stuart D. Warner and Stéphane Douard (South Bend, IN: St. Augustine's Press, 2001), p. 85.

200 **"almost wholly free from jealousy":** C. S. Lewis, *The Four Loves* (Orlando, FL: Harcourt, 1988), p. 77. These things do happen but such deeply painful episodes are less likely to occur between adults than between children.

200 **the friendships of children:** Aristotle took it that the ease with which such early bonds are made and broken shows that they are only inferior forms of *philia*—devoted to pleasure—and paid little attention to them; see *Nicomachean Ethics*, trans. and ed. Roger Crisp (Cambridge: Cambridge University Press, 2000), VIII.3, 1156a31–1156b6.

200 **Adults also abandon old friends:** "Adults . . . have a greater number of demands and more varied demands on their time. They are more likely to spend a large amount of time with their families and to have full-time jobs. Compared to college students, mature adults would be expected to interact with a wider variety of people and to have less time to socialize with friends. One would thus expect them to have fewer friends": Rosemary Bliezner and Rebecca G. Adams, *Adult Friendship* (Newbury Park, CA: Sage Publications, 1992), pp. 47–48.

201 **Losing a good friend hurts:** For the inadequacy of these traditional conceptions of the nature and importance of friendship, see Dean Cocking and Jeanette Kennett, "Friendship and the Self," *Ethics* 108 (1998): 502–527; I have learned a lot from their work, and my view, to a considerable degree, depends on, refines, and generalizes their own.

202 **Whenever they begin to develop:** The process goes in the other direction as well: making a new friend may provide the impetus for a personal change.

203 **"discover that they have in common":** Lewis, *The Four Loves*, pp. 65, 80, 86.

203 **"If I say, 'These are my friends'":** Ibid., p. 60.

203 **she rejects not only me:** That's why saying "It's not you, it's me," as we sometimes do in such situations, especially of course when a

love affair is ending, is no consolation. It's never just me: it's always, also, you.

203 **it is really something to mourn:** Sigmund Freud connected mourning with melancholia, by which he seemed to understand what psychiatry today classifies as both unipolar (major depression) and bipolar affective disorder (see Sigmund Freud, "Mourning and Melancholia," in *The Standard Edition of the Complete Psychological Works of Sigmund Freud*, ed. James Strachey, vol. 14 [London: Hogarth Press, 1986], pp. 237–258, at 243). Both mourning and melancholia, he argued, damage the capacity to love, inhibit activity, and undermine our interest in the outside world. Even more important, he attributed to melancholia a radical lowering of self-regard leading to "self-reproaches and self-revilings." Freud thought of mourning primarily as a reaction to the death of a loved person. But if we think of being abandoned by a friend as the death of who our friendship had made us, the end of a friendship is also, at least for the one abandoned, a reason for mourning. Just as separation and divorce lead to a serious increase in depression in many different countries, so there is every reason to believe that the breakup of a close friendship has similar effects (on separation and divorce, see Evelyn Bromet et al., "Cross-National Epidemiology of DSM-IV Major Depressive Episode," *BMC Medicine* 9 [2011]: 1–16; M. M. Weissman et al., "Cross-National Epidemiology of Major Depression and Bipolar Disorder," *Journal of the American Medical Association* 276 [1996]: 293–299; also, L. Andrade et al., "The Epidemiology of Major Depressive Episodes: Results from the International Consortium of Psychiatric Epidemiology [ICPE] Surveys," *International Journal of Methods in Psychiatric Research* 12 [2003]: 3–21). And the assurance "I can change," which we often give in such cases, is proof of self-reproach or even revulsion: it reveals that we ourselves believe that, being as we presently are, we are unworthy of love.

203 **friendship also separates us from everyone else:** See also Marilyn Friedman, *What Are Friends For?: Feminist Perspectives on Personal Relationships and Moral Theory* (Ithaca, NY: Cornell University Press, 1993), pp. 217–221.

204 **"Maybe the target nowadays":** Michel Foucault, "The Subject and Power," in *Power: Essential Works of Michel Foucault, 1954–1984*, ed. James Faubion (New York: New Press, 2000), p. 336.

207 **"Cause and effect"**: Friedrich Nietzsche, *The Gay Science*, trans. Walter Kaufmann (New York: Random House, 1974), sec. 112. Nietzsche may have been thinking of the Phi Phenomenon, first observed by Sigmund Exner in 1875, which he may well have known, but confirmed experimentally, by Max Wertheimer, only in 1910: when two dots at different ends of a screen are shown in quick succession, subjects report that they perceived one spot moving from one end of the screen to the other. More information and several other similar effects, including the Color Phi Phenomenon, which involves dots of different colors, can be found in Paul Kolers, *Aspects of Motion Perception* (Oxford: Pergamon Press, 1972). More sophisticated results, including further research on the perception of action, in Aaron F. Bobick, "Movement, Activity and Action: The Role of Knowledge in the Perception of Motion," *Philosophical Transactions of The Royal Society: Biological Sciences* 352 (1997): 1257–1265. Nietzsche may have taken Exner's observation to apply not just to apparent motion but also to actual motion, which presents considerably more complicated problems.

207 **"an arbitrary division and dismemberment"**: Nietzsche, *The Gay Science*, sec. 112. He does better in *The Will to Power*, trans. Walter Kaufmann and R. J. Hollingale (New York: Random House, 1967), sec. 666: "An action is never *caused* by a purpose; the purpose and means are interpretations whereby certain points in an event are emphasized and selected at the expense of other points, which, indeed, form the majority" (my emphasis).

207 **"I have already marked"**: Ian McEwan, *Enduring Love* (New York: Random House, 1997), pp. 20–21.

208 **"I do not correct my first imaginings"**: Michel de Montaigne, "On the Resemblance of Children to Fathers," in *The Complete Works of Montaigne: Essays, Travel Journal, Letters*, trans. Donald M. Frame (Stanford: Stanford University Press, 1958), II.37, p. 574.

208 **"I add but I do not correct"**: Montaigne, "Of Vanity," III.9, in Frame, *Complete Works*, p. 736. Like Nietzsche, who despised regret and forgiving, and who also believed that nothing, once it occurs, can change (a view connected with his idea of the eternal recurrence, according to which if anything occurred again in the world everything would have to occur in exactly the same way), Montaigne writes: "In all affairs, when they are past, however they have turned out, I have little regret. For this idea takes away the pain:

that they were bound to happen thus, and now they are in the great stream of the universe and in the chain of Stoical causes. Your fancy, by wish or imagination, cannot change a single point without overturning the whole order of things, and the past and the future," "Of Repentance," III.2, in Frame, *Complete Works*, p. 619. An illuminating and nuanced treatment of Montaigne's revisions is given by Paola Lemma, *Les repentirs de l'Exemplaire de Bordeaux (Montaigne, "Essais," Livre I)*, trans. Arlette Estève from the Italian (Paris: Honoré Champion, 2004).

212 **They did not discover their "real" self:** An excellent discussion of this issue, with a vivid example drawn from Jimmy Carter's autobiography, is provided by R. Lanier Anderson in "Nietzsche on Truth, Illusion, and Redemption," *European Journal of Philosophy* 13 (2005): 185–225.

213 **We may honor it on account of:** In "Love as Valuing a Relationship" (*Philosophical Review* 112 [2003]: 135–189), Niko Colodny identifies love in general with "a kind of valuing that . . . consists (a) in seeing a relationship in which one is involved as a reason for valuing both one's relationship and the person with whom one has that relationship, and (b) in valuing that relationship and person accordingly" (p. 150). In my opinion, that gives the relationship, important as it is, greater primacy than it deserves. After all, to value such a relationship is also to value the friend who, over time, made it what it was.

214 **"The person one loves at first":** John Williams, *Stoner* (New York: New York Review of Books, 2006; orig. pub. 1963), p. 194.

214 **"Life is a habit":** Tim Lott, *White City Blue* (London: Penguin Books, 2000), p. 2.

214 **"The minutest portion of a great composition":** John Ruskin, *Modern Painters*, vol. 5 (New York: John Wiley, 1869), chap. 2, para. 1, quoted by Ziyad Marar in his *Intimacy* (Durham: Acumen Publishing, 2012), p. 15.

215 **"The promise of intimacy":** Marar, *Intimacy*, p. 22.

215 **what counts as the self:** Marar's explanation is slightly different: "Our selves do not conceal an unwavering identity . . . Our innermost being is a subtle, shady and complex construct shifting across our lifetimes while providing the illusion of stability, even as we cling on to the hope of permanence and reliability" (p. 22). In my view, the self is variable not only over time, as Marar correctly notes, but also at the same time, from different points of view.

215 **"like all lovers":** Williams, *Stoner*, p. 196.

216 **they think that moral values are overriding:** Dissenting voices on
the supreme importance of morality for the value of life: Harry G.
Frankfurt, *The Importance of What We Care About* (Cambridge:
Cambridge University Press, 1988), *Necessity, Volition, and Love*
(Cambridge: Cambridge University Press, 1998), *The Reasons of
Love* (Princeton: Princeton University Press, 2006), and *Taking
Ourselves Seriously and Getting It Right* (Stanford: Stanford Univer-
sity Press, 2006); Bernard Williams, *Ethics and the Limits of Philos-
ophy* (Cambridge, MA: Harvard University Press, 1985), *Moral Luck*
(Cambridge: Cambridge University Press, 1981), and "Nietzsche's
Minimalist Psychology," in Richard Schacht, ed., *Nietzsche, Geneal-
ogy, Morality: Essays on Nietzsche's "Genealogy of Morals"* (Berkeley:
University of California Press, 1994), pp. 237–247; Susan Wolf,
Meaning in Life and Why It Matters (Princeton: Princeton University Press, 2010) and many of the essays in her *The Variety of Values.*
Moral philosophers sometimes acknowledge the importance of
other values but pass them over quickly. See T. M. Scanlon, *What
We Owe to Each Other* (Cambridge, MA: Harvard University Press,
2000).

216 **individuality is itself a value:** Individuality should not be confused
with individualism, which is commonly understood today as a kind
of libertarianism. It has nothing to do either with selfishness or
with the relationship between individuals and the state.

217 **great villains are individuals:** Susan Neiman, following Kant, argues that heroes must also be morally good individuals and uses the
abolitionist John Brown as an example of such a good hero in her
"Victims and Heroes," *The Tanner Lectures on Human Values*, vol. 31,
ed. Mark Matheson (Salt Lake City: University of Utah Press,
2012), pp. 65–92. Her treatment is often illuminating, but I have serious doubts about both her overall argument about heroism and
morality and her portrayal of John Brown.

217 **Titian's *Venus of Urbino*:** "What we call the *Venus of Urbino* is obviously an erotic representation of a female nude, but her typology as
a Venus figure can be called into play if the subject wants justification," Bette Talvacchia, *Taking Positions: On the Erotic in Renaissance Culture* (Princeton: Princeton University Press, 1999), p. 46.

217 **become attractive individuals themselves:** Strictly speaking, "attractive individual" is a pleonasm. Attraction, like love in all its
forms and degrees, is always focused on an individual.

217   **not often, in a moral sense:** Recall that individuality is in general a trivial feature of people: everyone is an individual. What matters is whether one is an attractive, important, or more generally unusual individual.

218   **I find C. P. Cavafy's poetry:** Cavafy was a Greek poet who lived most of his life in Alexandria. His works have been translated several times in English, in particular by Edmund Keeley and Philip Sherrard, *C.P. Cavafy: Collected Poems* (Princeton: Princeton University Press, 1975). The poem in question, "For the Shop," appears on p. 87.

218   **his idiosyncratic publishing habits:** Cavafy had his poems printed on single leaves, pinned several of them together in booklets, and distributed them among his friends. He would often add new ones to bundles that were already in circulation.

219   **I asked, for example, why Cavafy:** In "Not Text But Texture: C.P. Cavafy's Poems Unread, Unfinished, Unwritten," forthcoming. See also my "Memory, Pleasure and Poetry: The Grammar of the Self in the Writing of Cavafy," *Journal of Modern Greek Studies* 1 (1983): 295–319 and "Cavafy's World of Art," *Grand Street* 8 (1989): 129–146.

219   **"Art was not for him a need":** Quoted by Sonia Ilinskaya, *C.P. Cavafy* (Athens: Kedros, 1993), pp. 155–156 (in Greek).

220   **why would I love *Cavafy's* poetry:** Not that I don't love other poets as well. But in every poet—every artist—I love, I see something that no one else in the world does. That doesn't mean that I expect everyone to agree with me. Different people love different artists (or the same artists, though usually for different reasons) as they have different friends (or, as we saw in Chapter 4, the same friends, though for different reasons).

220   **To the extent that I could articulate:** Not here, though: here, I am only making some very elementary points—it is in my writing about him that I try to express as well as I can what I actually find so exciting about his work.

221   **what I find is in fact admirable:** Or his poetry: in this context, it makes no difference.

221   **in a way that is distinctly *my* own:** Strictly speaking, and as I argue in *Only a Promise of Happiness* (Princeton: Princeton University Press, 2007), chap. 4, if I not only accept someone else's interpretation of Cavafy (or anyone else) but work it out for myself, what I end up with is bound to be different from theirs. The reason is that to interpret something is to see how it is like and unlike other

things in the world. But, necessarily, the things in the world I will compare to, even if they overlap with those with which the original interpreter compared it, will have to be different not only in number but in importance as well. So, however similar our views turn out to be in the end, they won't be identical. But if the differences are only at the edges and not important, we are satisfied with saying that our interpretations are "the same." Once again, the issue is not whether there are differences between one view and another—there always will be: the issue is how important these differences are.

222 **"a great and rare art":** Nietzsche, *The Gay Science*, sec. 290.

223 **may or may not be "private information":** See Cocking and Kennett, "Friendship and the Self," p. 503.

223 **an interpretation of who we are:** This is close to what Cocking and Kennett call "the interpretation view of friendship" in "Friendship and the Self."

224 **what friends do together is less important than:** Stanley Cavell, *Pursuits of Happiness: The Hollywood Comedy of Remarriage* (Cambridge: Harvard University Press, 1981), p. 88; the passage is quoted in chap. 3.

224 **Nonmoral values—beauty, love, friendship:** See Annette Baier, "Trust and Antitrust," *Ethics* 96 (1986): 231–260, and Nietzsche, *The Gay Science*, sec. 344: in life, both are needed, "much trust *as well as* much mistrust."

224 **even intelligence:** See, most surprisingly, Plato, *Republic* VI, 494a–495c.

Index

Alexander Nehamas is a professor of philosophy and comparative literature at Princeton University and a fellow of the American Academy of Arts and Sciences. The author of books on art, literature, and authenticity, among other subjects, he lives in Princeton, New Jersey.